Basics for Communicating Effectively

Revised Edition

Christian Liberty Press   1996   Arlington Heights, Illinois

A publication of

Christian Liberty Press

502 West Euclid Avenue

Arlington Heights, Illinois 60004

Scripture references are conformed to The Holy Bible, New King James Version ©1982, Thomas Nelson, Inc., so that modern readers may gain greater comprehension of the Word of God.

Moes, Garry J.

    APPLICATIONS OF GRAMMAR, BOOK 1

    BASICS FOR COMMUNICATING EFFECTIVELY

    Includes glossary and index

    1. English Language—Grammar

Printed in the United States of America

PREFACE

This book is intended to lay a proper foundation for the student's effectiveness in communicating with the English language. The student will learn the basics of English grammar, including the definition and usage of verbs, nouns, adjectives, adverbs, and other parts of speech. In addition, the student will examine how these are to be properly used in phrases, clauses, sentences, paragraphs, and composition. The *Applications of Grammar* series is designed to develop students' skills in using the rules of grammar to communicate effectively for the glory of God.

While some today would discard the need for grammar, this text affirms that the learning of grammatical rules and their proper usage is foundational to good communication. The distinctions between words, their relation to each other in a sentence, and the rules that govern language are the basic building blocks of writing well.

This text is designed to be read carefully by the student so that he may review the grammar knowledge he has already learned and build upon it with new skills. Each lesson should be read carefully and reviewed as necessary. Some of the words used in the text may be new to the student's vocabulary, and their spelling unfamiliar. Therefore, a glossary and index are located at the back of this volume to provide students and teachers with additional reference material.

Many of the lessons will require use of a dictionary. While an unabridged dictionary would be useful, a standard, full-sized, collegiate-level dictionary will be more useful. Small, pocket-size, or greatly abridged desktop editions will likely not provide the amount of information which the student will need to complete many of the lessons in this book. It would also be helpful if the student had access to a set of encyclopedias or other reference works. These will be useful in the several writing assignments included in this textbook. If your school or home does not have adequate resources of this nature, you should visit your local library.

THE AUTHOR AND EDITOR

Garry J. Moes is a free-lance writer, textbook author, and editorial communications consultant from Murphys, California. He earned his B.A. in journalism from Michigan State University, East Lansing Michigan, and did postgraduate research at Scandinavian Christian University's Nordic College of Journalism in Sweden. He was a writer, reporter, and editor for The Associated Press for twenty-one years, and has been an essayist, international correspondent, and executive editor for several Christian periodicals.

Edward J. Shewan is an editor for Christian Liberty Press. He graduated from Valparaiso University with a B.S.E.E. degree in 1974. After a year of mission work in Africa, he attended the Moody Bible Institute's Advanced Studies Program in 1976. Subsequently, he served in Chicago city churches for ten years. In 1983 he graduated from Trinity Evangelical Divinity School with the M.Div. degree. He has also done free-lance editing for David C. Cook Publishing. Ed is married and has one daughter. He is the author of *How to Study: A Practical Guide from a Christian Perspective*, published by Christian Liberty Press.

TABLE OF CONTENTS

Introduction

Students often wonder why they have to study grammar and composition when they already know how to talk and write. Although basic communication skills may be evident, every student needs to thoroughly learn not only how language works but how to use it accurately. In order to speak and write well, students must acquire a proper understanding of grammatical definitions, functions, structures, and rules so that they may verbalize their thoughts with clarity and precision. Few skills are more important to Christian students than the ability to effectively communicate through the written and spoken word.

THE CHRISTIAN VIEW OF LANGUAGE

The student will be able to study language more purposefully if he begins with an understanding of the Christian view of language. Sadly, some students merely study language and grammar because they have been made to do so. They fail to grasp that, because we are made in God's image, good communication is essential to our service of God. As an image bearer of God, the student should consider how the Bible can direct his study of language. Through faith in Jesus Christ he can be reconciled to God and learn how to use language to the end for which it was created. Because language did not originate with us, we do not have the right to use it any way we wish. We must be guided by the Bible. Language skills are not neutral; they must be oriented toward reading, writing, and speaking the truth in love. Linguistic abilities should be developed as part of the student's chief end to glorify God and enjoy Him forever.

GOD IS THE ORIGIN OF LANGUAGE

> In the beginning God created the heaven and the earth. And the earth was without form and void; and darkness was upon the face of the deep. And the Spirit of God moved over the face of the waters. And God *said* … (Genesis 1:1-3).

God is the origin of language, for the three persons of the Trinity spoke to each other before time began. When the Father, the Son, and the Holy Spirit speak to each other eternally, their communication is perfect; there is never one word of misunderstanding! The Son of God is called the *Word* of God and the Holy Spirit searches the mind of God and communicates with spiritual words (1 Corinthians 2:10-13). When God created the heavens and the earth, He spoke it into existence by the Word of His power. When He spoke, He uttered a series of sounds—audible symbols which communicated His meaning and brought the creation into being. When God spoke, His Word conveyed both infinite power and eternal meaning—*infinite power* because He manifested His absolute will, and *eternal meaning* because He expressed His infinite mind. His infinite wisdom is revealed in creation, and the creatures He has made serve the purpose of communicating His glory. Thus the rock, for example, is used as a picture of God's unchanging character. Creation itself was designed to provide the basic terms and environment for language.

GOD GAVE MAN THE GIFT OF LANGUAGE

When God created man in His own image, He gave him the gift of language—the ability to communicate with words. He gave man the ability, like Himself, to convey meaning with his words, but He did not impart the infinite creative power of His speech. Thus, God's Word is the final authority, and men are to speak in submission to that Word. The language of man is to be subject to God, for man by his speech has no power to create or change what God has made. Yet there is a great power to human speech. It not only sets on fire the course of our lives but the course of history as well (James 3:6).

Because language is a gift of God, it has a purpose. It was given first of all as the means by which God would communicate to man. As such, it has a high and holy place in our lives. From the beginning God chose to communicate with man. The first words spoken to Adam and Eve were His charge, "Be fruitful, and multiply, and replenish the earth..." (Genesis 1:28). God's desire to communicate with Adam and Eve in the Garden of Eden was central to their fellowship. They "heard the voice of the Lord God walking in the cool of the day..." (Genesis 3:8). Secondly, language was given so that man would respond to God. God created mankind to praise His name and answer His call. Thirdly, it was given for men to communicate with each other in subjection to God's word. People were given the ability to talk to one another and thereby develop marriage, the family, and other social relationships. The primary instrument for building these relationships is verbal communication. God's purpose for language should direct our study of it.

RULES FOR COMMUNICATION

For many students, rules are a burden to be disregarded. But the student who is willing to submit to God's order will seek to develop precision in communicating. Because God is a God of order and truth, He has demonstrated the proper use of language in His speech from the dawn of history. For people to communicate properly and effectively with one another, God not only gave language but with it the basic principles of good communication. This does not mean that we have a divinely revealed set of rules from God, but we can learn from the Bible's use of language and build upon the principles that have been learned in the past. In particular, the Bible and the Christian religion have had a central role in molding the English language.

Consequently, the study of grammar—the body of rules for speaking and writing—should be based on the fact that God is the Creator of language and thereby the originator of its order. Good grammar reflects His logic and manifests the orderly structure of His mind. By learning the rules of proper usage, the student will know how to make his thoughts known and communicate in a compelling manner. His purpose is not simply to be able to communicate, however, but to use language effectively to communicate God's truth.

Language and grammar are not mere human conventions which spring from chance evolution to fill a human need. Language expresses a people's culture, religion, and history. This is why language changes over time. Each language has its own characteristics and rules of usage. But every language displays an underlying unity with other languages. Every language is a verbal system of communication. Each has similar patterns of grammar, though not expressed in exactly the same way. Yet at bottom, the basic principles of grammatical structure are common to every language, which is why writings from one language can be translated into another. While the basic principles of grammar may be adapted in unique ways, these are derived from the original language given by God to man.

LANGUAGE CORRUPTED BY SIN

After our first parents sinned, the same Voice that spoke the world into existence now stood in judgment over mankind. And the language that had been given as a gift to man by the Father of Truth had now been distorted by the Father of Lies. That which was created to praise and worship God had now been used to rebel against the Author of language. Man's fellowship with the Living God had been broken and he no longer desired to hear Him speak.

In addition, the Bible tells us that after the Great Flood, men united by a common language sought unity apart from God at the Tower of Babel. Seeing this, God confused their one language by dividing it into many, and scattered them over the face of the whole earth. Language was thus changed by God to keep men from disobeying His mandate. Because of these different languages there are now barriers between men when they communicate. And sin has continued to pervert the use of language, making it an instrument of lies and manipulation. Today, there are those who would reject all form and grammar and seek to justify any use of language and any breaking of the rules of grammar. As a result, confusion reigns in many quarters, and many people have great difficulty clearly articulating their thoughts in speech and writing.

THE RESTORATION OF LANGUAGE IN JESUS CHRIST

God chose to restore language in His Son. Jesus, as the second Adam, was sent into the world to undo the sin of the first Adam and its consequences (Romans 5:19). Jesus, who is the Word, was with God in the creation because He is God (John 1:1-3). Jesus is the *logos* or revelation of God to man, for God has spoken to us in His Son (Hebrews 1:1). There is no other name under heaven given among men, whereby we must be saved (Acts 4:12). God's will to communicate with man was one factor that motivated Him to restore language to its rightful state in Christ Jesus. By His death and resurrection, Christ not only provides forgiveness of sin, but also newness of life to those who receive Him by faith. As the Truth, Christ calls his disciples to speak the oracles of God (1 Peter 4:11), lay aside lies, and speak truth to one another (Ephesians 4:25). Jesus is the true source of the meaning of all things. He declared, "I am the Alpha and Omega, the beginning and the ending, saith the Lord, which is, and which was, and which is to come, the Almighty" (Rev. 1:8). As R. J. Rushdoony states:

> Christ's statement has reshaped Western languages and grammars, and, through Bible translation, is reshaping the languages of peoples all over the world. Bible translation is an exacting task, because it involves in effect the reworking of a language in order to make it carry the meaning of the Bible. This means a new view of the world, of God, time and language.... Our ideas of grammar, of tense, syntax, and structure, of thought and meaning, bear a Christian imprint.

Students who profess the Christian faith should have a unique appreciation of the role of verbal communication. It is the Christian, above all, who should seek to be clear and accurate

---

[1.]   Rousas J. Rushdoony, *The Philosophy of the Christian Curriculum* (Vallecito, CA: Ross House Books, 1985), p. 49-50.

in his use of the written word. His God-given duty is to use language with integrity and accuracy for the sake of promoting the gospel and Kingdom of Jesus Christ. Noah Webster saw this in his day when he wrote:

> If the language can be improved in regularity, so as to be more easily acquired by our own citizens, and by foreigners, and thus be rendered a more useful instrument for the propagation of science, arts, civilization and Christianity; if it can be rescued from the mischievous influence of ...that dabbling spirit of innovation which is perpetually disturbing its settled usages and filling it with anomalies; if, in short, our vernacular language can be redeemed from corruptions, and...our literature from degradation; it would be a source of great satisfaction to me to be one among the instruments of promoting these valuable objects.

To show that the Christian has the marvelous opportunity to employ language and its power for the service of the gospel, Gary DeMar asserts:

> Ideas put to paper and acted upon with the highest energy and uncompromising zeal can change the world. Even the worst ideas have been used for this very purpose. If minds are going to be transformed and civilizations changed, then Christians must learn to write and write well. Writing is a sword, mightier than all the weapons of war because writing carries with it ideas that penetrate deeper than any bullet. Writing about the right things in the right way can serve as an antidote to the writings of skepticism and tyranny that have plundered the hearts and minds of generations of desperate people around the world ...

Language as the gift of God needs to be cultivated for serving God. It will not only help the student in academic studies, but in every area of communication, at home, at church, and on the job. Proper English skills are a great asset in serving Christ effectively in one's calling. The student's skill in using English will make a good first impression when he sits for an interview and as he labors in the workplace. The student should take advantage of the time and opportunity he now has available to develop proficiency in English communication. May God bless you as you seek to glorify Him, not only by learning the proper use of English, but in using God's gift of language to spread His Word to every nation.

[2.] Noah Webster, *An American Dictionary of the English Language* (New York, NY: S. Converse, 1828); reprint by (San Francisco, CA: Foundation for American Christian Education, 1987), preface.

[3.] Gary DeMar, *Surviving College Successfully* (Brentwood, TN: Wolgemuth & Hyatt Publishers, Inc., 1988), p.225.

Unit 1
Start with Words

The basic building block of language is the WORD. A *written word* is a letter or combination of letters forming a stand-alone expression of a thought. A *spoken word* is a sound or combination of sounds capable of standing alone as a single unit of utterance. Words are classified according to their use in expressing a definite idea when combined in larger units of expression—phrases, clauses, and sentences. Another way to state this classification is to say that every word is a **part of speech**. In English, every word is at least one of the eight parts of speech: *noun, pronoun, verb, adjective, adverb, preposition, conjunction,* or *interjection.* In some cases, a word may be used in special ways so that it functions as more than one part of speech. For example, some verb forms can be used as nouns, adjectives, or adverbs; and some adverbs act as though they are conjunctions.

In this unit, we will classify words as follows:

❑ **Words that name — nouns and pronouns**

❑ **Words that assert — verbs (and verbals)**

❑ **Words that modify — adjectives and adverbs**

❑ **Words that join — prepositions and conjunctions**

❑ **Words that exclaim — interjections**

LESSON 1: WORDS THAT NAME—NOUNS

> **A NOUN is a part of speech that names a person, place, thing, quality, or idea.**

The English word *noun* comes from the Latin word *nomen,* meaning *name.* From this Latin word we also derive the English word *nominative,* which you will use on many occasions in your study of grammar. *Nominative* means "having the quality or character of a noun." Nominatives can be nouns, pronouns, phrases, or other groups of words that serve the purpose of a noun; that is, they **name** or **rename** *persons, places, things, qualities,* or *ideas.*

A noun is a word that "names" a person, place, thing, quality, or idea. The following are some examples of nouns in each of these five categories:

| PERSONS: | James, child, pastor, teacher, father, Mr. Harper, carpenter, president |
| QUALITIES: | politeness, warmth, friendliness, honesty, joyfulness, smoothness |

PERSONS: James, child, pastor, teacher, father, Mr. Harper, carpenter, president

PLACES: Alaska, London, home, avenue, Argentina, park, school, church, country

THINGS: bird, car, motorcycle, cereal, pole, telephone, computer, hand, lamp

QUALITIES: politeness, warmth, friendliness, honesty, joyfulness, smoothness

IDEAS: freedom, wisdom, hope, faith, worship, power, communism, democracy

KINDS OF NOUNS

There are two different kinds of nouns: *common* and *proper*. Common nouns name the general members of a common group: *tree, boy, building, automobile, radio, house, book*. These kinds of nouns are written without capital letters. Proper nouns name particular persons, places, things, etc.: *Mrs. Davis, Abraham Lincoln, Asia, Bible, Washington Monument, Yellowstone National Park*. These kinds of nouns are always capitalized.

Note: Nouns, especially proper nouns, can sometimes consist of more than one word, as the preceding examples show.

Every sentence has some kind of nominative, very often a noun. Here are some examples of sentences with both common and proper **nouns** (dark print).

The *book* I am reading before *bedtime* every *night* is interesting.

We plan to travel to the *desert* in *Arizona* for our *vacation*.

Millions of *men*, *women*, and *children* were killed during *World War II*.

The *Sydney Opera House* in *Australia* has an unusual *design*.

FUNCTIONS OF NOUNS

Nouns (and other nominatives) serve three basic functions, or uses, in sentences, phrases, or other sentence parts. These three functions are: *subject, object,* and *predicate nominative*.

> **The SUBJECT of a sentence is the noun (or other nominative) about which the sentence makes a statement.**

EXAMPLE: The *rain* usually begins in April.

> **An OBJECT is a noun (or other nominative) to which an action is done or which receives an action of a verb.**

EXAMPLE: The store sells *books*.

An object may also be a noun (or other nominative) which follows a preposition. A preposition is a word "positioned before" a noun or pronoun (the object) showing the relationship of that noun or pronoun to other words in the sentence.

  EXAMPLE: She walked *to* the *store*.

> **A PREDICATE NOMINATIVE is a noun (or other nominative) which follows a certain kind of verb called a *linking verb* (usually a form of *to be: is, am, are, was, were*) and *renames* the subject of the verb.**

  EXAMPLE: Robins are ***birds*.**

✎ **EXERCISE A** Write examples of nouns in the categories shown below.

100

Persons _Mom_____

Places __Rushville_____

Things_ _TV_____

Ideas or_ _purity_____
qualities

✎ **EXERCISE B** Fill the blanks in the follow sentences with nouns that fit the sense of the sentences. Do not use the same noun more than once.

100

1. In the _____fabric_____ , there are a few small _____flaws_____ .

2. My _____Sister_____ has red _____hair_____ .

3. His _____dog_____ likes to eat _____Crackers_____ .

4. She cooked _____pizza_____ for _____lunch_____ .

5. No one likes a _____jerk_____ .

6. Our _____meal_____ during _____Thanksgiving_____ was a great _____feast_____ .

7. _____Max_____ and _____Kola_____ are our _____pets_____ .

8. Put your _____money_____ in the _____bank_____ .

✎ **EXERCISE C** Underline all the nouns in the following sentences. Do not underline words which stand in the place of nouns, such as *we, he, it, they,* or verb forms used as nouns.

1. We had a very deep <u>snowfall</u> during <u>February</u> last <u>year</u>.

2. <u>God</u> is our <u>refuge</u> and our <u>strength</u>.

3. The <u>harvest</u> was large this <u>year</u>, but <u>prices</u> for <u>crops</u> were not high.

4. The <u>room</u> reserved for the <u>meeting</u> was crowded, so several <u>people</u> could not attend.

5. Serving the <u>Lord</u> has great <u>rewards</u>, both in this <u>life</u> and in <u>eternity</u>.

6. In this <u>exercise</u>, we are instructed to underline all <u>nouns</u>.

7. I sold my <u>bicycle</u> and <u>skateboard</u> to two <u>friends</u>.

8. In this <u>chapter</u>, the <u>hero</u> gets lost in the <u>forest</u>; but a <u>team</u> of <u>rescuers</u> find him.

9. The <u>factory</u> could hardly supply the <u>needs</u> of its <u>customers</u> because <u>materials</u> were scarce.

10. A young <u>lady</u> asked the <u>clerk</u> about the <u>price</u> of the <u>perfume</u>.

11. The <u>movie</u> was not able to hold my <u>attention</u> for more than a few <u>minutes</u>.

✎ **EXERCISE D** In the blank behind each of the nouns in dark print, write **S** if the noun is a subject, **O** if the noun is an object of a verb or preposition, or **PN** if the noun is a predicate nominative.

1. My *father* (_S_) is the *president* (_PN_) of the *committee* (_O_).

In this sentence, **father** is a noun about which the sentence is making a statement. The word is therefore the subject of the sentence. The word **president** renames the subject; that is, the words **father** and **president** refer to the same person. The word **president** is therefore a *predicate nominative.* The word **committee** follows the preposition **of** (it is the word to which **of** points) and it is therefore an object of a preposition.

2. *Jody* (_S_) learned her *lessons* (_O_) well.

In this sentence, **Jody** is a proper noun about which the sentence is making a statement. The word is therefore the subject of the sentence. The word **lessons** follows and receives the action of the verb **learned** and is therefore the *direct object* of the verb. A direct object usually answers the question "what?" about the verb.

3. **John** (S) finished his **composition** (O) on **Friday** (O).

4. **Birthdays** (S) are always happy **occasions** (PN).

5. At our **house** (O), everyone helps with the **work** (O).

6. Our **team** (S) defeated the **team** (O) from **Hope Christian School** (O).

7. His **name** (S) is **Mark** (PN).

8. The **teacher** (S) was proud of her **students** (O).

9. **Stores** (S) in our **town** (O) are usually closed on **Sunday** (O).

10. **Robbie** (S) and **Jamie** (S) enjoyed a **game** (O) of **chess** (O).

11. The **clerk** (S) stapled the **papers** (O) together.

LESSON 2: WORDS THAT SUBSTITUTE—PRONOUNS

> **A PRONOUN is a part of speech that is used in place of a noun.**

Pronouns can be thought of as **substitutes for nouns**. We use them so that we do not always have to keep repeating the same noun again and again when speaking or writing about a person, place, thing, idea, or quality. There are a number of different kinds of pronouns, each with a special use as noun substitutes. In this lesson, we will not go into detail about these special classifications of pronouns. The purpose of this lesson is to help you recognize various kinds of words that can be used in the place of nouns. Here are some examples of common pronouns:

PRONOUNS		
I, me, my, mine, myself	we, us, our, ours, ourselves	anybody, nobody, no one
you, your, yours, yourself	they, them, their, theirs	several, few, many, each, all
he, him, his, himself	themselves	somebody, someone
she, her, hers, herself	that, this, these, those	others, none, one, some
it, its, itself	who, whom, whose	both, either, neither

The following paragraph includes several pronouns.

Thinking about how the weather might affect *his* family's plans, Robert said to *himself*, "*We* could go the lake if *it* is not too cold." *He* hoped *everyone* would agree with *him*. *They* said *they* liked *his* idea, but *they* wondered if *his* father could get time off work.

Without pronouns, the paragraph would read as follows:

Thinking about how the weather might affect Robert's family's plans, Robert said to Robert, "The family could go to the lake if the weather is not too cold." Robert hoped all the members of the family would agree with Robert. The family members said the family liked Robert's plan, but the family members wondered if Robert's father could get time off work.

You can see how useful pronouns are in giving our communications variety, smoothness, and meaning. While pronouns are useful, they are also some of the most difficult words to use correctly, because they have so many different forms depending upon their exact function in the sentence. In future lessons, we will learn more about how to use pronouns properly and which forms to select.

For now, remember that *pronouns are substitutes for nouns.* As such, they, like nouns, refer to persons, places, things, ideas, or qualities. Like nouns, they may also be called *nominatives.* Like nouns, they can be used as *subjects, objects,* and *predicate nominatives.*

Note: Some forms of *pronouns* can also be used as adjectives.

✎ **EXERCISE** Underline the pronouns, as shown in the first line below, in the following paragraphs.

Before Squanto covered the hills of corn, <u>he</u> did a curious thing. What do <u>you</u> suppose <u>he</u> did? <u>He</u> caught a fish and put <u>it</u> into a hill of corn. <u>He</u> caught a great many fishes, so as to have <u>some</u> for each hill of corn. Then, after <u>he</u> had dropped fish into the hills with the grains of corn, <u>he</u> covered <u>them</u> with earth.

St. Valentine was a good <u>man</u> <u>who</u> lived in Europe nearly two thousand years ago. <u>He</u> was a Christian teacher. At that time, the emperor at Rome was not a Christian. <u>He</u> hated Christians and had <u>many</u> of <u>them</u> put to death. Those Christians <u>who</u> were put to death because of their faith in Christ are called martyrs. St. Valentine was a martyr, for <u>it</u> is said the emperor had <u>him</u> put to death because <u>he</u> kept on teaching men to be Christians.

One reason <u>we</u> love birds is because <u>they</u> sing, and the world loves people <u>who</u> sing. If <s>anybody</s> gives <u>us</u> a good song, <u>we</u> always remember <u>him</u> for <u>it</u>. <u>We</u> remember Francis Scott Key because <u>he</u> gave <u>us</u> "The Star-Spangled Banner"; <u>we</u> remember Samuel Francis Smith because <u>he</u> gave <u>us</u> "America."

Long ago in London a young man named Walter Raleigh had a handsome red velvet cloak. As he walked along the street, he saw a fine lady passing. She was Queen Elizabeth I of England. Just then the queen came to a muddy place in the road. She stopped a moment, not knowing what to do, for she had on a nice pair of shoes and she did not want to get them muddy. What do you think the young man did? He took off his handsome velvet cloak and spread it over the muddy place in the road. Then the queen could walk across without soiling her shoes.

I believe that we as Christians have the obligation to love our neighbors, and this love must be shown in action. When Christian brothers are suffering persecution, we must respond in prayer and action. We must publicize their plight. We must alert other Christians to the crisis. Each of us must pray for the persecuted. All of you must be generous in your support of those who are practically helping the persecuted. Encourage others to contribute any skills or resources they can towards helping those brothers and sisters in Christ who are suffering. And if God calls you to go and serve His people, be prepared to respond with wholehearted enthusiasm.

LESSON 3: WORDS THAT ASSERT—VERBS

> **A VERB is a part of speech that expresses action or a state of being, or that helps another verb complete its meaning.**

Every sentence must have a verb to make it complete. The purpose of a verb is to *tell something about the subject*. It may tell what the subject is, was, or will be doing. It may simply say that the subject exists, existed, or will exist. The verb or verb phrase in a sentence is also called the **predicate** of the sentence. A *simple predicate* consists of the verb or verb phrase alone. A *complete predicate* consists of the verb or verb phrase, plus all the words that are objects of the verb and all of the words that modify the verb and its objects.

Thus every sentence, in order to be complete, must have a *subject* and a *predicate*.

☞**EXAMPLE:**

|—subject and modifiers—| |———————complete predicate———————|
This *series* of books   *may be obtained* from your local library.

In this example, the noun *series* is the subject of the sentence. The main verb is *obtained*, expressing what action the subject has taken. The main verb has two "helping verbs," *may* and *be*. As you can see, the helping verbs do not express any "action" but merely assist the main verb in making its statement about the subject.

KINDS OF VERBS AND THEIR USES

There are three kinds of verbs: *action verbs, linking verbs,* and *helping verbs*.

■ *Action Verbs*

Action verbs may involve some kind of **physical action** (*walk, sit, beat, chop, mix, swallow*) or some kind of **activity in the mind or heart** (mental or emotional "action"—*believe, love, understand, sympathize, fear, dislike, accept*).

☞**EXAMPLES OF ACTION VERBS:**

She *jumped* when the door *slammed* shut.

The wind *swirled* around the farm buildings.

He *tasted* his food carefully because it was hot.

■ *Linking Verbs*

Other verbs do not show action. They express a **state of being** or **condition of existence**. Their purpose in the sentence is to **link** the subject to a word following the verb that describes the subject (predicate adjective) or renames the subject (predicate nominative). These verbs are therefore usually called *linking verbs*.

The most common linking verb is to be, along with its various forms: *am, is, are, was, were, been, being*. These verbs simply declare the "existence" of the subject.

Besides *to be*, other linking verbs are *appear, become, feel, grow, look, taste, remain, seem, smell,* and *sound*. Most of these verbs can also be action verbs. However, when they express a "state of being," they are linking verbs. You can usually tell if they are serving as linking verbs if you could substitute a form of the verb *to be* for them in the sentence.

☞**EXAMPLES OF LINKING VERBS:**

Mrs. Lindy *is* our teacher.

"Is" links the subject, "Mrs. Lindy," to the predicate nominative, "teacher."

She *seemed* happy to sing during the program.

"Seemed" could be replaced by "was"; both express the subject's "state of being."

This food *tastes* strange.

"Tastes" could be replaced by "is"; both "link" the subject, "food" to the predicate adjective, "strange."

■ *Helping Verbs*

The third type of verb is the *helping verb*, sometimes also called an *auxiliary verb* because it is mostly just an "extra" verb helping the main verb. Together, a helping verb and a main verb make up a **verb phrase**. Helping verbs do not express action or link the subject to other words in the predicate. Their purpose is to assist the main verb to complete its statement about the subject's action or state of being.

The most common helping verbs are *to have, to be,* and *to do.* Other common helping verbs are *can, could, may, might, must, ought, shall, should, will, would.* Less common are *dare, let, need, used.* Some helping verbs can stand alone as action or linking verbs.

☞**EXAMPLES OF HELPING VERBS:**

Mary *has* gone to bed for the night.

I *could* help you with that.

You *must* call the police at once.

We *shall be* going as soon as possible.

Jeremy *did* return the book as soon as he *could* (return it).

✎ **EXERCISE** Underline all the verbs in the following sentences. Above the verb, write **A** if the verb is an *action verb,* **L** if the verb is a *linking verb,* or **H** if the verb is a *helping verb.*

       H   H   A   L
1. I have been studying the Bible all my life because it is the source of much guidance.

           H H A
2. His name shall be called John.

           H L
3. His name shall be John.

      A
4. They have little money.

      H   A
5. They have had more money in the past.

     A   A
6. He does his homework immediately when he gets home from school.

          A   A   A
7. His mother does wonder what makes him so eager.

          H A
8. That bicycle was given to him by his grandmother.

           A   A
9. The telephone rang six times before he answered it.

     H A
10. I have lost all memory of that incident.

           A   A   A
11. The boys enjoyed computer games, but they knew that they wasted too much time with them.

     H   H A   L
12. We should have won the game, but the referee was unfair.

       L   A   A
13. Everyone was sad that the game ended the way it did.

        L   A
14. The day seemed brighter after we received the good news.

15. This bread <u>smells</u> moldy.
           L

16. Whenever the emergency crew <u>sounds</u> that alarm, it <u>sounds</u> frightening to me.

17. He <u>may</u> <u>find</u> himself in trouble if he <u>continues</u> that course of action.

LESSON 4: WORDS THAT MODIFY—ADJECTIVES

> **An ADJECTIVE is a part of speech that modifies a noun or pronoun.**

Adjectives are words that **modify** nouns or pronouns. The word *"modify"* means *to limit.* Therefore, a **modifier** is a word or group of words which describe or limit the meaning of other words or phrases. Adjectives modify or limit nouns and pronouns by making their meanings more exact. For example, the noun *car* is quite general and could refer to any of millions of cars in the world. If we modify the word *car* with the adjective *red*, we have eliminated from discussion all cars except those painted red. If we further modify the word *car* with the adjective *new*, we have narrowed the field even more. If we also add the adjective *my* (actually a pronoun used as an adjective), we have limited the subject to one automobile: *my new, red car.*

Adjectives answer the questions <u>*what kind?*</u> <u>*which one?*</u> <u>*how many?*</u> or <u>*how much?*</u> about the nouns or pronouns they modify or describe.

WHAT KIND?	WHICH ONE(S)?	HOW MANY?	HOW MUCH?
a **difficult** task	the **only** opportunity	**two dozen** oranges	**some** sugar
a **small** contribution	the **fourth** window	**one more** competitor	**less** rainfall
bottled water	the **youngest** child	**no** excuses	**more** sympathy
the **purple** flower	**those** people	a **thousand** times	**larger** amount
the **light, green** jacket	the **last** moment	a **few** candidates	the **most** credibility
the **cold, steel** blade	this **best** effort	**many** regulations	the **least** appeal

OTHER WORDS USED AS ADJECTIVES

Some words which may be other parts of speech are used as adjectives.

■ Possessive Pronouns

Certain pronouns, sometimes called **possessive pronouns**, function as adjectives, usually answering the question *which one(s)?*. These include: <u>*my*</u>, <u>*our*</u>, <u>*your*</u>, <u>*her*</u>, <u>*his*</u>, <u>*its*</u>, and <u>*their*</u>. Another class of pronouns, known as **demonstrative pronouns**, also may serve as adjectives, usually answering the question *which one(s)?* These include: *this, that, these* and *those.* Also, **indefinite pronouns**, such as <u>*many*</u>, <u>*some*</u>, <u>*every*</u>, <u>*most*</u>, etc., may be used as adjectives. (Demonstrative and indefinite pronouns are not always used as adjectives, however. Sometimes they are used strictly as pronouns; that is, as noun substitutes.)

■ *Articles*

The English language has three common small words called *articles*, which are technically *adjectives*. These three little words are *a, an,* and *the.* They are adjectives because they limit, or modify, nouns and pronouns. You can see some examples of their use in the table above. **In this workbook, when you are asked to identify adjectives, you may ignore all articles.**

■ *Numbers*

You will also notice from the table above that *numbers* can be adjectives when they modify nouns or pronouns. (Numbers are not *always* used as adjectives, however.)

■ *Nouns*

Sometimes *nouns* may function as adjectives when they limit or describe other nouns or pronouns. (Of course, nouns are not *always* used as adjectives.)

☞**EXAMPLES OF ADJECTIVES:**

The Smiths bought an *expensive, new* boat.

In this sentence, two adjectives modify the same noun, "boat."

Those small boys live in *my* neighborhood.

In this sentence, we have a demonstrative pronoun (those) and an adjective (small) modifying the noun "boys" and a possessive pronoun (my) modifying the noun "neighborhood."

We have a *video* player and a *television* set in *our entertainment* center.

In this sentence, the nouns "video," "television," and "entertainment" are used as adjectives. The possessive pronoun "our" is also used as an adjective.

✎ **EXERCISE A** Underline all the words that serve as adjectives in the following sentences. Draw an arrow to the noun or pronoun that each adjective modifies. *(Do not underline the articles.)*

1. It was a cold, snowy day when we left.

2. Unprotected hands can freeze on a blustery winter day.

3. Autumn leaves come in many colors.

4. Spring is my favorite time of year.

5. Summer days often include leisurely activities, but our work must also go on.

6. We sat on a quiet hillside for fifteen minutes, watching the brilliant sunset.

7. Thunder clouds arose on the distant horizon.

8. Most people enjoy some kind of outdoor sport during every season of the year.

9. A pleasant breeze blew along our tree-lined street.

10. The hand of a wise and provident God can be seen in the created world.

PREDICATE ADJECTIVES

Usually adjectives are placed right before the nouns or pronouns they modify. Sometimes, however, adjectives follow a linking verb and describe the subject of the verb. When adjectives follow linking verbs and modify the subject, they are called *predicate adjectives* because they are located in the predicate section of the sentence.

☞**EXAMPLES OF PREDICATE ADJECTIVES:**

My teacher is *patient*.

She became *sad* when she heard the bad news.

The disciples were *joyous* to learn of Jesus' resurrection, but some were *doubtful*.

✎ **EXERCISE B** Underline the predicate adjectives in the following sentences. Double-underline the linking verbs or verb phrases. Draw an arrow from the predicate adjective to the subject it modifies.

1. They are always late.

2. Synthetic rubber is useful for many products.

3. That pie smells delicious.

4. Food always seems tastier on a picnic.

5. Adjectives are usually easy to identify.

6. Everyone should be careful when crossing a street.

7. A man should not be wise in his own eyes.

8. She <u>was</u> unacquainted with the folk music of Bulgaria.

9. The hostages <u>remained</u> hopeful about their release.

10. That <u>sounds</u> encouraging.

11. She <u>was</u> lonesome during her weeks at summer camp.

12. Toby's comments <u>were</u> constructive.

✎ **EXERCISE C** Adjectives can sometimes (but not always) be identified by their *endings*. Below are a number of word endings which are commonly associated with adjectives. Some examples are given. Write another example for each in the blank.

-y	muddy, seedy,	*sunny*	*-ous*	vigorous, courageous,	*contagious*
-ful	sinful, helpful,	*useful*	*-ish*	brownish, Swedish,	*Polish*
-less	useless, faithless,	*sinless*	*-al*	optional, cordial,	*final*
-en	rotten, molten,	*eaten*	*-ic*	comic, artistic,	*Arabic*
-able	likable, desirable,	*trainable*	*-ary*	secondary, contrary,	
-ible	gullible, eligible,	*controlible*	*-some*	troublesome, lonesome,	*handsome*
-ive	passive, permissive,	*massive*	*-ly**	manly, lonely,	*friendly*

Note: Be careful not to confuse adjectives ending in *-ly* with the more common adverbs that have this same ending. We will study adverbs in the next lesson. REMEMBER: Adjectives are words that modify only nouns and pronouns. If the *-ly* word cannot be used to modify a noun or pronoun, it is not an adjective.

LESSON 5: WORDS THAT MODIFY—ADVERBS

> **An ADVERB is a part of speech that modifies a verb, adjective, or another adverb.**

Adverbs, like adjectives, are also words that modify (describe, limit, or in some other way make the meaning more nearly exact). Adverbs are distinguished from adjectives by the kinds of words that they modify. You will recall from the previous lesson that adjectives modify nouns and pronouns. Adverbs modify verbs, adjectives, or other adverbs.

Adverbs usually answer such questions as *how? how much? to what extent? how often? when? where?* or *in which way?* about the words that they modify. The chart below lists some examples of adverbs which answer these questions.

HOW? IN WHICH WAY?	HOW MUCH? TO WHAT EXTENT?	WHEN? HOW OFTEN?	WHERE?	OTHERS
happily, loudly, slowly, sadly, boldly, well, completely, lovingly, sinfully, patiently, warmly, somehow	very, more, only, quite, nearly, particularly, almost, somewhat, too, hardly, scarcely, so, especially, largely, not	always, never, now, once, later, yearly, often, annually, soon, twice, sometimes, then, usually, seldom, finally	here, nowhere, out, somewhere, away, back, around, there, outside, elsewhere, behind, anywhere, up	yes, no, perhaps, maybe, however, nevertheless, furthermore, moreover

☞**EXAMPLES OF ADVERBS IN SENTENCES:**

We went ***out*** for a walk in the woods. *(went where?)*

They ***always*** display ***such*** good manners. *(display how often?; good to what extent?)*

The apostles spoke ***boldly*** about Christ. *(spoke how?)*

You should ***not*** tell lies about me. *(should tell to what extent?)*

Take your wild stories ***elsewhere***. *(take where?)*

ADVERB ENDINGS

Adverbs can often, but not always, be recognized by their endings. The most common ending for adverbs is the suffix *-ly*. Almost any adjective can be changed into an adverb by adding the ending *-ly*. (Remember, however, not to confuse adjectives which themselves end in *-ly* with adverbs.) Adjectives ending with *-y* must sometimes have the "*y*" changed to "*i*" before the *-ly* is added. *(happy ⇒ happily; calm ⇒ calmly; neat ⇒ neatly; sudden ⇒ suddenly)*

Other endings for adverbs are *-wise* and *-ways*. Adding these endings to certain nouns will turn the nouns into adverbs. *(length ⇒ lengthwise; side ⇒ sideways)*

ADVERBS VS. PREPOSITIONS

Some words can be used as both adverbs and prepositions. You cannot tell the difference by their spelling. You can tell the difference only by the way they are used. If the word is followed by a noun, it is probably a preposition. If it is not followed by a noun, it is an adverb.

☞**EXAMPLES:**

> The smoke went *up*. (Adverb, answering *where?*)
>
> The smoke went *up* the chimney. (Preposition. The whole prepositional phrase is used as an adverb.)

INTENSIFIERS

Certain adverbs which answer the question *how much?* are sometimes called **intensifiers**. These adverbs include *very* and a number of other words which mean about the same thing as *very*. Adverbs in the *"very group"* include *really, so, exceedingly, quite, right, downright, extremely, rather, thoroughly,* and others.

☞**EXAMPLES OF INTENSIFIERS IN USE:**

The morning was *very* cold.	They behaved *so* wickedly.
You are *quite* wrong about that.	That was *really* stupid.
He was *rather* free with his insults.	Your song was *thoroughly* enjoyable.
They were *downright* nasty.	That slope is *extremely* dangerous.
You did a *right* fine job today, young man.	

✎ **EXERCISE A** Underline all the adverbs in the following sentences. Draw an arrow from the adverb to the verb (verb phrase), adjective, or adverb that it modifies.

1. Come <u>in</u>.

2. Leave your wet boots outside.

3. Place your empty cans here.

4. The rain fell heavily today, and more rain is expected tomorrow.

5. They lived happily in their new surroundings.

6. That accusation is not entirely new.

7. His help was voluntarily given, and he was highly praised for his compassion.

8. "Man is born unto trouble, as the sparks fly upward" (Job 5:7).

9. They left yesterday on an especially long vacation trip.

10. Our parents seldom quarrel.

11. They deal with each other's shortcomings patiently and lovingly.

12. "Sooner or later everyone sits down to a banquet of consequences" (R.L. Stevenson).

13. Jim is unusually quiet tonight.

14. She was very beautifully dressed for her portrait.

✎ **EXERCISE B** If the words in **dark print** in the following sentences are adverbs, write *adv.* above them. If they are adjectives, write *adj.* above them. When in doubt, look for the word(s) being modified. REMEMBER: Adjectives modify nouns or pronouns; adverbs modify verbs, adjectives, or other adverbs. Also, do not confuse predicate adjectives for adverbs just because they follow verbs.

1. The *adj.*
    The **early** bird gets the worm.

2. They awoke **early** this morning.

3. We ate our food **fast** because we were **late**.

4. He is a **fast** runner; I run **quite slowly** by comparison.

5. I have **not** practiced my **piano** lessons **very often lately**.

6. We took a **leisurely** walk around the park; our dogs trotted **leisurely** behind us.

7. My mother says that my father drives **too fast**.

8. She learned her lessons **well** and now feels **quite good** about it.

9. He walked **right** past me without saying a word.

10. Amy is **usually friendly** but **often** speaks **timidly** when she is with people she doesn't know.

11. Thank you for the **lovely** flowers you **so lovingly** sent for my birthday.

12. I **first** told you I could come, but, on **second** thought, I do not believe I can.

13. I am **still** waiting for a **more polite** reply.

✎ **EXERCISE C** Change the following adjectives into adverbs.

messy	_messily_	perfect	_____
clear	_____	hopeful	_____
careful	_____	smooth	_____
near	_____	violent	_____
plentiful	_____	patient	_____
easy	_____	large	_____
pretty	_____	uncanny	_____
rash	_____	dangerous	_____

LESSON 6: WORDS THAT RELATE—PREPOSITIONS

> **A PREPOSITION is a part of speech that shows the relationship of a noun or pronoun to some other word in a sentence.**

To show the relationship of ideas expressed in a sentence, we often need special words designed to indicate relationship. *Prepositions* often serve this purpose. The word *"preposition"* itself literally means *"position before,"* indicating that prepositions usually come before nouns or pronouns to show what relationship they have to other words or parts of the sentence. In this way, prepositions are in the class of words that "join."

Let's say, for example, that you wish to tell something about the relationship between a **book** and a **bookcase**. You could say that the book is **on** the bookcase, **under** the bookcase, **above** the bookcase, **behind** the bookcase, **near** the bookcase, **in** the bookcase, **beside** the bookcase, or **within** the bookcase. Each of these words—*on, under, above, behind, near, in, beside, within*—is a preposition showing a different positional relationship of the bookcase to the book.

The noun or pronoun following the preposition—that is, the word whose relationship is being shown—is called the **object of the preposition**. An object of a preposition must always be a noun or pronoun (or another word or group of words used as a noun, as you will learn later in your studies of grammar).

☞**EXAMPLES OF PREPOSITIONS IN SENTENCES:** *(Objects are underlined.)*

There was a skunk *underneath* the shed.

They bought a lovely home *near* the beach.

Inside the box was the most beautiful vase I have ever seen.

Here is a list of the most common prepositions:

PRESUPPOSITIONS			
aboard	beside	into	than
about	besides	like	through
above	between	near	throughout
across	beyond	notwithstanding	till
after	by	of	to
against	by reason of	off	toward
along	by way of	on	under
alongside	concerning	onto	underneath
amid	contrary to	opposite	until
amidst	despite	out of	unto
among	down	outside	up
around	due to	over	upon
at	during	past	with
atop	ere	per	within
because of	except	pertaining to	without
before	excepting	regarding	worth
behind	for	regardless of	
below	in	save	
beneath	inside	since	

A preposition and its object (together with any words which may modify the object) make up a *prepositional phrase.* Proper *word order* is important in a prepositional phrase.

Generally speaking, it is considered good grammar for the object to *follow* the preposition. In a few situations, however, this may result in some awkwardness. The best rule is: if the prepositional phrase can smoothly be written or spoken with the object following the preposition, use that arrangement. Be especially careful not to end a sentence with a preposition, unless awkwardness or lack of clarity dictates otherwise.

☞**QUESTIONABLE:**

Which house do you live *in*?

He is the man *whom* I am working *for*.

☞**BETTER:**

In which house do you live?

He is the man *for whom* I am working.

☞**AWKWARD:**

On which shirt do you have?

For what do you take me?

Do *of whatever* you are capable.

☞**ACCEPTABLE:**

Which shirt do you have *on*?

What do you take me *for*?

Do *whatever* you are capable *of*.

✎ **EXERCISE A** Fill the blanks with fitting prepositions. Try to use as many different prepositions as you can. Underline the objects of the prepositions you write.

1. We walked ____*across*____ the <u>bridge</u> which was built ____*over*____ the <u>river</u>.

2. They have eaten four bowls of popcorn _____ the past hour.

3. Hang that picture right _____ the other one.

4. Don't expect the shipment _____ Tuesday.

5. You have misused this word _____ your composition.

6. I used to hide _____ my blankets whenever it would thunder.

7. You are required to comply _____ all regulations.

8. _____ the sake _____ your reputation, don't do such things.

9. Our club collected trash which had been thrown _____ the highway.

10. They chose everyone _____ me.

11. Tell the cat to get _____ the couch.

12. Take the road that runs _____ the lake and the railroad track.

13. "Where two or three are gathered _____ my name, I will be _____ them," Jesus said.

14. "Walk _____ me, and be thou perfect," God said.

15. I have known _____ your illness _____ some time.

16. Since you came to be _____ me, I have been much happier.

17. "Who is sitting _____ us?" I asked, pointing over my shoulder.

18. That subject is _____ my understanding.

19. One picture is _____ a thousand words.

20. He was driving 55 miles _____ hour.

21. He stepped _____ the stage and _____ the spotlight.

22. He lives in the house just _____ the corner _____ ours.

✎ **EXERCISE B** Underline all the prepositional phrases in Psalm 1 *(NKJV)* below.

Blessed is the man who walks not <u>in the counsel</u> <u>of the ungodly</u>, nor stands in the path of sinners, nor sits in the seat of the scornful; but his delight is in the law of the Lord, and in His law he meditates day and night. He shall be like a tree planted by the rivers of water, that brings forth its fruit in its season, whose leaf also shall not wither; and whatever he does shall prosper.

The ungodly are not so, but are like the chaff which the wind drives away. Therefore the ungodly shall not stand in the judgment, nor sinners in the congregation of the righteous.

For the Lord knows the way of the righteous, but the way of the ungodly shall perish.

LESSON 7: WORDS THAT JOIN—CONJUNCTIONS

> **A CONJUNCTION is a part of speech used to connect words or groups of words such as phrases and clauses.**

A *conjunction* is a word—sometimes several words—used to link or connect words, phrases, clauses, or (occasionally) sentences. Conjunctions are classified into two main groups: *coordinating* and *subordinating*.

Coordinating conjunctions join elements which are of **equal** grammatical rank. By "equal," we mean that the elements do not depend upon each other grammatically but can stand alone with full meaning. *Subordinating* conjunctions join elements which are **unequal** in grammatical ranking. By "unequal," we mean that one of the elements joined is not complete on its own but depends upon the other element for its full meaning.

There are three types of coordinating conjunctions:

■ *Simple or pure conjunctions*

These are the best known and most commonly used conjunctions: *and, but, or, nor, neither* and (in some situations) *yet.*

■ *Correlative conjunctions*

These are always used in pairs. The most common are *both…and, either…or, neither…nor,* and *not only…but also.*

■ *Conjunctive adverbs*

These are adverbs that are used to join independent sections (clauses) of a sentence or to join two sentences. The most common are:

COMMON CONJUNCTIVE ADVERBS			
also	furthermore	likewise	otherwise
anyhow	hence	meanwhile	so
as a result	however	moreover	still
besides	in addition	namely	then
consequently	in fact	nevertheless	therefore
for example	indeed	notwithstanding	thus

In this lesson, we will consider only the three types of coordinating conjunctions. Subordinating conjunctions are more difficult and are used in a certain type of sentence which will be discussed in the next unit.

SIMPLE CONJUNCTIONS

When using simple coordinating conjunctions, be sure that you choose the right one to fit the meaning of your expression.

and	Used to connect elements that are *along the same line or in the same direction of thought*
but, yet	Used to connect *contrasting elements*

or	Used to connect elements showing *positive alternatives*
nor, neither	Used to connect elements showing *negative alternatives*

☞**EXAMPLES:**

WRONG: I thought you would like it, **but** you did.

RIGHT: I thought you would like it, **and** you did.

WRONG: I thought you would like it, **and** you didn't.

RIGHT: I thought you would like it, **but** you didn't.

WRONG: I did not think you would like it, **or** I did not want you to.

RIGHT: I did not think you would like it, **nor** (or **neither**) did I want you to.

CORRELATIVE CONJUNCTIONS

Use the *correlative conjunctions* **both...and** to "relate" only **two** elements or ideas.

☞**EXAMPLES:**

WRONG: **Both** the president, the secretary, **and** the treasurer were absent.

Some grammar experts also disapprove of the use of **neither...nor, either...or,** and **not only...but also** to relate more than two elements or ideas. Others find no fault with such use. Logic and clearness are the main yardsticks to use when deciding how to use these conjunctions.

QUESTIONABLE:

           Neither Utah, Kansas, Oregon **nor** Iowa are east of the Mississippi River.

BETTER: Utah, Kansas, Oregon, and Iowa are all west of the Mississippi River.

Neither and **nor** go together, but not **neither** and **or.**

WRONG: Miriam is **neither** the fastest **or** the slowest runner on the team.

The biggest problem people have with correlative conjunctions is using them to connect elements or ideas which are **not equal** (or "**parallel**").

WRONG: You may eat **either** the cake **or** you may eat the pie.

The conjunctions connect a noun [cake] with a clause [you may eat the pie].

RIGHT: You may eat **either** the cake **or** the pie.

           Either you may eat the cake **or** you may eat the pie.

CONJUNCTIVE ADVERBS

The only purpose of conjunctive adverbs is to join two independent clauses (stand-alone sections) of a sentence or to connect the thoughts in two separate sentences. **Do not** use conjunctive adverbs to join words or incomplete groups of words.

☞EXAMPLES:

WRONG: I like to eat hamburgers, pizza, *also* spaghetti.

Bob and Mary, *however* not Peter, are members of our team.

I did my homework, *then* went to bed.

RIGHT: I did my homework; *then* I went to bed.

He is not here now; *however*, he will be home in about an hour.

He is a good writer. *Indeed*, he is one of the best writers in our class.

You must learn the following special rules about **punctuating** conjunctive adverbs in a sentence. The rule has two parts:

Rule 1.1	If the CONJUNCTIVE ADVERB has *one syllable*, put a semicolon (;) ahead of it and no punctuation after it.

☞EXAMPLE:

It is important to keep teeth healthy; *so* brush them after every meal.

Rule 1.2	If the CONJUNCTIVE ADVERB has *two or more syllables*, put a semicolon (;) ahead of it and a comma (,) after it.

☞EXAMPLE:

I have lost my pencil; *however*, that is not my only problem.

To state these rules more concisely, **all** conjunctive adverbs are *preceded by a semicolon*, but only those with **two or more syllables** are *followed by a comma*.

INTERRUPTERS

Words that may be used as conjunctive adverbs are sometimes not used to directly connect independent clauses. In some cases, these adverbs are used merely as sentence **interrupters**. Even in these cases, they are usually indirectly connecting a thought in one sentence to a thought in another sentence. When used as interrupters, they are punctuated only with *commas*.

☞EXAMPLES:

She told me, *however*, that I should not worry.

The evidence, *moreover*, was clearly against him.

The woman's flower garden was, *in fact*, very pretty.

✎ **EXERCISE A** Fill the blanks with *a simple conjunction, correlative conjunctions,* or *a conjunctive adverb* that fits the meaning of the sentence. Watch for punctuation clues which may make a difference in which word you choose.

1. Benjamin _____*and*_____ Seth both have been elected as class officers.

2. You may choose _____ a red balloon _____ a blue one.

3. You are my friend, _____ I cannot show favorites.

4. You are my friend; _____, I cannot show favorites.

5. _____ rain _____ any other bad weather will discourage a determined football team.

6. Choose between him _____ me.

7. I will accept no if's, and's, _____ but's from you on this subject.

8. Anyone wishing to reproduce _____ quote portions of my book may do so.

9. This music is enjoyable; _____, it is very enjoyable.

10. Please pick up some milk at the store. _____ buy some bread.

11. Miss California is _____ pretty _____ talented.

12. She has betrayed me, _____ I love her.

13. Our school colors are aqua, black, _____ white.

14. You _____ I make a great team.

15. The glassy look in his eyes suggests that he is _____ dazed _____ day-dreaming.

16. I baptize you in the name of the Father, the Son, _____ the Holy Spirit.

EXERCISE B Underline the coordinating conjunctions in the following sentences. In the blanks, tell which kind of coordinating conjunctions they are: **SC** *(simple conjunction)*, **CC** *(correlative conjunctions)*, or **CA** *(conjunctive adverb)*. If there are two or more simple conjunctions or conjunctive adverbs in a sentence, identify them in the order in which they occur.

1. He cannot pitch well, <u>but</u> he is a good outfielder. __SC__

2. I will read the book; furthermore, I plan to do a book report on it. _____

3. She put not only chocolate syrup but also whipped cream on my sundae. _____

4. Please come either tomorrow or the next day. _____

5. My mother has two prayers; namely, that her children grow up to serve the Lord and that she and my father may live a long life together. _____ _____ _____

6. He reads his Bible and prays every morning. _____

7. I do not always understand what God is doing, yet I will trust in Him. _____

8. April did not want her sister's help, nor did she ask for it. _____

9. Both Jennifer and her cousin have red hair; in fact, they look alike in many respects. _____ _____

EXERCISE C Rewrite the sentences below, correcting the errors. You may add or subtract words to make the sentence correct.

1. Not only does he eat large meals but also desserts.

   _He eats not only large meals but also desserts._____

2. Neither my brother or I likes cauliflower.

   _____

   _____

3. Lenny, also Lynne, will serve on the committee.

   _____

   _____

4. You may have liked the book, and I certainly did not.

_____

_____

5. I could not attend the meeting tonight, however I will be there tomorrow night.

_____

_____

6. I hurt my foot, thus lost the race.

_____

_____

7. I told you not to eat my piece of cake, and you did.

_____

_____

8. It's raining; so, take your umbrella.

_____

_____

9. I saw one bird then two or three more came into view.

_____

_____

10. Both my legs, my back, and my neck ached after skiing.

_____

_____

11. They wondered; however; why no one came.

_____

_____

LESSON 8: WORDS THAT EXCLAIM—INTERJECTIONS

> **An INTERJECTION is a part of speech that makes an independent exclamation.**

The eighth part of speech is the *interjection*, a word that makes a mild or major exclamation but has little connection to the rest of the sentence in which it is contained. In fact, in some cases, it can stand alone as a "sentence" of its own.

☞**EXAMPLES:**

Oops!

Hey, why are you taking my suitcase?

Behold! I bring you good tidings of great joy!

It was then, *alas*, that our troubles began.

The following is a list of the most common interjections of the English language:

COMMON INTERJECTIONS				
ah	boo	halloo	listen	tush
aha	botheration	hello	lo	tut
ahem	bravo	hey	my	what
ahoy	certainly	ho	nonsense	why
alas	eh	ha	O	whoa
amen	encore	huh	off	whoopee
attention	eureka	hurrah	oh	woe
ay	excellent	hurray	ouch	yahoo
bah	goodbye	hush	pshaw	yea
behold	goodness	indeed	so	yippee

Various profanities, blasphemies, and vulgarities are also uttered as interjections by some writers and speakers who care little for the Bible's warnings against such speech (see Matthew 5:33-37, James 5:12).

The main grammatical consideration in using interjections is to **avoid overuse**. These words are intended to add special emphasis to our communications. Overusing them blunts their effectiveness and may be a sign of a strained or immature style of communication.

As you can see, some of the words in the list above can also be another part of speech. For example, *listen* is a verb; *nonsense* and *goodness* are nouns; *certainly* is an adverb; and *excellent* is an adjective. When such words are used as interjections, they may stand alone. However, even in such cases they may be serving their purpose as another part of speech, with the full context implied. Verbs used as interjections are often abbreviated sentences in which a subject is implied and the verb is in "command" (imperative) form.

☞**EXAMPLES:**

"Would you like to come to my party?"
"Certainly!" (Meaning: I *certainly* would like to come to your party.)

"How was my essay?"
"Excellent!" (Meaning: Your essay was *excellent*.)

"Listen!" (Meaning: [You must] *listen*.)

Pure interjections are those which do not double as some other part of speech: *aha, O, alas,* etc.

Interjections may be followed by an **exclamation point** or, in the case of a mild expression, by a **comma** or **period**. A few interjections may be followed by a **question mark**. If you use an exclamation point or question mark after an interjection, the next word should usually be capitalized.

☞**EXAMPLES:**

Aha! We now understand your scheme.

Oh, please don't feel embarrassed.

My! What a handsome little fellow you are!

What? You have never heard this song?

So? Am I supposed to care anything about that?

✎ **EXERCISE** Write five sentences using interjections. (See examples above.)

1. _____

_____

2. _____

_____

3. _____

_____

4. _____

_____

5. _____

_____

LESSON 9: UNIT REVIEW

✎ **EXERCISE A** In the blank following each sentence, identify which part of speech the word in **dark print** is. Identify this word as a *noun, pronoun, verb, adjective, adverb, preposition, conjunction,* or *interjection.*

1. There was a **calm** before the storm. _____*noun*_____

2. She has a **calm** spirit. _____

3. **Calm** yourself. _____

4. He takes a **daily** walk. _____

5. He walks **daily** for exercise. _____

6. Mother sent the children **outdoors** to play. _____

7. I love most **outdoor** sports. _____

8. Camping in the great **outdoors** is a good way to relax. _____

9. He showed great **strength** of character. _____

10. The carpenter tried to **strengthen** the stairway. _____

11. You have always been a good **friend** to me. _____

12. You have always been **friendly** to me. _____

13. I **will be** in the basement for a few minutes. _____

14. I will be in the basement **for** a few minutes. _____

15. **I** will be in the basement for a few minutes. _____

16. I will be **in** the basement for a few minutes. _____

17. I will be in the **basement** for a few minutes. _____

18. **Hello**. How are you today? _____

19. We are coming **down** to see you tomorrow. _____

20. He climbed **down** the ladder. _____

✎ **EXERCISE B** In the blank, tell which part of speech is needed to complete the sentence. **Do not write the missing word itself,** but write the name of the part of speech that is needed: *noun, pronoun, verb, adjective, adverb, preposition, conjunction,* or *interjection.*

1. It was a _____*adverb*_____ cold night.

2. Franklin is a _____ child.

3. She _____ the ball.

4. The birds built nests _____ the eaves of the barn.

5. Sunday is the _____ day of the week.

6. When Bob and I call for your answer, please give _____ one we can understand.

7. _____! What muddy feet you have!

8. Jenny's experience gives _____ many advantages over her competitors.

9. _____ the first time in my life, I have won a contest.

10. Jon _____ Jan are twins.

11. The Lord is _____ Shepherd; I shall not want.

12. The soldier died _____ in his buddy's arms.

13. The river runs _____ to the sea.

14. The moon _____ over the lake, casting bright sparkles on the waves.

15. Put your books _____ the table by the door.

16. It was a _____ concert.

17. "Give _____ all your money," the robber said.

18. The _____ is ringing.

19. That tree _____ larger than the other one.

20. She bought a _____ _____ for the party.

21. _____ _____ nouns are both nominatives.

✎ **EXERCISE C** Complete the following sentences.

1. A(n) _____ is the name of a person, place, thing, quality or idea.

2. A word used in place of a noun is a(n) _____.

3. A word that makes a statement concerning the action of a subject is a(n) _____.

4. A word that modifies a noun or pronoun is a(n) _____.

5. A word that modifies a verb, adjective, or adverb is a(n) _____.

6. A verb that expresses a state or condition of being is a(n) _____ verb.

7. A verb that assists an action verb or linking verb to complete its meaning is a(n) _____ verb.

8. A predicate _____ follows a linking verb and renames the subject.

9. A predicate _____ follows a linking verb and describes (modifies) the subject.

10. A group of words that begins with a preposition and ends with a noun or pronoun is called a _____ _____.

11. The noun or pronoun that follows a preposition is the _____ of the preposition.

12. A word that expresses an exclamation but is largely unrelated to the rest of the sentence is a(n) _____.

13. Adverbs that serve as conjunctions are called _____ _____.

14. Conjunctions that are always used in pairs are _____ _____.

15. Conjunctive adverbs with two or more syllables must be punctuated by preceding them with a _____ and following them with a _____.

Unit 2
Building Sentences

In the previous unit, we learned about the eight *parts of speech*. We learned that all words belong to one or more of these eight categories of utterance. When we use these parts of speech, however, we try to use them in a way that makes sense. Using words without any order results in gibberish or nonsense. Nonsense does not communicate our thoughts in ways which other people can understand. When we write or speak, therefore, we do so in an orderly way. We use sentences.

LESSON 10: WHAT MAKES A SENTENCE?

> **A SENTENCE is a group of words that expresses a complete thought.**

All word groups are not sentences. Below are four groups of words. Study them carefully.

1. to better himself
2. Tom's friend Rick
3. by studying hard
4. sincerely tries

Group No. 1 suggests that someone has a motive to do something for the purpose of bettering himself. But it does not tell us who that someone is or what he has done, is doing, or will do to better himself. It is not a complete thought.

Group No. 2 suggests that Tom has a friend named Rick. But we do not know anything about Rick or what he does or thinks. This group of words is not a complete thought.

Group No. 3 suggests that someone may be trying to accomplish something by working hard at his or her studies. But we do not know who is trying to do this or what he or she is trying to accomplish. This group of words is not a complete thought.

Group No. 4 suggests the idea of trying in a sincere way. But it does not tell us who or what is trying or what is being tried. It does not suggest a complete thought.

We can try to put these groups of words together in hopes that the incomplete thoughts might become more complete and express some meaning.

For example, we might write:

sincerely tried by studying hard Tom's friend Rick to better himself

While this might suggest something more to us than the individual groups of words alone told us, we still are confused. This larger grouping still does not express a meaningful, complete thought. It is close to being nonsense. To express a complete and meaningful thought in English requires us to put our words in a certain order. For example, if we put the four groups of words together as follows, we understand a complete thought:

Tom's friend Rick sincerely tried to better himself by studying hard.

We could also put the groupings together in the following ways, because the English language is flexible enough to allow for some variety of expression:

By studying hard, Tom's friend Rick sincerely tried to better himself.

Tom's friend Rick, by studying hard, sincerely tried to better himself.

Tom's friend Rick sincerely tried, by studying hard, to better himself.

You can see that at least one of the word groups—*by studying hard*—is capable of being placed in several locations with relation to the other groups. If you try to reshuffle the other groups, however, the result will be confusing. This shows us that when words and groups of words are put together, they must be done so in an orderly way if we hope to make a complete and meaningful statement. We call such a statement a *sentence*.

Two other things help us organize our thoughts into sentences. To show where a sentence (a complete thought) begins, we use a **capital letter** at the beginning of the first word. To show where the sentence (the complete thought) ends, we use a **punctuation mark** — a period (.), a question mark (?), or an exclamation point (!), depending on what kind of thought we are expressing.

We now have a complete definition of a sentence.

A sentence is a group of words that:
1. expresses a complete thought,
2. begins with a capital letter, and
3. ends with a mark of closing punctuation.

✎ **EXERCISE** Below are several groups of words without a beginning capital letter or any ending punctuation. In the blank at the left, write **S** if the group of words would be a sentence if properly capitalized and punctuated. Write **X** if the group of words are not a complete thought and therefore could not be a sentence.

___S___ 1. the message was a simple one

_____ 2. raised the microphone an inch or two

_____ 3. she began to sing a lovely melody

_____ 4. the man who owns the store

_____ 5. he was a person who enjoyed fishing

_____ 6. he reads several magazines every week

_____ 7. and have been sitting here ever since

_____ 8. in the following examples

_____ 9. she tries to study and get good grades

_____ 10. the telephone rang several times

_____ 11. we can be sure God hears us when we pray

_____ 12. my brother Bill is a good swimmer

_____ 13. fell from her horse

_____ 14. down by the old mill stream

_____ 15. white-water rafting is one of the most exciting sports

_____ 16. a smile is better than a frown

_____ 17. a wise son heeds his father's instruction

_____ 18. there goes one now

_____ 19. the way of the unfaithful is hard

_____ 20. a ring of gold on her finger

_____ 21. but as for me

_____ 22. they sang, praising and giving thanks to the Lord

_____ 23. some of the dogs

_____ 24. for a skater to fall occasionally

_____ 25. spoken words are remembered with more difficulty

_____ 26. made a list of the people in the class

_____ 27. make a list of the people in the class

_____ 28. did you say where you found your belt

_____29. now is the time for all good men to come to the aid of their party

_____30. the best-selling novel for this month

LESSON 11: SUBJECTS AND PREDICATES

To make a complete statement, a group of words must have a *subject* and a *predicate*. From this rule, we can say that every sentence must have at least these two elements.

> **The SUBJECT of a sentence is the word or group of words about which something is being said or written.**
>
> **The PREDICATE of a sentence is the word or group of words which says something about the subject.**

All of the words in a sentence belong either to the subject or the predicate. As the examples below show, the subject may be long or short and the predicate may consist of one word or many. The *length* of the subject or predicate—that is, the number of words in either—is not important. The important consideration is the *function* the words have in the sentence. Are they the words about which something is being said? If so, they are part of the subject. Are they the words which say something about the subject? If so, they are part of the predicate.

SUBJECT (Always includes at least one noun, pronoun, or group of words used as a noun)	PREDICATE (Always includes at least one verb)
His **temper**	**was** always on the verge of erupting.
The **boys** and **girls** in the seventh grade	**will have** their gym classes on separate days.
Jesus	wept.
Tomorrow	**is** another day.

✎ **EXERCISE A** Draw a vertical line (|) between the subject and the predicate of each of the following sentences.

1. My mother | baked me a birthday cake.

2. This toothpaste is my favorite.

3. Always happy, Trudy was a pleasant person to be around.

4. He is my only brother.

5. The members of the club agreed to meet again next week.

6. Smoke billowed out of the windows of the burning warehouse.

7. The youth group at church spent two weeks preparing for their mission trip.

8. A sentence consists of a subject and a predicate.

9. Dr. McDonald is a family physician.

10. A flashing red traffic signal means that drivers must stop before proceeding.

11. My brother and his wife are members of Valley Presbyterian Church.

12. We all had a hearty laugh after falling into the swimming pool.

13. Vigorous massage will improve blood circulation.

14. I was very nervous about my performance.

15. Nobody cares about anything anymore.

16. The gnats in our backyard are extremely bothersome.

17. You are cordially invited to attend the recital.

18. You can find him in his workshop on just about any evening.

19. The subject of a sentence must contain at least one noun, pronoun, or a group of words used as a noun.

20. My dog is lovable.

21. The company offered free samples to help promote its new product.

✎ **EXERCISE B** In the blank at the left of each sentence, write **S** if the word in **dark print** is part of the subject or **P** if it is part of the predicate.

_S_ 1. My history **book** has several interesting pictures about Civil War battles.

____ 2. The lost hikers **were found** safe but tired.

_____ 3. The train rolled on during the entire **night**.

_____ 4. Having been elected chairman, **Bob** called the meeting to order.

_____ 5. A motion **was made** to adjourn the meeting.

_____ 6. **Traveling** by car is usually cheaper than flying.

_____ 7. The Lord is **in His holy temple**.

_____ 8. He **flew** to Los Angeles with his parents.

_____ 9. I have no **objection** to your proposal.

_____10. Timothy hoped to find a summer **job**.

LESSON 12: MORE ABOUT SUBJECTS AND PREDICATES

In the previous lesson, you learned to identify the subjects and predicates of sentences. You learned that every word in a sentence must belong either to the subject or to the predicate.

The subjects and predicates you worked with in Lesson 10 are called *complete subjects* and *complete predicates* because each contains all the words in their share of the sentence. You should also learn to identify the *simple subject* and *simple predicate* of a sentence. Learn the following four definitions:

A SIMPLE SUBJECT is the main noun, pronoun (or group of words used as a noun) about which the sentence makes a statement.

A COMPLETE SUBJECT is the simple subject and certain words that modify it.

A SIMPLE PREDICATE is the main verb or verb phrase in the sentence.

A COMPLETE PREDICATE is the simple predicate and all the other words that make a statement about the subject.

Consider the following sentence:

Mary / sneezed.

This sentence is as simple as a sentence can get. It is a sentence because it contains the two necessary elements of a sentence—a **simple subject** *(Mary)* and a **simple predicate** *(sneezed)*.

Now consider this sentence:

Poor little Mary, who suffers from allergies in the springtime, / sneezed repeatedly into the handkerchief given to her by her grandmother.

This sentence is much longer, but all the words belong to one or the other of the two necessary elements of a sentence—the subject or the predicate.

The **complete subject** consists of the same simple subject *(Mary)*, plus two adjectives *(poor, little)* and a group of words used as an adjective *(who suffers from allergies in the springtime)* that all modify the simple subject. The simple subject is the main word naming the person about whom the sentence is making a statement. The rest of the words in the complete subject relate in some way to the simple subject.

The **complete predicate** consists of the same simple predicate *(sneezed)*, plus adverbs, phrases that are used as adverbs, and other groups of words related to the simple predicate and its modifiers *(repeatedly in the handkerchief given to her by her grandmother)*. The simple predicate is the verb which makes the main statement about the subject. The other words in the complete predicate relate in some way to the action of the verb and help the verb complete its statement about the subject.

COMPLETE SUBJECT	COMPLETE PREDICATE
All of your money	will be refunded if you are not fully satisfied.
Our after-school art club	is planning an exhibit of members' works.
My parents, who have been married for fifteen years,	are very precious to me.
All of the members of our basketball team	are tall.

A simple predicate may consist of a **single verb** or a **verb phrase**. A verb phrase is a main verb and any helping verbs connected to the main verb.

☞**EXAMPLES OF VERB PHRASES FORMING SIMPLE PREDICATES:**

Your radio **has been playing** nonstop all day.

The sound **was heard** throughout the building.

We **could see** the stage easily from our seats.

The Ten Commandments **should be memorized** by everyone.

✎ **EXERCISE** Underline the *complete subject* in each of the following sentences. Double-underline the *complete predicate*. Circle the *simple subject* and *simple predicate* in each sentence.

1. The(children) (left)the building in an orderly fashion during the fire drill.

2. Christian morality is important for self-government.

3. Uncle Anthony has promised to pay for my college education.

4. Zeal without knowledge often leads to fanaticism.

5. Truth will always be truth regardless of lack of understanding, disbelief, or ignorance. *(Stone)*

6. It is good to have things settled by faith before they are unsettled by feeling. *(Cowman)*

7. They that sow in tears shall reap in joy. *(Psalms)*

8. No army can withstand the strength of an idea whose time has come. *(Hugo)*

9. We consume our tomorrows fretting about our yesterdays. *(Persius)*

10. Our family has fond memories of our last vacation.

11. The time is 4 o'clock.

12. The quality shows in every product they make.

13. All of the children in kindergarten are under 6 years old.

14. Western civilization has been influenced profoundly by Christianity.

15. Some modern computers can be operated by the human voice.

16. My dog's name is Bushy.

17. Charles Dickens is the author of *Oliver Twist* and *David Copperfield*.

18. Documentary programs are becoming more popular on television.

19. Our flight will be arriving in San Francisco at 9:10 p.m.

20. The students at our school call their Bible-study group Campus Club.

LESSON 13: COMPOUND SUBJECTS AND PREDICATES

Many sentences have more than one subject and/or more than one verb. We call these subjects *compound subjects* and these verbs *compound verbs* or *compound predicates*.

> **A COMPOUND SUBJECT** consists of two or more subjects having the same verb.
>
> **A COMPOUND PREDICATE** consists of two or more verbs having the same subject.

☞**EXAMPLES OF COMPOUND SUBJECTS:**

Football and *baseball* are two of America's favorite sports.

Love, joy, peace, and *patience* are called "fruits of the Spirit."

A box *wrench* or a socket *wrench* can be used for this job.

A clean *sheet* of paper and a sharp *pencil* are all you will need for the test.

Compound subjects are usually joined by the simple conjunctions *and, or,* or *nor.* They may also be joined by correlative conjunctions such as *both...and, neither...nor,* or *either...or.*

☞**EXAMPLES OF COMPOUND PREDICATES:**

She *kissed* and *hugged* her parents before getting on the plane.

She *flew* to her destination but *took* a train back.

He *opened* the book, *read* a few words, and *closed* it again.

I neither *accept* your position nor *appreciate* it.

Compound predicates (verbs) are joined by the simple conjunctions *and, or, nor,* or *but,* or by correlative conjunctions.

Note: Notice that *commas* are used to separate compound subjects and compound verbs with *more than two* elements.

✎ **EXERCISE** Underline any compound subjects you find in the following sentences. Double-underline compound verbs or verb phrases. If a sentence has neither, leave it as it is.

1. My brother and I mowed and raked the lawn.

2. Wind and rain have caused erosion on that hillside.

3.   Swimming, canoeing, hiking, and archery were some of the activities offered at camp.

4.   Randy found a lost wallet and returned it to its owner.

5.   The money was missing and was never found.

6.   "Heaven and earth shall pass away, but my words shall not pass away" (Matthew 24:35).

7.   He has few enemies and many friends.

8.   Martin Luther, John Calvin, and John Knox led the Reformation and remain in high regard today among many Christians and other scholars.

9.   A boy and his dog are always good friends.

10. My cousins came for a visit and stayed for a week.

11. Mother washed, dried, and ironed my clothes.

12. The car was damaged beyond repair and was sent to the junkyard.

13. Both men and women played in the tournament.

14. The flood waters receded and returned to their normal channels.

15. Gary did his research, prepared an outline, wrote his composition, and submitted it.

16. We drove through Ohio, Indiana, Illinois, and Iowa.

17. The cultures of the eastern and western hemispheres are quite different.

18. The librarian unpacked several new books, catalogued them, and placed them on a shelf.

19. My dad gave me my allowance but warned me not to spend it foolishly.

20. English and history are my favorite subjects.

21. I promise to repay your loan and will do so next week.

22. The telephone rang and rang but went unanswered.

23. Three boys and three girls were chosen to participate in the geography contest.

24. The science fair opened on Monday and closed on Thursday.

25. "Give me liberty or give me death!" (Patrick Henry).

26. Rob and Carl know the rules but have ignored them.

LESSON 14: SIMPLE AND COMPOUND SENTENCES

One way to classify sentences is by their structure. Sentences are classified three ways, according to their structure: *simple sentences, compound sentences,* and *complex sentences.* In this lesson, we will consider only *simple* and *compound sentences.*

> **A SIMPLE SENTENCE has one complete subject and one complete predicate, although either or both may be compound.**
>
> **A COMPOUND SENTENCE has two or more simple sentences joined by a conjunction or semicolon.**

A *simple sentence* may be long or short. It can have a single subject or a compound subject. It can have a single verb or a compound verb. But it will have only *one complete thought.*

☞**EXAMPLES OF SIMPLE SENTENCES:**

All of the following simple sentences have one complete subject and one complete predicate. (The complete subject and complete predicate are separated by a slash mark.)

Jane / talked all night. *(single subject and single verb)*

Jane and **Kelly / talked** all night. *(compound subject and single verb)*

Jane / talked and **laughed** all night. *(single subject and compound verb)*

Jane and **Kelly / talked** and **laughed** all night. *(compound subject and compound verb)*

A *compound sentence* may be long or short. It has two or more complete subjects and two or more complete predicates. It therefore has *two or more complete thoughts.* In other words, it is like two or more simple sentences joined together into one sentence. Each of the complete thoughts can have a single or compound subject and a single or compound verb.

In a compound sentence, each of the complete thoughts is called an **independent clause.** That means that if you separated the complete thoughts, each could stand alone (be independent) as a complete simple sentence in itself.

> **A CLAUSE is a group of words including a *subject* and *predicate* and forming a *part of a sentence.***

☞**EXAMPLES OF COMPOUND SENTENCES:**

All of the following compound sentences have *two complete thoughts* or *independent clauses*. In the illustrations, the clauses are separated by vertical lines (|). Each of the independent clauses has one complete subject and one complete predicate. In the illustrations, the subjects and predicates are separated by slash marks (/). The two clauses are joined by a simple conjunction, conjunctive adverb, or a semicolon. Notice that when a conjunction is used, it is preceded by a comma. When a conjunctive adverb is used, it is preceded by a semicolon and followed by a comma if it has two or more syllables. If no connecting word is used, the clauses are separated only by a semicolon.

The **grass** / **is** green, | *and* | the **sky** / **is** blue.

John and **Jim** / **are** in the seventh grade, | *but* | **Jane** and **Kelly** / **are** in the sixth grade.

Jesus / **was, is**, and always **will be** God; | **He** / **is** also a man.

Casey / **was** sick yesterday; | *however*, | **she** / **feels** better today.

Notice that if you eliminate the connecting word or semicolon, start each independent clause with a capital letter, and end each clause with a period, each clause would be a complete thought in itself. Each would therefore be a simple sentence. Compare the simple sentences below with the compound sentences above.

The grass is green. The sky is blue.

John and Jim are in the seventh grade. Jane and Kelly are in the sixth grade.

Jesus was, is, and always will be God. He is also a man.

Casey was sick yesterday. She feels better today.

Note: In addition to simple conjunctions, conjunctive adverbs, and semicolons, *correlative conjunctions* may be used to join independent clauses in a compound sentence.

☞**EXAMPLE:**

He did sing. He danced. *(two simple sentences)*

Not only did he sing, *but* he *also* danced. *(one compound sentence)*

✎ **EXERCISE A** Underline each independent clause in the following compound sentences. Circle the connecting word or punctuation mark. (The connecting word is considered to be part of the clause which follows it.)

1. The sky is cloudy, (and) rain is falling.

2. There was a power outage in our area; therefore, we lit our wood-stove to keep warm.

3. Your order was received, and we will mail the merchandise immediately.

4. The temperature is dropping; it may be snowing soon.

5. My book is here, but you left yours at school.

6. Finish your supper, or go to bed hungry.

✎ **EXERCISE B** Combine the simple sentences below into compound sentences.

1. We caught six fish. We cleaned and cooked them for supper.

    _____*We caught six fish, and we cleaned and cooked them for supper.*_____

2. Jenny swept the floor. Gina dusted the furniture.

    _____

    _____

3. Columbus sailed to the New World. Magellan's expedition circumnavigated the globe.

    _____

    _____

4. Oil and water do not mix. Alcohol and water do.

    _____

    _____

5. He is not here. He has risen.

    _____

    _____

6. The door was left open again. The dog got out.

    _____

    _____

✎ **EXERCISE C** Write four compound sentences of your own. Use simple conjunctions in two of them, a semicolon in one of them, and a conjunctive adverb in the other.

1. _____

   _____

2. _____

   _____

3. _____

   _____

4. _____

   _____

LESSON 15: SENTENCE FRAGMENTS AND RUN-ON SENTENCES

In Lesson 10 we saw that not all groups of words form complete sentences. A group of words may logically go together, but if they do not express a complete thought with a subject and a predicate, they are not a complete sentence. They are a *sentence fragment*—something less than a complete sentence. They express only part of an idea, not a complete thought, because either the subject or the predicate is missing (or both are missing).

> **A SENTENCE FRAGMENT is a part of a sentence that does not express a complete thought.**

☞**EXAMPLES OF SENTENCE FRAGMENTS:** *(Fragments are in dark type.)*

We visited the Statue of Liberty. **A famous landmark in New York Harbor.**

I saw a man. **Painting a picture.**

A woman known for her pie-making abilities.

In Lesson 14, we saw that two simple sentences can be joined together into a compound sentence. We learned that when we join two sentences together, we must use a connecting word or a semicolon. An error is made when writers and speakers try to combine two sentences without using a connecting word or the proper connecting punctuation. This error is called a *run-on sentence*. It is especially incorrect when the two sentences are not closely related in thought to each other.

> **A RUN-ON SENTENCE is one consisting of two or more sentences joined without the proper connecting word or punctuation.**

If two or more sentences are joined only by a comma or by no connecting device at all, they form a run-on sentence. Sentences must be **properly joined** or **not joined at all**. When they do not belong together, the first must be ended with a period, question mark, or exclamation point; and the second must be started with a capital letter. Run-on sentences confuse us because we cannot tell where one thought ends and another begins, as the following examples show.

☞**EXAMPLES OF RUN-ON SENTENCES:**

What was he trying to say I don't know.

We went hiking on Monday the next day we went swimming.

Why he said that, I don't know it certainly is puzzling to me.

I think I need new eyeglasses I can't see very well anymore.

I don't know the answer I will find it.

Jim ate a hot dog his dog ate one too.

The above run-on sentences could be corrected by *separating* the parts into two sentences or *properly joining* the parts with conjunctions, conjunctive adverbs, or semicolons. You can see below that if we use the proper separators or joining devices, the confusion disappears. We can then understand where one thought ends and the next begins.

What was he trying to say? **I** don't know.

We went hiking on Monday. The next day we went swimming.

Why he said that, I don't know; it certainly is puzzling to me.

I think I need new eyeglasses; I can't see very well anymore.

I don't know the answer; **however**, I will find it.

Jim ate a hot dog, **and** his dog ate one too.

✎ **EXERCISE A** In the blanks at the left, write **F** if the words that follow are a sentence fragment. Write **S** if they form a complete sentence. Write **R** if they form a run-on sentence.

_F_ 1. A famous author from the sixteenth century.

_____ 2. I do believe this is an answer to prayer.

_____ 3. He liked thick pillows she didn't.

_____ 4. Please do not send any more information we have all we need.

_____ 5. The book on the desk.

_____ 6. In order to properly understand me.

_____ 7. My dentist appointment is at 9 o'clock my sister's is a half hour later.

_____ 8. She went shopping yesterday she hoped to find some new clothes for her trip.

_____ 9. She went shopping yesterday, hoping to find some new clothes for her trip.

_____10. Some people. Never learn how to obey.

_____11. Some people never learn.

_____12. Some people never learn how to obey.

✎ **EXERCISE B** Find all of the sentence fragments and run-on sentences in Exercise A. Add words to change the sentence fragments into complete sentences. Correct the run-on sentences by properly separating the parts or properly joining them in a compound sentence.

1. _____

   _____

2. _____

   _____

3. _____

   _____

4. _____

   _____

5. _____

   _____

6. _____

   _____

7. _____

   _____

8. _____

   _____

LESSON 16: FUNCTION OF SENTENCES

In Lesson 14, you learned that sentences can be classified according to their structure—*simple, compound,* and *complex.* Sentences can also be classified according to their *function* or *purpose.* In this lesson, you will study four kinds of sentences: *declarative, interrogative, imperative,* and *exclamatory.*

> **A DECLARATIVE sentence makes a statement and ends with a period.**
>
> **An INTERROGATIVE sentence asks a question and ends with a question mark.**
>
> **An IMPERATIVE sentence gives a command or makes a request. It ends with a period or exclamation point.**
>
> **An EXCLAMATORY sentence shows strong feeling and ends with an exclamation point.**

A *declarative* sentence makes a straightforward statement. It may be a simple, compound, or complex sentence. It simply declares facts, opinions, or ideas. It always ends with a period.

☞**EXAMPLES OF DECLARATIVE SENTENCES:**

In 1652, the founding father of South Africa, Jan van Riebeck, landed in Table Bay and knelt on the shore of what was to become Cape Town.

His prayer was that the settlement he was about to establish would be for the glory of God.

An *interrogative* sentence asks a question and always ends with a question mark. It may be a simple, compound, or complex sentence.

☞**EXAMPES OF INTERROGATIVE SENTENCES:**

What was the vision of the Dutch Reformed settlers who accompanied him?

Was it not that they desired to spread the light of the Gospel throughout the "dark continent" of Africa?

An *imperative* sentence gives a command or makes a statement of request (not a question). It usually ends with a period, but it may end with an exclamation point if the command or request is especially forceful. The subject of an imperative sentence usually is *"You,"* but it is usually *implied,* rather than expressed.

☞**EXAMPLES OF IMPERATIVE SENTENCES:**

(You) Do not believe everything you have heard about South Africa.

(You) Please give me your report about the missionary influence of the Afrikaners.

Thy will be done on earth as it is in heaven.

An *exclamatory* sentence expresses strong feeling or makes an exclamation. It always ends with an exclamation point.

☞**EXAMPLES OF EXCLAMATORY SENTENCES:**

What an amazing story the history of the Great Trek makes!

The determination of the Boers was astonishing!

✎ **EXERCISE A** In the blank, identify the kind of sentence that follows as *declarative, interrogative, imperative,* or *exclamatory*. If the sentence expresses strong feeling *in the form of a command*, label it *imperative*. Place the appropriate punctuation mark at the end of each sentence.

_____*declarative*_____	1.	Thank you for your recent letter.
_____	2.	The smoke filled the room, causing everyone to gasp for breath
_____	3.	What was the name of that book you were reading
_____	4.	How great was their joy when they first believed in Christ
_____	5.	Do you understand what an interrogatory sentence is
_____	6.	Do unto others what you would have them do unto you
_____	7.	Never, never, never do such a terrible thing again
_____	8.	When did Jan van Riebeck land in South Africa
_____	9.	I will mail you a letter tomorrow
_____	10.	My only hesitation is whether we can raise enough money for this project

✎ **EXERCISE B** Write four sentences illustrating the types below.

1. **Declarative**

_____

_____

2. **Interrogative**

_____

_____

3. **Imperative**

_____

_____

4. **Exclamatory**

_____

_____

LESSON 17: UNIT REVIEW

✎ **EXERCISE A** Complete the following definitions.

1. A sentence is a group of words that _____.

2. The subject of a sentence is the word or group of words about which _____
   _____.

3. The predicate of a sentence is the word or group of words which _____

   _____.

4. A compound subject consists of _____.

5. A compound predicate consists of _____.

6. A simple sentence has one complete _____ and one complete _____, although
   either or both may be _____.

7. A compound sentence has two or more simple sentences joined by a _____,
   _____ _____, or _____.

8. A sentence fragment is a part of a sentence that does not _____

   _____.

9. A run-on sentence is one consisting of two or more sentences joined without the proper
   _____ _____ or _____.

✎ **EXERCISE B** Read the following paragraph and follow the instructions below it.

The Crucifixion of Jesus Christ took place on Friday of the Passover week of the Jews, in the year A.D. 30. This day is known and now generally observed by Christians as Good Friday. Crucifixion, as a means of inflicting death in the most cruel, lingering, and shameful way, was used by many nations of antiquity. The Jews never executed their criminals in this way, but the Greeks and Romans made the cross the instrument of death to malefactors. The cross was in the shape either of the letter T or the letter X, or was in the form familiar in such paintings of the Crucifixion as the well-known representation of [Flemish painter, Peter P.] Rubens. It was the usual custom to compel the criminal to carry his own cross to the place of execution. The cross was then set up and the criminal was usually tied to it by the hands and feet and left to perish of hunger and thirst. Sometimes he was given a narcotic drink to stupefy him. In the case of the crucifixion of Jesus Christ, the victim was fastened to the cross by nails driven through his hands and feet.

—Frederic William Farrar

1. Write the first sentence of the above paragraph. Then underline the *complete subject* and double-underline the *complete predicate.*

   _____

   _____

2. Find the *first* sentence in the above paragraph that has a *compound predicate.* Write the sentence below.

   _____

   _____

3. Find a *compound sentence* in the above paragraph. Write the sentence below.

   _____

   _____

4. Find a sentence which has a *compound subject.* Write the sentence below.

   _____

   _____

5. Find a *simple sentence* in the paragraph. Write the sentence below.

_____

_____

6. Write the last sentence in the paragraph. Then underline the *simple subject* and double-underline the *simple predicate.*

_____

_____

✎ **EXERCISE C** In the blank at the left of each sentence, write **T** if the sentence is true or **F** if the sentence is false.

_____ 1. A simple sentence cannot have a compound subject.

_____ 2. Independent clauses in a compound sentence may be separated by a semicolon.

_____ 3. Independent clauses must be separated by only a comma.

_____ 4. A compound sentence must have a compound subject and a compound verb.

_____ 5. An independent clause is a sentence part which could stand alone as a sentence.

_____ 6. A run-on sentence is any sentence that takes up more than two lines.

_____ 7. Independent clauses may be joined by a conjunctive adverb.

_____ 8. A subject must be a noun.

_____ 9. A complete predicate must have at least one verb.

_____10. All words in a sentence are part of the complete subject or the complete predicate.

_____11. An imperative sentence asks a question.

_____12. An exclamation point may be placed at the end of either an imperative sentence or an exclamatory sentence.

_____13. An interrogatory sentence can never be a compound sentence.

Unit 3
Sentence Design

Sentences, like clothes, come in many, many different designs. They can be extremely simple in their design, or they can be extremely complicated. Contrast the two sentences below:

Airplanes fly.

The city of God we speak of is the same to which testimony is borne by that Scripture, which excels all the writings of all nations by its divine authority, and has brought under its influence all kinds of minds, and this not by a casual intellectual movement, but obviously by an express providential arrangement.

—Augustine, *The City of God.*

As you can see, sentence designs can vary a great deal, from the simple two-word design in the first example to the highly complex design of the second. Most sentence designs fall somewhere between these two extremes. In this unit, you will learn some of the **basic** designs of sentences. Understanding sentence design will help you understand your language so that you can communicate your ideas more clearly to others. Clear communication is an important way to prevent confusion and conflict when you write or speak with others.

Grammar textbooks use a number of different terms to describe sentence designs. Some refer to the "sentence base" and list "two-part," "three-part," and "four-part" sentence bases. Some refer to "sentence frameworks" and some to "sentence diagrams." In this workbook, we will look at five different designs. We will call them simply Designs A, B, C, D, and E. To simplify our study, we will deal first with *simple sentences* in each of these five designs. We will then see how these simple-sentence designs apply to compound sentences, since compound sentences are really combinations of two or more simple sentences.

LESSON 18: SENTENCE DESIGN A

The most simple sentence design, which we call Design A, has two basic parts:

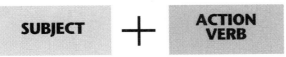

Many of the simple sentences you have studied so far in this workbook are constructed along the lines of Design A. Here are two more:

Frogs croak.

Crickets and grasshoppers chirp and hop.

This design consists of a *subject (simple or compound)* and an *action verb (simple or compound)*. Both the subject and the action verb may be modified. The subject may be modified by adjectives or by prepositional phrases used as adjectives. The verb may be modified—by adverbs or prepositional phrases used as adverbs.

Green **frogs** *on the bank of the lake* **croak** *steadily in the spring.*

In the above sentence, the subject "frogs" is modified by an adjective, "Green," and a prepositional phrase, "on the bank," used as an adjective. The prepositional phrase, "of the lake," serves as an adjective modifying "bank." The verb "croak" is modified by the adverb "steadily" and the prepositional phrase, "during the spring," used as an adverb.

We can diagram this sentence design as follows:

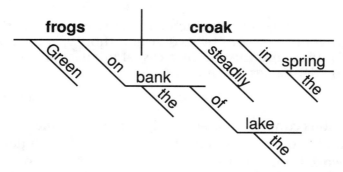

This diagram shows that the ***sentence base*** *(the main horizontal line)* of sentences in Design A consists of two main elements: the subject *(frogs)* and the verb *(croak)*. All other sentence elements are related to one or the other of these two base elements. Notice that if you eliminated all of the elements except the two main ones (Frogs croak), the sentence still would make complete sense. **Study the diagram carefully. Identify all the sentence parts. Notice how subjects, verbs, adjectives, adverbs, and prepositional phrases are arranged.**

✎ **EXERCISE A** Underline **only** the **two essential elements** (subject and action verb) in the following Design-A sentences. Remember, an action verb can be a *verb phrase*, consisting of a main verb plus a helping verb.

1. The <u>population</u> <u>has increased</u> slowly.

2. Rivers overflow from melted snow.

3. Wild horses live on prairies in several western states.

4. Coyotes roam in open pastures.

5. Droughts have come regularly.

6. The railroads helped with westward migration.

7. Wild animals in parts of the West roam freely on the open plains.

✎ **EXERCISE B** Draw diagrams similar to the one on the previous page for each of the following sentences. Remember that the sentence base for Design-A sentences has only two elements, a subject and an action verb. **Use a ruler to draw lines for these and all future diagrams.**

1. Airplanes fly in the sky.

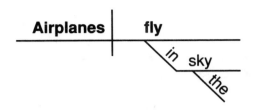

2. The sun rises in the morning.

3. Fallen leaves decompose during the winter.

4. The story was told in an interesting way.

5. The plant died from a lack of water.

LESSON 19: SENTENCE DESIGN B

The next simple-sentence design, which we call Design B, has three basic parts.

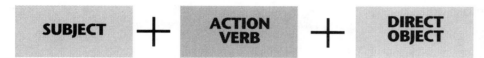

You have already learned about subjects and verbs. Design-B sentences have a third basic element—a ***direct object***. The subject tells *who* or *what* is acting. An action verb tells us *that* the subject is doing, saying, or thinking something. A direct object tells us *what* the subject is doing, saying, or thinking. A direct object answers the question *what?* or *whom?* about the action verb. If the direct object is a person, it will answer the question *whom?* about the verb. If the direct object is a place, thing, quality, or idea, it will answer the question *what?* about the verb. You will notice from this description that a direct object will be a person, place, thing, quality, or idea. In other words, a direct object will always be a *noun* or *pronoun*, or an *expression functioning as a noun.*

> **A DIRECT OBJECT is a noun, pronoun, noun phrase, noun clause, or other noun-like expression that either receives the action of a verb or is the result of the verb.**

☞**EXAMPLES OF DESIGN-B SENTENCES:**

Luke sold tickets. *(Luke sold **what?**)*

Luke saw her. *(Luke saw **whom?**)*

My mother baked a cake. *(Mother baked **what?**)*

My hungry family quickly ate the birthday cake. *(Family ate **what?**)*

You can see from the last example above that all of the basic three elements in a Design-B sentence may have modifiers. The subject "family" is modified by "my" and "hungry." The verb "ate" is modified by "quickly." The direct object "cake" is modified by "the" and "birth-day."

We would diagram this sentence as follows:

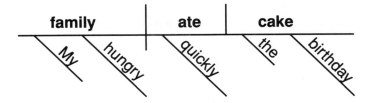

Note: When placing the *direct object* on the diagram baseline, separate it from the verb by a vertical line that does NOT extend through the baseline

---

✎ **EXERCISE A** Underline the subject in each sentence below. Double-underline each verb. Circle each direct object. HINT: To find the direct object, ask *whom?* or *what? about the verb.*

1. The <u>park</u> <u><u>attracts</u></u> many (tourists.)

2. Fur traders established trading posts in the West.

3. Some businesses temporarily employ students during the summertime.

4. I have heard that song somewhere before.

5. My friend from Australia sent a postcard yesterday.

6. Jeannie received many compliments on her new dress.

7. Bob liked swimming.

8. The rain brought an end to the drought.

✎ **EXERCISE B** Diagram the following sentences, following the example found above and other previous examples.

1. The park attracts many tourists.

2. My friend from Australia sent a postcard yesterday.

3. Jeannie received many compliments on her new dress.

4. Explorers have discovered rich deposits of coal in Montana.

5. Kerry has always loved skiing in powdery snow.

6. Students in our class brilliantly performed our class play.

✎ **EXERCISE C** Write five sentences styled according to Design B. Each must have a subject, an action verb, and a direct object. (You may also add any modifiers you need.)

1. _____

   _____

2. _____

   _____

3. _____

   _____

4. _____

_____

5. _____

_____

LESSON 20: SENTENCE DESIGN C

The third design that can be used for simple sentences, which we call Design C, has four basic parts.

SUBJECT + **ACTION VERB** + **INDIRECT OBJECT** + **DIRECT OBJECT**

The new element in Design-C sentences is the ***indirect object***. It is a noun, pronoun, or group of words used as a noun that shows *to whom or what* or *for whom or what* the action of the verb is done. The indirect object is the *receiver of the direct object*. The direct object is the *receiver of the verb's action*.

One of the best ways to find an indirect object is to put an imaginary *"to"* or *"for"* in front of a noun or pronoun that comes after an action verb and before the direct object.

My parents gave (to) **me** a fine birthday present.

Brian does (for) **Tim** many favors.

The teacher assigned (to) her **class** six chapters in their history book.

Because the implied "to" and "for" would be prepositions if expressed, we diagram indirect objects in the same way we diagram prepositional phrases, although we do not need to write the implied "to" or "for" in the diagram. (It is shown below just to illustrate the idea.)

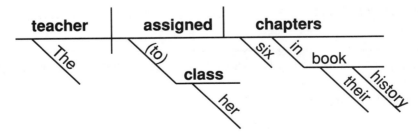

In this sentence, "class" is the *indirect object* because it is the group of people *to whom* the verb's action of assigning is directed. The noun "chapters" is the *direct object* because it is *what*

was assigned. Remember: **Direct objects** answer the questions *whom?* or *what?* about the verb; and **indirect objects** answer *to whom? for whom? to what?* or *for what?* about the verb.

> An **INDIRECT OBJECT** is a noun, pronoun, or other noun-like expression that precedes a direct object and indicates the *receiver of the direct object* of the verb.

✎ **EXERCISE A** Underline the direct objects in the following sentences. *Double-underline* the *indirect objects.*

1. The Nineteenth Amendment gave American <u>women</u> the <u>right</u> to vote.

Note: In this sentence, the complete direct object is actually a phrase, "the right to vote," used as a noun. The main word in the phrase is "right." The noun "women" is the indirect object because "women" were the receivers of the direct object, "the right to vote."

2. The children served their mother breakfast in bed on Mother's Day.

3. Mother told them a story.

4. The pamphlet gave us detailed instructions.

5. A vacation in Yellowstone National Park always offers visitors many great memories.

6. The grassy fields provided the sheep plenty of food.

7. The rehearsal afforded the actors much-needed practice.

8. We always feed our dogs nutritious food.

9. The man sold my father a new car.

10. The committee allotted the parents ninety tickets for the school play.

✎ **EXERCISE B** Diagram the following Design-C sentences. (See example on the previous page.)

1. Mother told the children a story.

2. The grassy fields provided the sheep plenty of food.

3. We always feed our dogs nutritious food.

4. The man sold my father a new car.

5. The pamphlet gave us detailed instructions.

6. Mother allowed the girls an extra hour of sleep.

LESSON 21: SENTENCE DESIGN D

The fourth sentence design, which we call Design D, also has four parts.

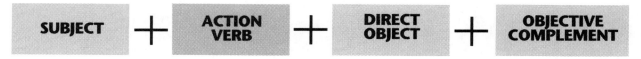

A *complement* is something that *"completes."* In grammar, a *complement* is a word or expression used to *complete* an idea stated in a sentence or clause. English has four sentence designs that use complements. You have already studied two of them, Design B and Design C. Direct objects and indirect objects are called *verb complements.* In this lesson, you will learn to identify the third kind: sentences with *objective complements.* **Objective complements** complete the meaning of the direct object. We refer to sentences which use objective complements as Design-D sentences. In the next lesson, we will learn to identify *subjective complements,* which are used in sentences styled according to Design E.

Note: Do not confuse the word "complement" with the word "compliment," which means "an expression of regard or praise."

> **An OBJECTIVE COMPLEMENT is a noun, pronoun, or adjective following a direct object and completing its meaning.**

☞**EXAMPLES OF SENTENCES WITH OBJECTIVE COMPLEMENTS:**

Jake painted his bicycle *red*.

The class elected Terry their first *president*.

We named our cat *Fritzie*.

You are driving me *crazy*.

You can see that the adjectives and nouns in dark print in the examples above add important information about the direct object in order to complete the meaning. Because they complete the meaning of a grammatical *object*, they are called *objective* complements.

Notice that the position of the complement—following the direct object—is very important. In the case of adjectives used as objective complements, the meaning of the sentence would change if the adjective were placed before the direct object. Saying *"Jake painted his red bicycle"* (it was already red before he painted it) has quite a different meaning than saying *"Jake painted his bicycle red"* (he changed the color to red). Similarly, saying *"You are driving me crazy"* means something quite different from saying *"You are driving crazy me."* You will notice similar confusion of meaning or resulting nonsense if you try to place nouns used as objective complements before the direct objects.

We diagram objective complements in the following way:

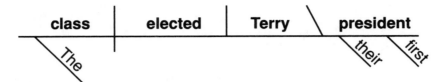

✎ **EXERCISE A** Underline any nouns used as objective complements in the following sentences. Double-underline any adjectives used as objective complements.

1. My parents named my newborn sister <u>Rachel</u>.

2. His behavior has made his reputation bad in the community.

3. Our team chose Josh captain.

4. Consider yourself scolded.

5. Your accusations make me angry.

6. The teacher found his composition very commendable.

7. The umpire called the runner "safe."

8. She considered the pattern in the blouse fabric too elaborate for wearing with a striped skirt.

9. The assistant principal designated Sam hall monitor for this week.

10. We elected Todd vice president of our class.

✎ **EXERCISE B** In the space below, diagram the odd-numbered sentences from Exercise A. (HINT: The prepositional phrase at the end of Sentence 9 is used as an adverb.)

1.

3.

5.

7.

9.

LESSON 22: SENTENCE DESIGN E

In the previous lesson, you learned about *objective complements*, which complete the meaning of direct objects. You learned that objective complements can be either *adjectives* or *nouns*. In this lesson, you will learn about *subjective complements*. **Subjective complements** complete the meaning of the subject of the sentence. Like objective complements, they may be adjectives, nouns, or pronouns. Because they are located in the predicate half of the sentence, we call these subjective complements *predicate adjectives* and *predicate nominatives*. A predicate nominative may be a noun, pronoun, or other expression used as a noun.

Predicate adjectives and predicate nominatives **always follow linking verbs**. Sentences using these complements are written according to Design E. Design-E sentences have a three-part sentence base and are the only ones which use *linking verbs*.

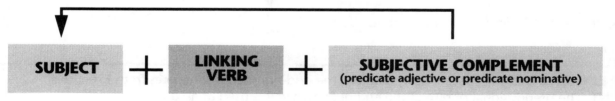

SUBJECT   +   LINKING VERB   +   SUBJECTIVE COMPLEMENT
(predicate adjective or predicate nominative)

> **A PREDICATE ADJECTIVE is an adjective placed in the predicate after a linking verb and used to modify the subject of a sentence or clause.**
>
> **A PREDICATE NOMINATIVE is a noun, pronoun, or other noun-like expression used in a predicate after a linking verb to rename or identify the subject.**

☞**EXAMPLES OF DESIGN-E SENTENCES WITH PREDICATE ADJECTIVES:**

I am *hungry.*

The man with the umbrella is still *dry.*

She was *happy* to see her cousin again.

The leaves of most maple trees turn *red* in the autumn.

This cheese smells *awful.*

In all of the above sentences, the words in dark print are adjectives which modify the subjects of the sentence and they all follow *linking verbs.* Review the discussion in Lesson 3 to refresh your memory about linking verbs.

☞**EXAMPLES OF DESIGN-E SENTENCES WITH PREDICATE NOMINATIVES:**

George Washington was the first *president* of the United States.

Wuthering Heights is a *novel* by Emily Brontë.

That red-leaf tree is a *maple.*

The most common linking verb is *"to be."*

Our new car is a Japanese *model* made in an American factory.

We diagram subjective complements in the following way:

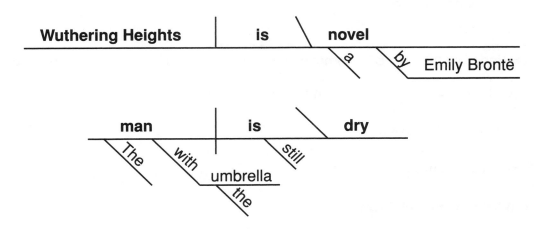

───

✎ **EXERCISE A** Underline all predicate adjectives in the following sentences. Double-underline all predicate nominatives.

1. Dinner will be <u>ready</u> soon.

2. My mother is a good cook.

3. Her food always tastes good.

4. Do what seems best.

5. A linking verb is not an action verb.

6. The tallest building in our town is City Hall.

7. God is love.

8. Jesus is the second Person of the Trinity.

9. All honorable forms of work can be a calling from God.

10. Your words are very wise.

11. Three of the buildings on campus are dormitories.

12. This exercise is easy.

13. Your report looks fine to me.

14. Everyday life in some countries of the southern hemisphere is difficult for many people.

15. The test will not be hard for you.

✎ **EXERCISE B** Underline the subjective complements describing God in the following Bible verses:

1. "I am thy <u>shield</u> and thy exceeding great <u>reward</u>" (Genesis 15:1).

2. "I am the Almighty God…" (Gen. 17:1).

3. "…I am the Lord in the midst of the earth" (Exodus 8:22).

4. "…I the Lord thy God am holy" (Leviticus 19:2).

5. "The Lord of Hosts is His name" (Isaiah 51:15).

6. "God is not the God of the dead, but of the living" (Matthew 22:32).

7. "I am the Son of God" (Matthew 27:43).

8. "I am the bread of life" (John 6:35).

9. "I am the good shepherd" (John 10:11).

10. "I am the resurrection and the life" (John 11:25).

11. "I am the true vine" (John 15:1).

12. "I am Alpha and Omega, the beginning and the end, the first and the last" (Revelation 22:13).

GOD'S PREDICATE NOMINATIVE

(Read Exodus 3:13-15)

Israel couldn't believe that God was finally speaking to them after 400 years of silence. The Lord asked Moses, an exile from Israel, to go back to Egypt and to describe Him as "I AM" to the religious leadership of the Jews. The sentence seems incomplete. I AM...what? Wasn't there a word in the entire Hebrew language that Moses could use to describe God? Did he have to leave them with an incomplete sentence? Was there no noun he could use to follow a simple linking verb and explain God?

Israel's leaders were skeptical of Moses' message. When things got worse instead of better, they grumbled. But then, through a series of miracles, God finished the I AM sentence about Himself with one amazing demonstration of His power after another.

People today assume that if their minds cannot conceive of God, then God cannot be known. Or if God doesn't come to them personally, then He cannot come at all. Sound like an ego problem? How typical of us! How pathetic!

Moses believed God. But he also understood human nature. And he had the challenge of convincing the most respected, most critical leaders of Israel that God had spoken. No wonder Moses wanted to stay in the desert!

How would Moses finish the I AM...sentence to us? I think he would leave the sentence incomplete, and fill in the missing predicate nominative with evidences of God's awesome power and love in our daily experience with Him.

—Doug Pearson, *Campus Journal* (Grand Rapids: Radio Bible Class), April 12, 1995.

LESSON 23: COMPOUNDS IN SENTENCE DESIGNS

So far in this unit, you have studied five designs for *simple* sentences. Most of the simple sentences you have studied have had single subjects, verbs, direct object, indirect objects, objective complements, and subjective complements. Since *compound* sentences are actually two or more simple sentences joined together, the same grammatical and diagramming rules that apply to simple sentences also apply to the independent clauses of compound sentences.

Compound sentences are diagrammed as follows:

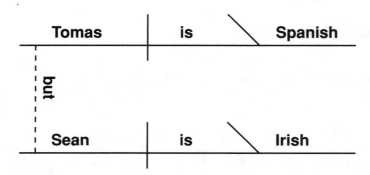

The example above illustrates a compound sentence styled according to Design E for predicate adjectives. Sentences of Designs A, B, C, and D may also be compounded.

Furthermore, all of the single elements of these sentence designs can themselves be compound. You can write sentences with compound subjects, verbs, direct objects, indirect objects, objective complements, and subjective complements. When diagramming compound sentence elements, we use divided lines joined by dotted lines, as shown in the following illustration:

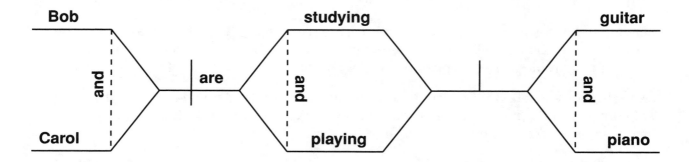

The example above illustrates compound subjects, verbs, and direct objects in a Design-B sentence. Compound elements can also be used in the other sentence designs. The diagram below shows compound complete predicates:

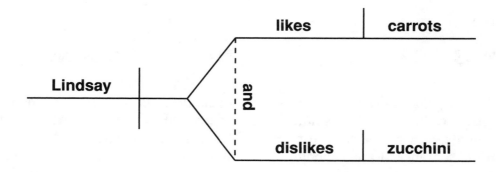

The following illustrates how to diagram compound adjectives and adverbs.

The Museum workers packaged the rare and very valuable antiques slowly and carefully.

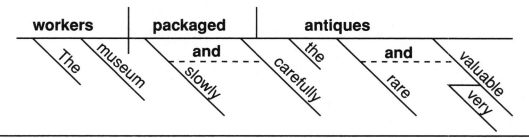

Note: The diagram above shows how to diagram an adverb (*very*) that modifies an adjective.

The following illustrates how to diagram compound prepositional phrases. In this example, the prepositional phrases are used as adverbs.

She placed a bouquet of flowers on the shelf and between two sets of books.

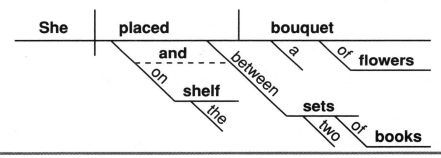

✎ **EXERCISE** Diagram the following sentences:

1. We will need a shovel and a rake.

2. My grandfather has home movies, but we now have home videos.

3. The weather is becoming warmer and more sunny.

4. She dropped everything and came immediately to my aid.

5. Linda wore her new sweater, and Carrie wore her old sweat shirt.

6. Larry drives carefully, but Joe is reckless.

7. The tornado warning sent us to the basement and under a table.

8. Softly and tenderly, Jesus is calling.

9. Marsha was elected secretary and treasurer.

LESSON 24: UNIT REVIEW

✎ **EXERCISE A** Fill in the blanks below:

1. Name the two parts of a Design-A sentence.

    _____ + _____

2. Name the three parts of a Design-B sentence.

    _____ + _____ + _____

3. Name the four parts of a Design-C sentence.

    _____ + _____ + _____ + _____

4. Name the four parts of a Design-D sentence.

    _____ + _____ + _____ + _____

5. Name the three parts of a Design-E sentence.

    _____ + _____ + _____

6. What three parts of speech may serve as objective complements?

    _____, _____ and _____

7. What are the two kinds of subjective complements?

    _____ and _____

8. A direct object is a noun, pronoun, or other noun-like expression that answers the questions
    _____? or _____? about the verb.

9. An indirect object is a noun, pronoun, or other noun-like expression that answers the questions
    _____? _____? _____? or _____? about the
    verb.

10. Direct objects and indirect objects are _____ complements.

11. Complements in the predicate which modify or rename the subject are called _____
    complements.

12. Complements in the predicate which complete the meaning of a direct object are called
    _____ complements.

13. Sentence Design E is the only design that uses _____ verbs rather than action verbs.

✎ **EXERCISE B** In the blanks at the left, write A, B, C, D, or E to tell which sentence design is used.

_____ 1. Our God is an awesome God.

_____ 2. The magazine held a contest for the best essay.

_____ 3. I consider him a valuable friend.

_____ 4. He is a valuable friend.

_____ 5. He is very friendly.

_____ 6. He helps his friends at every opportunity.

_____ 7. The sun rises every morning and sets every evening.

_____ 8. My pastor gave me a valuable book about moral behavior.

_____ 9. Charity is a Christian duty.

_____10. The Sunday school teacher told the children the story of Noah's Ark.

_____11. I received a letter from the company in answer to my questions.

_____12. They named their pet frog Hoppy.

_____13. The name of their pet frog was Hoppy.

_____14. Their pet frog seemed happy.

Unit 4
Forming Phrases

Sentences are made up of words, each of which is classified as one of the eight parts of speech. Words may also be combined into groups which form less than a full sentence. These groupings are called phrases and clauses. Clauses are groups of words that include both a subject and a predicate but form only part of a sentence. Phrases are groups of words that do not include both a subject and a predicate.

> **A PHRASE is a group of related words that does not contain both a subject and a predicate but which is used as a single part of speech.**

Phrases may be used as nouns, pronouns, verbs, adjectives, adverbs, conjunctions, prepositions, or interjections, and are often *identified* by their use or their *most prominent grammatical feature*. We speak of *prepositional phrases, verb phrases, noun phrases, infinitive phrases, gerund (or gerundial) phrases, participle (or participial) phrases, adverb (or adverbial) phrases,* and *adjective (or adjectival) phrases*.

In this unit, we will study the ***prepositional phrase***, which was introduced to you in Lesson 6. Review that lesson to refresh your memory about prepositions and the parts of prepositional phrases. You will recall from Lesson 6 that a ***preposition*** is a part of speech that shows the relationship of a noun or pronoun to some other word in a sentence. You learned that a ***prepositional phrase*** is a group of words that begins with a preposition and ends with a noun or pronoun called the ***object of the preposition***. A prepositional phrase may also include words that modify the noun or pronoun.

A sentence may include many prepositional phrases. They are often strung together, one after another, to provide a detailed expression relating one word to another in the sentence.

☞**EXAMPLE:**

The night air is filled ***with** the sound **of** thousands **of** crickets **from** field and meadow **during** the summer **in** the midwestern part **of** our country.*

In the preceding example, the words "The night air" form a *noun phrase* used as the subject of the sentence; and the words "is filled" form a verb phrase used as the simple predicate of the sentence. All of the other words are part of a series of prepositional phrases beginning with the prepositions in dark print.

LESSON 25: ADJECTIVE PHRASES

The first type of prepositional phrase we will study is the adjective phrase.

> **An ADJECTIVE PHRASE is a prepositional phrase used as an adjective to modify a noun or pronoun.**

A noun or pronoun may be modified by a single adjective or by a group of words that function as an adjective, making the meaning of the noun or pronoun more definite. As you will recall from Lesson 4, adjectives usually answer the questions *what kind? which one? how many? or how much?* about the nouns or pronouns they modify. Those questions may also be answered by prepositional phrases.

☞**EXAMPLES:**

The man *in the middle* is my father. *(Which man is my father? The one "in the middle.")*

The War *Between the States* is often called the Civil War.
(Which war is often called the Civil War? The War "Between the States.")

I prefer bananas *without bruises.*
(Which kind of bananas do I prefer? The ones "without bruises.")

Read the above sentences without the prepositional phrases. You will notice that they are still complete sentences expressing a complete thought. But you will also notice that the prepositional phrases make the nouns they modify much more definite and therefore give important additional meaning to the sentence. The purpose of adjectives and adjective phrases is to supply that extra meaning.

✎ **EXERCISE A** Underline the adjective phrases in the following sentences. Put parentheses around the nouns or pronouns they modify. *Do not mark any prepositional phrases that are* **not** *adjective phrases.* Some are adverb phrases, which should not be marked. It might be helpful to review the list of prepositions in Lesson 6 before you start so that you can more easily recognize the prepositional phrases. Remember also that a prepositional phrase must include a noun or pronoun as an object.

1. Charles Dickens wrote a (book) <u>about the French Revolution</u> called A (Tale) <u>of Two Cities</u>.

2. The old car in our driveway belongs to my brother.

3. The woman talking to my mother is a person of very fine character.

4. We are excited about the prospect of a new member among us.

5. A day without laughter is like a day without sunshine.

6. "Go ye therefore into all the world and make disciples of all nations."

7. She wore leather gloves on her hands for protection from the thorns.

8. Zane Grey wrote stories about the American West of the nineteenth century.

9. I sent two letters during April to my cousin in Arizona.

10. He selected several of various sizes and colors.

11. Grandpa rested in the shade of the old oak tree in the backyard of our house.

12. Grandma canned vegetables from her garden.

13. The sound of children playing is a pleasure to both of them.

14. Aunt Lily pressed a rose between the pages of a book.

15. The old sofa in the garage will be donated to a thrift store.

16. The clock on the wall tells me it is time to go.

17. Men from the Street Department were repairing the pavement in front of our house.

18. "Worship the Lord in the beauty of holiness."

19. Works by Rembrandt are the most beautiful of all the paintings in the National Museum of Art in Amsterdam, in my opinion.

✎ **EXERCISE B** Write an adjective prepositional phrase in the blanks in the following sentences. Make sure the phrase makes sense in the context of the sentence.

1. The last gift _under the Christmas tree_ is for Mother.

2. The tree _____ will be cut down next week.

3. The people _____ are very friendly.

4. The book _____ is one of my favorites.

5. My uncle _____ will be visiting us during Christmas vacation.

6. We live in a house _____.

7. The food _____ is for our guests.

8. The scuff marks _____ were caused by my shoes.

9. The troops marched to the accompaniment _____.

10. The space _____ is reserved.

LESSON 26: ADVERB PHRASES

Like single adverbs, prepositional phrases can be used to modify verbs, adjectives, and other adverbs.

> **An ADVERB PHRASE is a prepositional phrase used as an adverb to modify a verb, adjective, or other adverb.**

Prepositional phrases used as adverbs often answer such questions as *when? where? how? why? how much? to what extent? how long?* or *how often?*

☞**EXAMPLES:**

We talked *for two hours*. *(How long?)*

They travel mostly *for enjoyment*. *(Why?)*

We usually do our homework *after dinner*. *(When?)*

He speaks *with great conviction* whenever he expresses his opinions. *(How?)*

Unlike adjective phrases, which almost always follow immediately after the word they modify, adverb phrases can often be placed in various locations in a sentence.

☞**EXAMPLES:**

In the morning, we will start to do that project.

We will start to do that project *in the morning*.

We will start *in the morning* to do that project.

✎ **EXERCISE A** Underline prepositional phrases used as adverbs in the following sentences. Draw arrows to the verbs, adjectives, or adverbs they modify. Some sentences may have more than one adverb phrase modifying the same word.

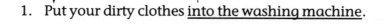

1. Put your dirty clothes <u>into the washing machine</u>.

2. These leftovers have been sitting in the refrigerator for a week.

3. I always think about you on your birthday.

4. Jesus taught that we should build our houses on a rock.

5. He meant by this that our lives should depend on things that last for eternity.

6. They left in a hurry after church.

7. Independence Day in Mexico is called *Cinco de Mayo* and is celebrated on May 5th.

8. It was too early in the morning.

9. His conclusions are based on false information.

10. Children living in colonial days sometimes did their schoolwork by candlelight.

✎ **EXERCISE B** Underline all the prepositional phrases in the following paragraph. Above the phrase, write *adj.* if the phrase is used as an adjective or *adv.* if it is used as an adverb.

At 11:25 p.m., Patrolman Tom Charles flicked the switch on the dashboard of his patrol car. Ahead of him in an old truck covered with rust drove a young man. Officer Charles did not know at first that the young man was wanted by police in a neighboring state. Behind them, in the other state, a terrible crime had been committed. Officer Charles knew about it through police communications. His immediate concern was the young man in the car before him. The license plate of the car was missing. When Officer Charles obtained identification of the owner, he realized the young man was a fugitive from justice. He brought the suspect to a halt with his flashing lights. It was a time for reckoning with the law.

✎ **EXERCISE C** An adverb phrase can sometimes be used to replace a single adverb. Conversely, a single adverb can sometimes replace an adverb phrase. Rewrite the following sentences, using an adverb phrase or single adverb in place of the word or words in **dark print**. You may rearrange, add, or subtract words, if necessary, for smoothness and readability.

1. They left **hurriedly**.

    They left in a hurry.

2. They did their work **in a satisfactory way.**

    _____

3. They behaved **dangerously** in the boat.

    _____

4. His eyes drooped **in a sleepy manner.**

    _____

5. She called to him **loudly.**

    _____

6. The girls crept **with silence** out of the room.

    _____

7. He does his homework **in** too **much haste.**

    _____

8. He prays **at regular times** for his son.

    _____

9. She described the scene **accurately.**

    _____

10. **Under normal conditions**, I would be happy to come.

    _____

11. **On occasion**, I hear a song I like on that station.

    _____

LESSON 27: NOUN PHRASES

Occasionally, a prepositional phrase can be used as a noun (*see note below*). These types of phrases are not as common as adjective and adverb phrases, but you should be aware of this grammatical device in order to give variety to your communications and better understand the expressions of others. The most common use of a noun prepositional phrase is as the *subject* or *predicate nominative* of a sentence or clause in sentences with linking verbs.

Note: Grammar experts do not all agree that prepositional phrases may be used a nouns. Some consider phrases such as those illustrated above to be **adverb** phrases. If so, the sentences would be considered "delayed subject" sentences. In the sentence diagrammed below, the subject would be "*time.*" The phrase "*after dinner*" would modify the verb "*is.*" The phrase then would be diagrammed as any other adverb phrase is diagrammed.

On the other hand, some experts teach that only *action verbs* can be modified by adverbs or adverb phrases. This is why some of them consider phrases such as those shown above—those used with *linking verbs*—to be **noun phrases**. In this book, we will consider this type of phrase to be a noun phrase. (See also Lesson 36, page 104, "Sentences Beginning With Phrases.")

☞**EXAMPLES OF NOUN PHRASES:**

   After dinner is a good time for a nap. *(subject)*

   The habitat for fish is ***under water***. *(predicate nominative)*

Prepositional phrases used as nouns are diagrammed as follows:

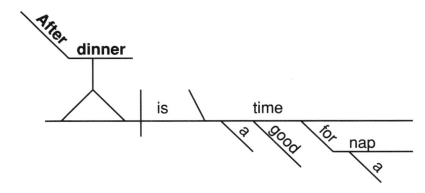

✎ **EXERCISE A** Underline the noun phrases in the following sentences.

1. Along the roadside were thousands of wildflowers.

2. What you are saying is beside the point.

3. Among my suggestions is the following one.

4. During the next song would be a good time to slip out of the auditorium.

5. That old toy is worth money.

6. Your tardiness is without excuse.

7. Beyond the horizon are many interesting adventures.

8. He is out of his mind.

9. His request was against all reason.

10. Near the center of the park is a playground.

11. Within this dish are many types of bacteria.

12. Amid the crowd was one lost boy.

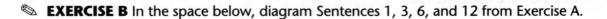

✎ **EXERCISE B** In the space below, diagram Sentences 1, 3, 6, and 12 from Exercise A.

1.

3.

6.

12.

LESSON 28: MISPLACED PHRASES

Where you place a prepositional phrase is important for a clear understanding of what you say or write. As you learned in Lesson 25, adjective phrases almost always must be placed immediately after the word they modify. Adverb phrases are more flexible; they can often be placed in a variety of locations. Misplacing your phrases can result in confusion or strange meanings.

Consider these two sentences containing prepositional phrases:

> Jerry read an article ***about crime***. *(adjective phrase modifying "article")*

> Jerry read an article ***in the school library***. *(adverb phrase modifying "read")*

If we combine these two sentences, we must be careful where we place the two phrases. Consider this arrangement:

> Jerry read an article ***about crime in the school library***.

Is this sentence telling us where Jerry was when he read the article or is it telling us that there is crime in the school library? We cannot tell. Consider this arrangement instead:

> ***In the library***, Jerry read an article ***about crime***.

This sentence makes it clear that Jerry was in the library when he was reading the article about crime. It does not suggest that the crime was in the library.

When we place any modifier in a location that makes it appear to modify the wrong word, the modifier is called a ***misplaced modifier***. Corrections can often be made by simply relocating the modifier.

> **WRONG:**   The road was closed for repairs to drivers.

> **BETTER:**   The road was closed to drivers for repairs.

Sometimes it is best to completely rephrase a sentence in order to avoid confusion with misplaced prepositional phrases.

> **WRONG:**   I repainted our bedroom with my sister.

> **BETTER:**   My sister and I repainted our bedroom.

The best rule to remember is this:

Rule 4.3	**Place prepositional phrases where they make the most sense or rewrite the sentence to eliminate the confusing phrase.**

✎ **EXERCISE** Correct the following sentences by relocating the misplaced phrase or rewriting the whole sentence.

1. We need a van for our family with three seats.

    _____

2. A teacher explained about the volcano in our school.

    _____

3. A man dug a hole in the street with a hard hat.

    _____

4. The snake bit the hiker with long fangs.

    _____

5. We saw the house of our neighbors with two stories.

    _____

6. The tourists saw the homes of movie stars on the tour bus in Beverly Hills.

    _____

7. The bicycles were ridden by two boys with ten gears.

    _____

8. I could hardly see the bridge with my poor eyesight.

    _____

9. I fondly recalled the squirt-gun battle we boys waged in my mind.

    _____

10. We watched the stars falling from our back deck.

_____

LESSON 29: PREPOSITIONS OR ADVERBS?

Take special care not to mistake certain adverbs for prepositions. The mistake occurs in the way certain English expressions are commonly spoken or written, giving the false appearance of a prepositional phrase.

☞**EXAMPLES OF ADVERBS OFTEN MISTAKEN FOR PREPOSITIONS:**

Don't forget to turn *off* the light.

She tried to blow *out* all the candles.

They waited until the storm was *over*.

Turn *down* the volume of your radio.

The cost will be ten dollars or *under*.

Some driftwood washed *up* on the beach.

I lift *up* my eyes unto the hills.

The rain drenched us *through and through*.

Read your book *through* to the end.

The sound of the explosion could be heard for miles *around*.

Remember that a *preposition* is a word that is used to show the relationship of its object to some other word in the sentence. An adverb modifies a verb, adjective, or other adverb and usually answers questions such as *how? how much? to what extent? how often? when? where?* or *in which way?* Confusion often occurs because prepositional phrases can be used as adverbs which answer these same questions. To avoid confusion, you must carefully examine how the word in question is being used and what is the sense of the expression in which it is found.

❏ **One way to determine if the word is a preposition or an adverb is to move it elsewhere in the expression. If it can be moved,** *it is likely* **not** *a preposition.*

☞**EXAMPLES OF ADVERBS:**

Don't forget to turn *off* the light. ⇒ Don't forget to turn the light *off*.

She tried to blow *out* all the candles. ⇒ She tried to blow all the candles *out*.

Turn *down* the volume of your radio. ⇒ Turn the volume of your radio *down*.

❏ **Another clue is to look for nouns or pronouns that follow the word in question. Check if they are truly objects of a preposition being related to another word in the sentence.**

☞**EXAMPLES OF PREPOSITIONS:**

> We walked *down* the *road.*

> He climbed *up* the *fence.*

> Her insults cut *through and through* my *heart.*

> They jogged *around* the *block.*

> Get your feet *off* the *table.*

> Keep them *under* the *table.*

✎ **EXERCISE** In the blanks at the left, write **P** if the word in **dark print** is a preposition or **A** if it is an adverb.

_____ 1. Look **up** that word in a dictionary.

_____ 2. After dinner, he turned **on** the television to watch the evening newscast.

_____ 3. He plowed **under** the weeds in his garden.

_____ 4. He found weeds growing **under** the porch.

_____ 5. She went to the hospital to cheer **up** her friend.

_____ 6. They looked **out** across the valley to the mountains on the other side.

_____ 7. They looked **out** the window to the mountains on the other side of the valley.

_____ 8. Mother sent the children **outside** to play.

_____ 9. The mailman waited **outside** the gate until the dog was taken inside the house.

_____10. The owners tied **up** their dog.

_____11. He was falling **behind** in the race.

LESSON 30: UNIT REVIEW

✎ **EXERCISE A** Underline the prepositional phrases in the following sentences. Above the phrase write **adj.** if the phrase is used as an adjective, **adv.** if it is used as an adverb, or **noun** if it used as a noun.

                      adv.   *adv.*
1. We are going <u>to an Italian restaurant</u> <u>for dinner</u>.

2. Under the mattress is where he hid some of his money.

3. She is a woman of many moods.

4. Raise your hand into the air if you have a question for me after my speech.

5. A hand in the air will be easily noticed.

6. They often spoke to each other by telephone.

7. In this book are many interesting stories about the Pilgrims.

8. The tree in the backyard of our house was struck by lightning.

9. We found several sand dollars on the beach of the Sea of Cortez in Baja California.

10. The color of a person's skin was not a matter of importance to him.

11. She tried to picture herself with red hair.

12. God examines what is in our hearts.

13. In Sunday school we learned what to do about our bad habits.

14. I am underlining one prepositional phrase in this sentence.

15. She was a teacher of handicapped adults.

16. The number of prepositional phrases in a sentence can be many.

17. Jesus taught the crowds about the Kingdom of God.

18. The explorer wrote a book about his experiences in the Amazon Basin.

19. The song being played on the radio is familiar to me.

20. Your advice was very valuable to me on that occasion.

✎ **EXERCISE B** Put parentheses around the word(s) being modified by the prepositional phrases in **dark print**. Above the *word being modified*, indicate which part of speech it is. Write **N** if it is a noun, **P** if it is a pronoun, **V** if it is a verb (or verb phrase), **adj.** if it is an adjective, or **adv.** if it is an adverb.

       V

1. She (gave) the bottle **to the baby.**

2. The wagon was red **in color.**

3. The scientist poured the solution **into a beaker.**

4. The woman **with the red hair** is my aunt.

5. The fence was blown down **to the ground.**

6. The river winds **through a narrow canyon.**

7. The author **of that book** has had many interesting experiences.

8. Barbarians **from northern Europe** defeated the Romans.

9. The purpose **of the Ten Commandments** is to show us our sinfulness and teach us how to please God.

10. Put only fresh vegetables **into your soup.**

11. The vegetables **in your soup** should be fresh.

12. I feel lonely **at night** when you are away from me.

13. I feel lonely at night when you are away **from me.**

14. Anyone **with an illness** may be excused from duty.

15. Because I love my family, I want to do whatever I can to make life better **for them.**

16. **In reading the Bible,** we will find many answers to our questions about life.

17. In reading the Bible, we will find many answers **to our questions** about life.

18. In reading the Bible, we will find many answers to our questions **about life.**

19. Earthquakes are not unusual **to us** in California.

20. Earthquakes are not unusual to us **in California.**

Unit 5
Do They Agree?

One of the things that makes people sound illiterate in their speech and writing is using subjects and verbs that do not agree with each other in grammatical form. For example, it sounds uneducated to say: *"The boys has their coats with them."* Most people for whom English is a native language have learned instinctively to make their subjects and verbs agree in form. However, there are a number of common problems areas which need careful study. Sometimes when a phrase comes between a subject and its verb, we can become confused about which form of the verb to use. Indefinite pronouns, contractions, and compound subjects also cause confusion for many people, as do "turnaround" (or "delayed-subject") sentences beginning with *"Here"* or *"There."* We will study these problem areas in this unit. But first we must understand two related grammatical concepts: *number* and *person*.

LESSON 31: SINGULAR AND PLURAL (NUMBER)

> **NUMBER is the form taken by a noun, pronoun, or verb indicating whether it refers to one or more than one.**
>
> **When a word refers to one person, place, thing, idea, quality, action, or condition, it is SINGULAR in number.**
>
> **When a word refers to more than one, it is PLURAL in number.**

All nouns, pronouns, and verbs are either *singular* or *plural* in *number.* Most nouns, pronouns, and verbs show which number they are by a change in their form. Learn the following rules about singular and plural forms of *nouns*:

Rule 5.1	**Most singular nouns are changed to plural by adding -s or -es.**
Rule 5.2	**When a singular noun ends with a -y preceded by a consonant, the -y is changed to -i before the plural ending is added.**

Rule 5.3	When a singular noun ends with a -*y* preceded by a vowel, the -*y* is NOT changed before the plural ending is added.
Rule 5.4	When a singular noun ends with -*ss, -x, -ch,* or -*sh,* the plural is usually formed by adding -*es.*
Rule 5.5	Some singular nouns change their spelling or add other endings to form their plurals.
Rule 5.6	Some nouns have the same form for both singular and plural.

☞**EXAMPLES:** (Numbers refer to the rule above that applies.)

SINGULAR	PLURAL	RULE	SINGULAR	PLURAL	RULE
boat	boats	1	knife	knives	5
house	houses	1	scarf	scarves	5
bully	bullies	2	ox	oxen	5
monkey	monkeys	3	goose	geese	5
fox	foxes	4	man	men	5
class	classes	4	mouse	mice	5
church	churches	4	deer	deer	6
bush	bushes	4	sheep	sheep	6

Personal pronouns (including their possessive forms) use entirely different words for singular and plural, except for *"you,"* which stays the same.

SINGULAR	PLURAL
I, me, my, mine	we, us, our, ours
you, your, yours	you, your, yours
he, him, his, she, her, hers, it, its	they, them, their, theirs

The singular and plural forms of most *action verbs* follow a pattern which is the opposite of the pattern for nouns. The singular of action verbs usually ends with -*s* or -*es*, while the plural does not.

☞**EXAMPLES:**

SINGULAR	PLURAL	SINGULAR	PLURAL
he *gets*	they *get*	balloon *rises*	balloons *rise*
cow *eats*	cows *eat*	horse *gallops*	horses *gallop*
pastor *preaches*	pastors *preach*	he *empties*	they *empty*
contestant *exhibits*	contestants *exhibit*	musician *plays*	musicians *play*

Linking verbs have various forms for singular and plural. You must simply memorize them. Here are some examples of the singular and plural forms of *to be* and some other linking verbs:

SINGULAR	PLURAL
am, are, is, was, were, (shall/will) be, (have/has) been	are, were, (shall/will) be, (have) been
seem, seems, seemed	seem, seemed
taste, tastes, tasted	taste, tasted
become, became	become, became
feel, feels, felt	feel, felt

✎ **EXERCISE** In the blanks, write **S** if the word is singular, **P** if the word is plural, or **B** if the word could be both singular and plural. Nouns and verbs are included. NOTE: This exercise continues on the following page.

____ 1. clowns (noun)

____ 2. clowns (verb)

____ 3. computer

____ 4. computes

____ 5. paint (verb)

____ 6. paint (noun)

____ 7. whispers (noun)

____ 8. whispers (verb)

____ 9. cabinet

____ 10. lamps

____ 11. Popsicle

____ 12. train (verb)

____ 13. train (noun)

____ 14. knife (noun)

____ 15. knives

____ 16. knifes (verb)

____ 17. were

____ 18. woman

____ 19. they

____ 20. crosses (noun)

____ 21. crosses (verb)

____ 22. coupon

____ 23. asked

____ 24. said

____ 25. beaches (noun)

____ 26. dollar

____ 27. sofa

____ 28. floors (noun)

____ 29. sale

____ 30. sail (noun)

____ 31. sails (verb)

____ 32. radios (noun)

____ 33. radios (verb)

____ 34. lice

____ 35. children

____ 36. birds

____ 37.	leaves (noun)	____ 47.	books (noun)	____ 55.	had
____ 38.	leaves (verb)	____ 48.	books (verb)	____ 56.	watched
____ 39.	ribbon	____ 49.	printer	____ 57.	agrees
____ 40.	cloud (noun)	____ 50.	staplers	____ 58.	dances (noun)
____ 43.	bicycle (noun)	____ 51.	crouches (verb)	____ 59.	dances (verb)
____ 44.	losses	____ 52.	like (verb)	____ 60.	boxes (noun)
____ 45.	loses	____ 53.	bypasses (noun)	____ 61.	boxes (verb)
____ 46.	speakers	____ 54.	bypasses (verb)	____ 62.	us

LESSON 32: PERSON

> **PERSON is a term describing the form taken by PRONOUNS indicating whether the person or thing represented by the pronoun is the one speaking (first person), the one spoken to (second person), or the one spoken about (third person).**
>
> **VERBS also have PERSON. When used with pronouns, the form of verbs varies according to the person of the pronoun with which they are associated.**

Before we go on to study agreement between subjects and verbs, we need to learn about the grammatical concept of *person*. This is only important when the subject is a *personal pronoun*. We do not usually speak about nouns having person, although when it comes to choosing the right verb to go with a noun subject, we could say that all nouns are in the *third person* (the person, thing, etc., *spoken about*) and therefore nouns take a verb in the *third person*. Most of our problems with subject-verb agreement come when the subject is a personal pronoun, because personal pronouns have three distinct persons; and we must learn to choose the correct corresponding verb form.

The chart below shows the forms that personal pronouns take according to person. Since we are primarily concerned right now about subject-verb agreement, the **subjective** form of the pronoun is highlighted with dark print; other forms are in parentheses.

PERSON	SINGULAR	PLURAL
First Person	**I** (me, my, mine)	**we** (us, our, ours)
Second Person	**you** (yours, you, your, thou, thee, thine, thy)	**you** (yours, you, your, ye)
Third Person	**he, she, it** (him, her, his, hers, its)	**they** (them, their, theirs)

✎ **EXERCISE** Underline the personal pronouns in the following sentences. Above them, write **1, 2,** or **3** to indicate whether they are in the *first, second,* or *third* person.

      1   *2*   *1*

1. <u>We</u> would like to invite <u>you</u> to <u>our</u> party.

2. "Thine is the kingdom, and the power, and the glory." *(The Lord's Prayer)*

3. She always gives them a lecture when they misbehave.

4. You were on my mind this morning when I received your greeting card.

5. "Give me your tired, your poor, your humble masses yearning to be free." *(Statue of Liberty in-scription)*

6. You may give them whatever they want.

7. We will be eternally in your debt for the kindness you have shown us.

8. It has come to my attention that you are related to my best friend.

9. "Mine, Mine was the transgression, but Thine the deadly pain." *(Bernard of Clairvaux)*

10. He is stronger than I.

11. "They were expected to defeat us, but we defeated them instead," he and I reported.

12. We need to have the death of Christ applied to our account if we are to be forgiven of our sins.

13. "Will you tell us another story?" they asked her.

14. He told him, "Believe on the Lord Jesus Christ, and thou shalt be saved."

15. "I have asked you not to borrow my clothes without consulting me first," she complained to her sister.

16. "Thou shalt not covet thy neighbor's house." *(Tenth Commandment)*

17. She took them to her room to show them its new decor.

18. "I was in the bathtub when you called me," he told their friend.

LESSON 33: SUBJECT-VERB AGREEMENT

Rule 5.7	SUBJECTS and VERBS must agree with each other in number and person.

When a subject is singular, the verb must be singular also. When the subject is plural, the verb must be plural. All *noun* subjects take the third person form of the verb, either singular or plural. Verbs used with *pronoun* subjects must have the same person and number as the pronouns. These rules apply to all kinds of verbs: action, helping, and linking.

Perhaps the most commonly heard mistake is the use of the singular form of the verb *to be* with the plural pronoun *they*, as in the following sentence: *They was on their way to our house when the accident occurred.* In fact, most errors with subject-verb agreement occur when personal pronouns are used with a form of the verb *to be*. Because this is so, it would be good to memorize the various possible forms of *to be* as shown in the following chart*:

SINGULAR	PLURAL	SINGULAR	PLURAL
I am	we are	I have been	we have been
you are	you are	you have been	you have been
he, she, it is	they are	he, she, it has been	they have been
I was	we were	I had been	we had been
you were	you were	you had been	you had been
he, she, it was	they were	he, she, it had been	they had been
I shall be	we shall be	I shall have been	we shall have been
you will be	you will be	you will have been	you will have been
he, she, it will be	they will be	he, she, it will have been	they will have been

Note: *There are other forms, in addition to the above, which you will learn later in your studies of grammar.

✎ **EXERCISE A** Underline the correct form of the verb in parentheses in each of the following sentences:

1. Dogs (<u>chase</u>, chases) cats.

2. They (has eaten, have eaten) at that restaurant before.

3. My friends (plan, plans) to visit me during Christmas vacation.

4. He (come, comes) over to our house frequently.

5. The sun (shine, shines) through my window early every morning.

6. He (own, owns) two horses.

7. Parties often (become, becomes) rowdy when Duane and his friends arrive.

8. That apple pie (taste, tastes) delicious.

9. They (was coming, were coming) sometime after 9 p.m.

10. Several spiritual revivals (has occurred, have occurred) in our country's history.

11. You (was, were) among the guests, (was, were) you not?

12. We (was, were) late for church this morning.

✎ **EXERCISE B** Rewrite the following sentences, changing the *number* of the subjects and verbs from singular to plural or from plural to singular. (You may have to change other words in the sentence also.)

1. The women were discussing the pros and cons of motherhood.

_____*A woman was discussing the pros and cons of motherhood.*_____

2. The states have certain rights under the Constitution.

_____

3. We are privileged to live in this country.

_____

4. The trees were cut down to make way for a new road.

_____

5. Several old records were broken during our track meet yesterday.

_____

6. He has a collection of antiques.

   _____

7. The tables were purchased at a local furniture store.

   _____

8. The encyclopedia belongs to our school library.

   _____

9. Plural subjects take plural verbs.

   _____

LESSON 34: STUMBLING OVER PHRASES AND COMPOUNDS

When a verb comes right after its subject, most people have no trouble making the two of them agree in number and person. However, there are two grammatical situations which often cause stumbles in subject-verb agreement. One is when a prepositional or other phrase comes between the subject and the verb.

Rule 5.8	The number or person of a subject is not changed by any phrase that may come between the subject and its verb.

Most English speakers have a tendency to make a verb agree with the noun that is closest to it. That tendency can be helpful, as we shall see in a moment; but it causes problems for some people when a phrase coming between the subject and verb contains a noun of a different number and/or person than that of the subject.

☞**EXAMPLES:**

    WRONG: One *player* (from all the teams playing in the tournament) *were* injured.

    RIGHT: One *player* (from all the teams playing in the tournament) *was* injured.

Compound subjects can also cause errors with subject-verb agreement, especially when a compound subject consists of nouns or pronouns that are different in number and/or person. Learn these rules:

Rule 5.9	Compound subjects joined by the conjunction 'AND' take a *plural* verb UNLESS they refer to a *single* entity.

Rule 5.10	**Singular compound subjects joined by OR, NOR, EITHER...OR, or NEITHER...NOR take a singular verb. Plural compound subjects joined by these conjunctions take plural verbs.**
Rule 5.11	**If a compound subject consists of both a singular word and a plural word and these are joined by OR, NOR, EITHER...OR or NEITHER... NOR, the verb should agree with the subject closest to the verb.**

The rules in the previous boxes refer to differences in number. Similar rules apply when the compound subjects have elements that differ in *person*.

☞**EXAMPLES:**

Bill and Charlene *are* coming for dinner tonight.

The band **director and** softball **coach** *is* Mr. Potts. (Mr. Potts has both positions.)

Neither he nor we *understand* the instructions.

Either she or I *am* going.

✎ **EXERCISE A** Underline the correct verb in the following sentences.

1. Katie and she (is, <u>are</u>) the best of friends.

2. Either one 12-inch pipe or two 6-inch pipes (fill, fills) the gap.

3. Neither the book nor its movie version (have, has) a good plot.

4. Both public and private schools (were, was) invited to participate in the track meet.

5. The local public school and local Christian schools (has, have) equal numbers of students.

6. A truck and five cars (were, was) blocking the intersection.

7. You and I never (quarrels, quarrel).

8. The boys in the back of the bus ahead of us (were, was) waving at us.

9. Two eggs in the carton of twelve (was, were) cracked.

10. Scores of Canada geese or a flock of ducks (stop, stops) at our pond on their way south every fall.

11. One teacher from both schools (was, were) chosen to attend the conference.

12. Hopes for the success of our team in the tournament (are, is) fading with every game.

13. Cows and horses (graze, grazes) in the same pasture.

14. The pigeons in the park (are, is) both an attraction and a nuisance.

15. Neither my parents nor I (have, has) blond hair.

16. Either red and white or blue and gold (is, are) the favorite combination for school colors.

17. *People and Places* (is, are) the name of my geography book.

✎ **EXERCISE B** Unless a prepositional phrase is used as a subject itself, the subject of the sentence will not be found in a prepositional phrase. Find the subjects in the following sentences and underline them. If the verb does not agree in number and person with the subject, cross it out and write the correct form above it.

attend

1. <u>Ten</u> of the women on the committee from our church ~~attends~~ regularly.

2. The hayfields toward the back of our farm needs mowing.

3. All of the boys in the third row from the front is the same height.

4. The magazine with the article about nutrition contains several other interesting stories.

5. Classes at the school in our neighborhood starts at 8:30 a.m.

6. We, the people of the United States of America, has much for which to be thankful.

7. Scientists and engineers at a laboratory in Ohio have been testing several new devices.

8. That joke about the boy from Brooklyn visiting his cousin in Iowa makes me laugh.

9. The hamsters in the cage in our classroom has escaped.

10. The length of the two books are about the same.

11. A delegation of students usually attend the school board meeting.

12. Heather, Lonnie, and Molly, the three youngest members of our class, has won awards.

13. A person with glasses rarely are accepted into jet-pilot training school in the Air Force.

14. The puffy, white clouds below the aircraft resembles a bowlful of popcorn.

15. For a joke, the boys sometimes walk up to my door, ring the doorbell, and then runs off.

16. The can of oil and the box of tools in the trunk belongs to my brother.

17. The winner of both events at the track meet receive a blue ribbon.

18. In the late summer, the children from our church and from several other churches attend Bible camp at the lake.

19. Compound verbs should both agree with the subject of the sentence.

20. Light from stars in distant galaxies take many years to reach earth.

LESSON 35: VERBS WITH INDEFINITE PRONOUNS

There is a certain class of noun substitutes called *indefinite pronouns*. They are called "indefinite" because they seem to refer to no particular person, place, or thing named elsewhere in the sentence that contains them. This quality of "indefiniteness" makes choosing the correct verb form difficult when they are used as subjects of sentences, especially when they are modified by prepositional phrases. The problem is that it is sometimes difficult to determine if they are plural or singular.

The best way to avoid mistakes is to memorize which of these indefinite pronouns are usually plural and which are usually singular.

The following indefinite pronouns usually require *singular verbs* because, in most cases, they imply the idea of "one":

INDEFINITE PRONOUNS + SINGULAR VERBS			
anybody anyone each	either everybody everyone	neither nobody no one	one somebody someone

☞**EXAMPLES:**

Each of the boys *has* his own room.

Neither of you *seems* to understand my problem.

Someone is knocking at my door.

The following indefinite pronouns usually require *plural verbs* because they imply the idea of "more than one":

INDEFINITE PRONOUNS + PLURAL VERBS			
both	few	many	several

☞**EXAMPLES:**

Both of the books *are* overdue at the library.

Many are called, but *few are chosen*.

Several of the children *are* from Japan.

The following indefinite pronouns may require *either singular or plural verbs*. You must look at the context of the sentence to determine which number of verb to use. Clues as to the number of these pronouns can usually be determined from the number of any nouns used as objects of prepositions in phrases that modify these pronouns or from the number of any other words in the sentence. In the illustrations that follow, the underlined words in the adjective phrases provide the context needed to determine the number of the pronouns.

INDEFINITE PRONOUNS + SINGULAR OR PLURAL VERBS				
all	any	most	none	some

☞**EXAMPLES:**

Some of the <u>milk</u> *was spilled*.

Some of the <u>hunters</u> *were* successful.

All of the <u>water</u> *has evaporated*.

All of the <u>trees</u> *are* maples.

Most of the <u>girls</u> in the second grade *are* taller than the boys.

Most of the <u>air</u> *was removed* from the vacuum tube.

In some cases, context may not be available in the sentence that contains the indefinite pronoun. If the sentence is part of a larger narrative, the number of the pronoun may have to be found in a preceding sentence, for example. Otherwise, the intent of the speaker or writer governs the choice of verb forms.

☞**EXAMPLES:**

The <u>girls</u> vowed to keep the secret. *None* [implied: "of <u>them</u>"] *have* ever *told*.

It would also be acceptable to say:

The girls vowed to keep the secret. *None* [meaning: "no one"] *has* ever *told*.

✎ **EXERCISE A** Underline the correct verb in parentheses.

1. One of these pens (<u>is</u>, are) out of ink.

2. Both of these checks (need, needs) endorsement.

3. Neither of the candidates (seems, seem) to understand the issues.

4. Either of your ideas (is, are) acceptable to the committee.

5. Everyone, from the young to the old, (enjoys, enjoy) a good joke.

6. Few of those who enter that battle ever (survive, survives).

7. Someone (know, knows) who did it.

8. No one in the room (was, were) willing to admit it.

9. Each of the winners (receives, receive) a certificate of merit.

10. Several of England's monarchs (has, have) been women.

11. Anyone who buys this car (deserve, deserves) to be forewarned about its problems.

✎ **EXERCISE B** Some of the verbs in the following sentences do not agree with their subjects. Cross out any incorrect verb and write the correct form above it. If the verb is correct, leave the sentence as it is.

1. Neither of the two colors ~~go~~ *goes* well with her skin complexion and hair.

2. Everyone in those churches enjoy singing this song.

3. Some of the clouds have moved eastward.

4. Any of the students who pass the first test is eligible for the next round.

5. Not all of the students are eligible.

6. Many of the students proceeds to the next round after passing their first test.

7. "No one, having put his hand to the plow and looking back, is fit for the kingdom of God" *(Luke 9:62, NKJV).*

8. It seems that someone in the two groups always arrive late.

9. Both of their sons are more than six feet tall.

10. One of these paintings are a fake.

11. A flu outbreak has hit many of the students in our school. Most has missed several days of attendance.

12. One of the most popular patriotic songs are "America the Beautiful."

LESSON 36: OTHER PROBLEMS WITH AGREEMENT

CONTRACTIONS

A *contraction* is a word made up of two words, with one or more of the letters omitted and replaced by an apostrophe. Certain contractions cause problems with subject-verb agreement for many people. The biggest offenders are *don't*, *doesn't*, and *aren't.*

Some people commonly confuse *don't* and *doesn't*. To avoid this confusion, remember that *don't* is short for *do not* and must be used with *plural subjects and the singular pronouns "I" and "you." Doesn't* is short for *does not* and must be used with *singular subjects, except "I" and "you."* Study the chart below.

SINGULAR	PLURAL
I don't	we don't
you don't	you don't
he, she, it doesn't	they don't
the dog doesn't	the dogs don't

☞**EXAMPLES:**

WRONG: George *don't* know what to do next.

RIGHT: George *doesn't* know what to do next.

WRONG: The questions you ask *doesn't* matter as much as the answers you give.

RIGHT: The questions you ask *don't* matter as much as the answers you give.

Another verb contraction that is commonly abused is *aren't*, especially when it is used with the subjective personal pronoun *"I"* in the form of a question.

WRONG: *Aren't I* going along with you?

I'm the logical choice, *aren't I*?

It is curious that people who would never think of saying *"I are not"* often make the mistake of saying *"Aren't I?"* To avoid this problem, keep in mind that *aren't* is short for *are not*. The personal pronoun *"I"* is singular and requires the first-person, singular form of "to be," which is *"am."*

Much of the problem with this idiom comes from the fact that the contraction for *am not* is *ain't*. This word traditionally has been considered to be substandard speech and therefore has been discouraged. Speakers and writers who wish to avoid the use of *ain't* should use the expression *am not* rather than its contraction.

☞**EXAMPLE:**

SUBSTANDARD: I'm the logical choice, *ain't I?*

Ain't I going along with you?

PREFERRED: I'm the logical choice, *am I not?*

Am I not going along with you?

THE WORD "NUMBER" AS A SUBJECT

When the word *"number"* is used as a subject, it requires a *plural* verb if preceded by the article *"a."*

☞**EXAMPLE:**

A *number* of us *are* disappointed.

When the word *"number"* is used as a subject, it requires a *singular* verb if preceded by the article *"the."*

☞**EXAMPLE:**

The *number* of winners *is* to be announced on Saturday.

To help you make the right choice, use this memory device: Remember that the article *"a"* means *"any of a large group"* (plural = more than one), while the article *"the"* means *"that particular one"* (singular = one).

"HERE" AND "THERE"

Some sentences beginning with the words *here* or *there* are called "turnaround" sentences. One of the features of such sentences is that the subject comes after the verb. For this reason, the subjects are sometimes referred to as "delayed subjects." This arrangement means that special care must be taken to determine the subject and to match it to the proper form of the verb. To avoid errors with subject-verb agreement, you must "think ahead" to select the proper verb form.

☞**EXAMPLES:**

There *are* several *problems* to consider. *(Plural subject—"problems"; plural verb—"are")*

Here *is* a *list* of things to avoid. *(Singular subject—"list"; singular verb—"is")*

Here *are* a *number* of rules to learn. *(Plural subject—"number"; plural verb—"are")*

Is there a *problem*? *(Singular subject—"problem"; singular verb—"is")*

The same rules apply when the contracted forms **here's**, **here're** *(here are)*, **there's**, and **there're** *(there are)* are used.

SENTENCES BEGINNING WITH PHRASES

You must also "look ahead" when a prepositional phrase begins a sentence. Refer to Lesson 27 for a discussion about some such phrases, which some grammar experts consider to be noun phrases and others consider to be adverb phrases. When an *action verb* is used, such phrases clearly appear to be adverb phrases. Whatever they are called, they raise a potential problem for selecting the correct verb. To choose the correct verb, you must "look ahead" to the noun or pronoun which follows.

☞**EXAMPLES:**

Down the aisle *walk* the **bride and groom**. *(The **bride and groom walk** down the aisle.)*

At the top of the pile *was* my **notebook**. *(My **notebook was** at the top of the pile.)*

Up in the sky is where some children point when asked where God lives.

Under the table were two sleeping cats. *(Two sleeping **cats were** under the table.)*

INTERROGATORY SENTENCES

The subject often comes after the verb in sentences that ask questions. In some interrogatory sentences, the subject may come between the parts of a verb phrase. These arrangements make it necessary to give careful thought to subject-verb agreement. It may be helpful to mentally change the word order around, so that the subject comes first.

☞**EXAMPLES:**

What *is* your **name**? *(Your **name is** what?)*

Do you and Jane want your lunch now? *(**You and Jane do want** your lunch now.)*

Have they changed their minds? *(**They have changed** their minds.)*

✎ **EXERCISE A** Underline the subject(s) in the following sentences. Then underline the correct choice in parentheses.

1. Here (come, <u>comes</u>) my <u>brother</u>.

2. (Have, has) you seen my sunglasses anywhere?

3. The humidity during the summer months (don't, doesn't) bother me.

4. Under the tree (is, are) a large number of fallen apples.

5. The largest number of people ever to fill our stadium (was, were) disappointed by our team's defeat.

6. (Do, does) your parents approve of your friends?

7. (Where's, Where are) the books I gave you?

8. On the street following the accident (was, were) many pieces of broken glass.

9. There (have, has) been a record rainfall this season.

10. (Here's, Here are) the magazines you ordered.

11. (What's, What're) those dogs eating?

12. A number of us (disagree, disagrees) with you.

13. Down the street (is, are) my friend's house.

14. (Has, Have) any of the class members heard of the French composer Claude Debussy?

LESSON 37: UNIT REVIEW

✎ **EXERCISE A** Put an ✓ in the box next to the best answer.

1. _____ is a term describing the form taken by nouns, pronouns, and verbs to indicate one or more than one.

    ❑ Number   ❑ Person   ❑ Nominative

2. The form of a pronoun indicating the person, place, or thing *spoken about* is the _____ person.

    ❑ first   ❑ second   ❑ third

3. When a singular noun ends with *-ss, -x, -sh,* or *-ch,* the plural is usually formed by adding
   _____.

   ❑ the letter "s"   ❑ the letters "es"   ❑ nothing

4. Some nouns use the same form for both singular and plural.

   ❑ True   ❑ False

5. Subjects and verbs must agree in _____.

   ❑ person only   ❑ person and number   ❑ number only

6. The word "number" requires a plural verb if it is preceded by the article _____.

   ❑ "a"   ❑ "the"

7. The number and person of a subject is _____ by any phrase which comes between
   it and its verb.

   ❑ changed   ❑ not affected   ❑ determined

8. Two subjects joined by the conjunction "and" require _____
   verb.

   ❑ a singular   ❑ either a singular or plural   ❑ a plural

9. Which of the following groups of indefinite pronouns require a singular verb?

   ❑ none, most, several   ❑ all, some, few   ❑ anybody, one, everyone

10. The contraction "don't" may be used with a _____ subject.

    ❑ singular   ❑ plural

11. Sentences beginning with "here" or "there" are called _____ sentences.

    ❑ "turnaround"   ❑ "delayed-subject"   ❑ either of the previous

✎ **EXERCISE B** Underline the correct verb(s) or contraction(s) in parentheses.

1. Each of us (has, have) a responsibility to pray for our leaders.

2. One of the most common birds (is, are) the sparrow.

3. Some of the most common birds (is, are) sparrows and starlings.

4. Here (is, are) several suggestions for composition topics.

5. His collection of matchbook covers (was, were) stolen.

6. It (is, are) a sad fact that more and more children in our day and age (live, lives) with a single parent.

7. Many (are, is) the times I have wanted to visit Hawaii.

8. Jennifer, Casey, and I (is, are) glad you and Stacey (is, are) joining us.

9. On the table beside the sofa (is, are) my mother's favorite lamp.

10. On the table beside the sofa there (is, are) two new magazines.

11. (There's, There're) two gentlemen in the hallway waiting to see you.

12. (Wasn't, Weren't) you happy to see me?

13. The oxen (isn't, aren't) used much for pulling wagons anymore.

14. In the grass (crawl, crawls) thousands of insects.

15. In the grass (crawl, crawls) a thousand insects.

16. There (was, were) too many people to fit into the elevator.

17. (Don't, Doesn't) you think there (is, are) several possible answers?

18. Either "A" or "B" (is, are) correct.

19. Here finally (is, are) the answers for which you (has, have) been seeking.

20. Who among the great philosophers really (know, knows) the truth?

21. (Have, Has) God ever promised Christians a life of ease?

22. Happy (is, are) the nation whose God (is, are) the Lord.

✎ **EXERCISE C** Refer to the introductory paragraph for Unit 5 to answer the following:

1. *Write* the first sentence from that paragraph below. Underline the subject of the sentence. Double-underline the main verb of the sentence.

    _____

    _____

2. *Write* the third sentence from that paragraph below. Underline the subject of the sentence. Double-underline the main verb of the sentence.

    _____

    _____

3. *Read* the fourth sentence of that paragraph. What is the subject of the sentence? Why is the main verb ("are") plural?

    _____

    _____

4. *Read* the sixth sentence. Why is the verb in the second clause (...as *do* "turnaround"...) plural rather than singular (*"does"*)?

    _____

    _____

Unit 6
Using Words

In Unit 1, we noted that the word is the smallest unit of speech or writing that can stand alone as a meaningful utterance. We learned that every word can be classified as one of the eight parts of speech common to the English language. In addition to the problem of *identifying* words, users of English also face the problems of *spelling* and *diction*.

Correct spelling is absolutely essential to effective communication. Even the smallest errors can mark the writer as substandard and are a source of irritation and distraction to readers. For this reason, not only your teachers but also your future employers, businessmen, and professional associates will evaluate your competence on the basis of your commitment to high performance in spelling. Admittedly, spelling the English language is difficult, but correctness is very important.

> *Diction reveals the man even more clearly than dress or manners. A person's choice of words is not accidental but is an organic part of him—of his education, his environment, his background, his occupation. Listen to someone for a few minutes, or read something he has written, and you will learn much about the kind of person he is. Thus, we frequently say of some, "He talks like a lawyer," or a physician, or a scientist, or a sailor. A novelist or a dramatist makes each of his characters use words that are suitable, "in character."*
>
> *Since diction is basic in all writing, and since it is clearly indicative of what we are and what we wish to express, every one who puts words on paper, who even opens his mouth to speak, must keep in mind the necessity for regular effort to improve in the choice and use of words.*
>
> — George S. Wykoff, Harry Shaw, *The Harper Handbook*

Diction refers to the choice of words for the expression of ideas. This also is an important aspect of effective communication. Individuals with a strong command of words are able to communicate their ideas precisely and are thus better able to influence people and accomplish their own goals. Christians, who have been charged by God to communicate the Gospel, should be especially concerned about their overall ability to express ideas effectively.

LESSON 38: THE DICTIONARY

One of the most useful tools for achieving good diction is the "*diction*-ary." When you study grammar or spelling or when you write, you should always have immediate access to a good dictionary. The English poet and essayist Samuel Johnson once advised: "Give your days and nights to wise study of your dictionary." Noah Webster, who wrote the first dictionary of American English, said he compiled his dictionary "to ascertain the true principles of language," to purify it from errors, to reduce its irregularities, and to pass on to future generations of Americans a consistent and standardized "tongue." Perhaps your school or curriculum provider has already recommended a quality dictionary for you to use. If not, here are some guidelines for choosing and using a dictionary.

1.   CHOOSE A RELIABLE DICTIONARY

There are hundreds of different types of dictionaries available on the market. Some are useful study tools; some have only minimum value. The name Webster on the cover is no longer a reliable guide, since virtually any publisher may use the name. In choosing a dictionary, consider the following:

■ **Has the dictionary been recently published or revised?**

While newness may not always be the best test of the dictionary publisher's commitment to purity of language and language heritage, currency is important in helping you understand the language of your day. Noah Webster's 1828 dictionary is still useful, especially for Christians, but even Webster acknowledged that times, circumstances, and cultures change and dictionaries are necessary both to preserve continuity with the past and to keep current with what is "new and peculiar."

■ **What are the qualifications of those who have compiled it, and what is the scholarly reputation of the publisher?**

■ **Is it sufficiently large, with at least 60,000 to 100,000 entries?**

■ **Does it have complete or detailed explanations and word background information?**

■ **Does it maintain high standards of usage or does it include vulgar and incorrect usage without comment?**

Among the commonly recognized quality desk-size dictionaries are the following: *Webster's New World Dictionary of the American Language, Webster's New Collegiate Dictionary, The American College Dictionary, The Random House College Dictionary, Funk & Wagnall's Standard College Dictionary, The American Heritage Dictionary of the English Language,* and *The Thorndike-Barnhart Comprehensive Desk Dictionary.* Larger, unabridged works (with 300,000 to 600,000 entries) include *Webster's Third New International Dictionary of the English Language; Webster's New International Dictionary of the English Language, Second Edition;* and *The Random House Dictionary of the English Language.*

2.   LEARN HOW TO USE YOUR DICTIONARY

A dictionary has many uses. Before trying to use it, you should become familiar with its contents. Examine the table of contents and look over the explanatory notes at the front of the book. The notes will tell you how the dictionary itself describes things. It will probably have a sample of word entries, with explanations about abbreviations, pronunciation, symbols, and other devices it uses to help you understand words. The dictionary may have illustrations, appendixes, and various tables and listings with special information.

3.   FIND THE WORD

The words in the main body of the dictionary are listed alphabetically, of course. The first help available to you are the guide words at the top of each page. The word on the left will be the first word listed on the page; the word on the right will be the last word on the page. Look at the guide words and determine if the word you are seeking falls alphabetically between the two guide words. All entries are listed letter by letter in alphabetic order, including compound and hyphenated words.

4. FIND THE DEFINITION

Many words have more than one meaning and some can be more than one part of speech. Check the word entry for abbreviations indicating which part of speech the word is. If you are looking for a definition of a verb, make sure you are not reading a definition of the noun version of that word. Review all the various definitions listed under a given part-of-speech listing for that word. Find the exact definition that best suits the context for your particular use of the word. Look for usage notes such as *"slang," "obs."* (obsolete), *"vulgar,"* or *"archaic."* These labels describe non-standard usage, and you should be forewarned about using a word which may not be appropriate for your intended communication. Here is a sample of three entries in *Webster's New Collegiate Dictionary*:

re•li´gion (re•lij´*un*), *n.* [OF., fr. L. *religio*, prop., taboo, restraint.] **1.** The service and adoration of God or a god as expressed in forms of worship. **2.** One of the systems of faith and worship. **3.** The profession of practice of religious beliefs; religious observances collectively; *pl.*, rites. **4.** Devotion or fidelity; conscientiousness. **5.** An awareness or conviction of the existence of a supreme being, arousing reverence, love, gratitude, the will to obey and serve, and the like; as, man only is capable of *religion*.

state´ly (stat´li), *adj.*; STATE´LI•ER (-li•er); STATE´LI•EST. Evincing state, or lofty dignity.—**Syn.** See GRAND. —*adv.* In a stately manner. — **state´li•ness,** *n.*

thwart (thwôrt; *naut.* thôrt), *adj.* [ME. *thwert,* adv., fr. ON, *thvert,* orig. neut. of *thverr* athwart, transverse.] **1.** Situated or placed across something else; transverse; oblique. **2.** *Obs.* Perverse; intractable. —*adv.* Athwart. —*n. Naut.* A rower's seat reaching athwart a boat. —*v.t.* **1.** *Obs.* To pass through or across. **2.** To oppose or baffle, as a purpose; hence, to frustrate or defeat; block. —**Syn.** See FRUSTRATE. —**thwart´er,** *n.*

Take note of all the items of information in these listings. Most dictionaries include such pieces of information as the following:

■ Vocabulary entry

The main word is usually printed in bold (dark) type. Other words associated with the main entry often follow, also in bold type. Sometimes these associated words are listed only by the prefixes or suffixes which distinguish them from the main word.

■ Spelling

The main word and associated words are spelled. Usually plurals are indicated by their suffixes or alternative spellings. Various forms of adjectives, adverbs, and verbs are spelled or indicated by their endings. Compound words are spelled either with hyphens or as solid words, according to their nature. When more than one spelling is acceptable, the preferred is given first.

■ *Syllables*

Syllables are separated by dots (•) unless the word normally is spelled with a hyphen, in which case both dots and hyphens may be used in their appropriate places.

■ *Pronunciation*

Primary and secondary accent marks are placed behind syllables to indicate emphasis. Dictionaries use a variety of symbols over vowels to indicate how those vowels are to be properly pronounced. Check the notes and pronunciation guides at the beginning of the dictionary for explanations of the meaning of these symbols and the sounds they are intended to indicate.

■ *Part of speech*

After every word entry is an abbreviation such as *n., adj., adv., v.t., v.i., conj., interj., prep., pron.,* etc., indicating which part or subpart of speech the word is. As mentioned before, many words are listed as multiple parts of speech.

■ *Origins*

Most of the better dictionaries include background information tracing the early origins of the word. The word may have come, for example, from Latin (L.), Greek (Gr.), Old English (OE), Middle French (MFr.), or Sanskrit (Skr.). The meaning(s) of the word in the language of origin is also usually given.

■ *Meanings*

Historical and current meanings, in all their shadings and varieties, are given. Each meaning is preceded by a number, usually in bold type.

■ *Special usages*

Some word entries also include indications of special or unusual usage, indicating archaic, obsolete, slang, dialect, geographical, poetic, colloquial, literary, or other uses. In the example on the previous page, for instance, the entry for **thwart** contains the notation, *Naut.,* meaning that the word has a special usage in the nautical realm. Other notations may indicate that the word has special meaning in the realm of biology, religion, baseball, etc.

■ *Synonyms and antonyms*

Often the word entry will include listings of synonyms (words with similar meanings) and antonyms (words with opposite meanings). Sometimes dozens or even hundreds of words with similar or opposite meanings will be included.

✎ **EXERCISE A** Check the spelling of the following words in your dictionary. If the word below is spelled incorrectly, write the correct spelling in the blank. If it is spelled correctly, place a check mark (✓) in the blank.

1.	sieze	_____	7.	sacrilegious	_____
2.	liquify	_____	8.	villian	_____
3.	perserverance	_____	9.	embarrass	_____
4.	questionaire	_____	10.	morgage	_____
5.	temperment	_____	11.	supersede	_____
6.	weird	_____	12.	mosquitos	_____

✎ **EXERCISE B** Each of the following words has at least two pronunciations, depending upon which part of speech it is. Look them up in your dictionary. Place an accent mark (´) at the end of the accented syllable in each case and indicate in the blank which part of speech it is.

1.	re • cord´	_*verb*_	7.	reb • el	_____
	rec • ord	_____		re • bel	_____
2.	mod • er • ate	_____	8.	con • test	_____
	mod • er • ate	_____		con • test	_____
3.	pro • duce	_____	9.	min • ute	_____
	pro • duce	_____		mi • nute	_____
4.	sub • ject	_____	10.	re • fuse	_____
	sub • ject	_____		ref • use	_____
5.	ad • dress	_____	11.	con • trast	_____
	ad • dress	_____		con • trast	_____
6.	ob • ject	_____	12.	pro • gress	_____
	ob • ject	_____		prog • ress	_____

✎ **EXERCISE C** Learn the correct pronunciation for these words. Be prepared to say them orally to your teacher, parent, or other helper. Write a brief definition for each.

1. **gnome**

_____

_____

2. **amateur**

_____

_____

3. **data**

_____

_____

4. **beret**

_____

_____

5. **subtle**

_____

_____

6. **superfluous**

_____

_____

7. **often**

_____

_____

8. **impugn**

_____

_____

9. **victuals**

_____

_____

10. **advertisement**

_____

_____

11. **suite**

_____

_____

12. **coupon**

_____

_____

13. **valet**

_____

_____

14. **indefatigable**

_____

_____

15. **adult**

_____

_____

16. imperturbable

_____

_____

17. juvenile

_____

_____

18. isthmus

_____

_____

LESSON 39: SYNONYMS

> **SYNONYMS are words that have the same or similar meanings.**

To give variety to your expressions, learn to use synonyms effectively. While synonyms are defined, as above, as words with the same or similar meanings, they often have very subtle differences in meaning as well. Choosing a word which expresses exactly the meaning you intend will help you get your ideas across to others with the utmost precision.

There are two sources of help with finding synonyms. As you learned in the previous lesson, dictionaries often list synonyms. A more complete reference book for finding synonyms is a **thesaurus.** The best known is _Roget's International Thesaurus of English Words._ Others include _Webster's Dictionary of Synonyms_ and _Crabb's English Synonyms._ Most modern electronic word processors include a computerized thesaurus, as well, making alternative word selection as simple as pushing a button or two.

✎ **EXERCISE** Write synonyms for the following words. If you cannot think of one from your general vocabulary knowledge, use a dictionary or thesaurus. NOTE: This exercise continues on the next page.

1. small   _____little_____   4. difficult   _____
2. apparent   _____   5. street   _____
3. ascend   _____   6. know   _____

7.	joyous	_____	18. grasp	_____
8.	reduce	_____	19. answer	_____
9.	cordial	_____	20. house	_____
10.	defame	_____	21. vital	_____
11.	kindle	_____	22. grace	_____
12.	avenge	_____	23. emphasize	_____
13.	rebuke	_____	24. vacate	_____
14.	yield	_____	25. hostile	_____
15.	effort	_____	26. meager	_____
16.	beat	_____	27. arrogant	_____
17.	blemish	_____	28. frank	_____

LESSON 40: ANTONYMS

ANTONYMS are pairs of words that have the opposite or negative meanings.

Sometimes we can convey the most precise meaning by choosing a word that is the opposite of a word that might normally or readily come to mind. Our intention may be best expressed by using an antonym.

You will discover, when you study antonyms, that a given word may have a number of opposites, each with a different meaning. Notice the various possible opposite meanings for the word *"man"* in the following illustration:

☞**EXAMPLE:**

man ⇔ woman   man ⇔ boy   man ⇔ beast   man ⇔ God

✎ **EXERCISE A** The following words have at least two possible antonyms with meanings completely different from each other. See the example above. Write two antonyms for the following words. NOTE: this exercise continues on the following page.

1. right _____   2. short _____

_____   _____

3. hard   _____   4. light   _____

    _____   _____

✎ **EXERCISE B** Write a single antonym for the following words.

1. arrive   _____   8. temporary   _____

2. affirmative _____   9. accept   _____

3. arrogant   _____   10. understand   _____

4. rise   _____   11. gentleman   _____

5. rough   _____   12. refined   _____

6. huge   _____   13. talkative   _____

7. decrease   _____   14. loud   _____

Sometimes antonyms are formed by the simple addition of a *prefix* which changes the meaning of a word to its opposite. Each of the prefixes below means *not*.

☞**EXAMPLES:**

un-	**+**	true	⇒	*un*true
dis-	**+**	like	⇒	*dis*like
mis-	**+**	understand	⇒	*mis*understand
in-	**+**	sincere	⇒	*in*sincere
im-	**+**	perfect	⇒	*im*perfect
ir-	**+**	reverent	⇒	*ir*reverent
il-	**+**	legal	⇒	*il*legal
a-	**+**	moral	⇒	*a*moral

Adjectives with the *suffix -**ful*** can often be changed to their antonyms by substituting the *suffix -**less***.

☞**EXAMPLES:**

joy***ful***   ⇒   joy***less***

sin***ful***   ⇒   sin***less***

fear***ful***   ⇒   fear***less***

✎ **EXERCISE C** Write antonyms for the following words, either by adding one of the negative prefixes listed above or substituting a negative suffix. If a word is listed twice, change the suffix in one case and add a negative prefix in the other.

1.	helpful	_____	15.	favor	_____
2.	respect	_____	16.	admissible	_____
3.	happy	_____	17.	graceful	_____
4.	religious	_____	18.	graceful	_____
5.	complete	_____	19.	adequate	_____
6.	faithful	_____	20.	qualify	_____
7.	faithful	_____	21.	qualified	_____
8.	harmful	_____	22.	patient	_____
9.	fruitful	_____	23.	millennial	_____
10.	licit	_____	24.	heedful	_____
11.	advisable	_____	25.	thankful	_____
12.	loyal	_____	26.	thankful	_____
13.	sensitive	_____	27.	reconcilable	_____
14.	theist	_____	28.	legitimate	_____

LESSON 41: HOMONYMS AND HOMOGRAPHS

HOMONYMS are pairs of words that sound alike but are spelled differently and have different meanings.

☞**EXAMPLES:**

scene — what is revealed to the vision or can be seen

seen — past participle form of the action verb *to see* which means *to behold*

not — negative word meaning *no*

knot — a fastening made by tying together lengths of material such a string or rope

✎ **EXERCISE A** Write at least one homonym for each of the following words. Some of these words may have two homonyms. Write them both if you can.

1.	role	_____	17.	right	_____
2.	deer	_____	18.	wrest	_____
3.	would	_____	19.	shear	_____
4.	herd	_____	20.	sew	_____
5.	know	_____	21.	whether	_____
6.	two	_____	22.	weak	_____
7.	sore	_____	23.	shone	_____
8.	new	_____	24.	shutter	_____
9.	scent	_____	25.	led	_____
10.	flue	_____	26.	passed	_____
11.	site	_____	27.	their	_____
12.	hole	_____	28.	peace	_____
13.	rap	_____	29.	stationary	_____
14.	reign	_____	30.	then	_____
15.	fare	_____	31.	who's	_____
16.	wring	_____	32.	you're	_____

✎ **EXERCISE B** Define the following homonyms and near-homonyms.

complement_____*something that completes*_____

compliment_____*an expression of regard or praise*_____

1. bare   _____

   bear   _____

2. beat _____

   beet _____

3. slay _____

   sleigh _____

4. threw _____

   through _____

5. principle _____

   principal _____

6. course _____

   coarse _____

7. counsel _____

   council _____

   consul _____

8. do _____

   due _____

9. capital _____

   capitol _____

10. accept _____

    except _____

✎ **EXERCISE C** Use the following homonyms correctly in sentences.

1. fourth _____

   _____

   forth _____

   _____

2. medal   _____

_____

metal   _____

_____

mettle   _____

_____

3. therefore   _____

_____

therefor   _____

_____

4. want   _____

_____

wont   _____

_____

5. pail   _____

_____

pale   _____

_____

6. latter   _____

_____

ladder   _____

_____

7. allusion   _____

_____

illusion   _____

_____

8. allude   _____

_____

elude   _____

_____

9. aisle   _____

_____

isle   _____

_____

10. affect   _____

_____

effect   _____

_____

11. hour   _____

_____

our   _____

_____

are   _____

_____

12. already   _____

_____

all ready   _____

_____

HOMOGRAPHS

> **HOMOGRAPHS are two or more words that are spelled alike but which have different meanings and may have different pronunciations.**

Try to avoid using homographs together in the same sentence.

☞**EXAMPLES:**

AVOID: He was a terrible *bore*, but we *bore* with him as long as we could.

BETTER: He was a terrible *bore*, but we *put up* with him as long as we could.

AVOID: The *sole* reason for buying new shoes is that the *sole* of one of them has a hole.

BETTER: The *only* reason for buying new shoes is that the *sole* of one of them has a hole.

✎ **EXERCISE D** Define the following homographs according to their various meanings. As you look them up in a dictionary, take note of any differences in pronunciations associated with each meaning.

1. row   _____

   row   _____

   row   _____

2. air   _____

   air   _____

   air   _____

3. bow   _____

   bow   _____

   bow   _____

   bow   _____

4. fair   _____

   fair   _____

5. lead   _____

    lead   _____

LESSON 42: UNIT REVIEW

✎ **EXERCISE A** Underline the correct word in parentheses to fit the meaning of the sentence.

1. The Old Testament Tabernacle included an (altar, alter) on which incense was burned.

2. We agreed to (meet, meat) our friends at the school flagpole.

3. I cannot (hear, here) what you are saying.

4. A proverb is a statement of (principle, principal) more than a rule of law.

5. His favorite (course, coarse) is history.

6. He (sent, scent, cent) me to the school nurse.

7. Her name was printed at the top of her (stationery, stationary).

8. Jimmy accidentally (through, threw) the ball over the fence.

9. Rome is the (capital, capitol) of Italy.

10. When you carry in the groceries, try not to (break, brake) the eggs.

✎ **EXERCISE B** In the blank at the end of each sentence, write a synonym for the word in **dark print**.

1. A holiday is always a big **event** in our family's life. _____

2. The **sense** of this word is hard to discern. _____

3. The **job** of building a skyscraper is immense. _____

4. You must learn the **rules** of our club if you wish to be a member. _____

5. The mall has more than one hundred **stores**. _____

6. The **main** reason I cannot come is that I am sick. _____

7. She felt quite **fatigued** after her long walk. _____

8. We **consumed** the pizza in five minutes. _____

9. What **vocation** do you plan to pursue after college? _____

10. The dog **pursued** the rabbit for nearly half a mile. _____

11. Can you give me a **hint** as to where you hid my gift? _____

12. They **constructed** their house in the suburbs. _____

✎ **EXERCISE C** Write these words in alphabetical order.

oral	brutal	lonesome	disunity	orchestra
inferior	feature	button	sausage	fortress
distress	brush	novice	camper	November
novel	confetti	saturate	irritate	linoleum
pyramid	interior	quartet	canine	federal

1. _____   10. _____   19. _____

2. _____   11. _____   20. _____

3. _____   12. _____   21. _____

4. _____   13. _____   22. _____

5. _____   14. _____   23. _____

6. _____   15. _____   24. _____

7. _____   16. _____   25. _____

8. _____   17. _____

9. _____   18. _____

✎ **EXERCISE D** Assume that the words to the left and right of each blank below are **guide words** on a page in a dictionary (see illustration below). In the blanks, write *one* word from the box on the right that would fit on the page between the guide words.

capitalize	201	captivate

cap·i·tal·ize (kap/i t⁹līz/; *Brit. also* kə pit/⁹līz/), *v.t.* **-ized, -iz·ing. 1.** to write or print in capital letters or with an initial capital. **2.** to authorize a certain amount of stocks and bonds in the corporate charter: *to capitalize a corporation.* **3.** *Accounting.* to set up (expenditures) as business assets in the books of account instead of treating as expense. **4.** to supply with capital. **5.** to estimate the value of (a stock or an enterprise). **6.** to take advantage of; turn to one's advantage (often fol. by *on*). Also, *esp. Brit.,* **cap·italise.** —**cap/i·tal·iz/a·ble,** *adj.* —**cap/i·tal·iz/er,** *n.*
cap/ital lev/y, a tax based on capital, as distinguished from a tax on income.
cap·i·tal·ly (kap/i t⁹lē), *adv.* excellently; very well.
cap/ital pun/ishment, punishment by death for a crime; death penalty.
cap/ital ship/, one of a class of the largest warships; a battleship, battle cruiser, or aircraft carrier.
cap/ital stock/, 1. the total stock authorized or issued by a corporation. **2.** the book value of the outstanding shares of a corporation.
cap·i·tate (kap/i tāt/), *adj.* **1.** *Bot.* having a globular head; collected in a head. **2.** *Biol.* having an enlarged, headlike termination. [< L *capitāt(us)* headed = *capit-* (s. of *caput*) head + *-ātus* -ATE¹]
cap·i·ta·tion (kap/i tā/shən), *n.* **1.** a poll tax. **2.** a uniform fee or payment for each person. [< LL *capitātiōn-* (s. of *capitātiō*) = L *capit-* (s. of *caput*) head + *-ātiōn-* -ATION] —**cap/i·ta/tive,** *adj.*

ca·pri·cious (kə prish/əs, -prē/shəs), *adj.* **1.** subject to, led by, or indicative of caprice or whim; erratic. **2.** *Obs.* fanciful or witty. [< It *capriccioso = cappricci(o)* CAPRICE + *-oso* -OUS] —**ca·pri/cious·ly,** *adv.* —**ca·pri/cious·ness,** *n.*
Cap·ri·corn (kap/rə kôrn/), *n.* **1.** *Astron.* the Goat, a zodiacal constellation between Sagittarius and Aquarius. **2.** *Astrol.* the 10th sign of the zodiac. See diag. at **zodiac. 3.** tropic of. See under **tropic** (def. 1a). Also, **Capricornus** (for defs. 1, 2). [ME *Capricorne* < L *Capricorn(us)* (trans. of Gk *aigókerōs* goat-horned) = *capri-* CAPRI- + *corn(ū)* HORN + *-us* adj. suffix]
Cap·ri·cor·nus (kap/rə kôr/nəs), *n., gen.* **-ni** (-nī). Capricorn (defs. 1, 2). [< L]
cap·ri·fi·ca·tion (kap/rə fə kā/shən), *n.* the pollination of figs by fig wasps attracted by the caprifig fruit hung in the branches of the trees. [< L *caprificātiōn-* (s. of *caprificātiō*) = *caprificāt(us)* pollinated from the wild fig tree (ptp. of *caprificāre;* see CAPRIFIG) + *-iōn- -ION*] —**cap/ri·fi·ca/tor,** *n.*
cap·ri·fig (kap/rə fig/), *n.* a fig, *Ficus carica sylvestris,* bearing an inedible fruit used in caprification. [< L *caprific(us)* the wild fig tree, lit., the goat-fig = *capri-* CAPRI- + *ficus* FIG¹]
cap·ri·fo·li·a·ceous (kap/rə fō/lē ā/shəs), *adj.* belonging to the *Caprifoliaceae,* plants including the honeysuckle, elder, etc. [< NL *caprifoliāce(ae)* honeysuckle family (*caprifoli(um)* honeysuckle (genus) < ML = L *capri-* CAPRI- + *folium* leaf + NL *-acea* -ACEAE) + *-ous*]

bugle	_____	**bumblebee**
dot	_____	**drafty**
everyday	_____	**example**
house	_____	**huckleberry**
pawn	_____	**peddler**
railing	_____	**ramification**

bulb	drab
enemy	ramify
hub	bureau
excite	peerless
ratify	rally
drastic	hostage
bunk	exact
pearl	horse

✎ **EXERCISE E** Test your vocabulary and spelling ability by underlining the correct word in parentheses in each of the following sentences. Check a dictionary if necessary.

1. A (dairy, diary) is a book used to record (personal, personnel) thoughts.

2. There is a (statue, statute, stature) of Stonewall Jackson on the grounds of the West Virginia State (Capitol, Capital) building.

3. Christians have formed many interpretations of the (prophecy, prophesy) of Daniel.

4. Animals should be treated (humanly, humanely).

5. The Seventh Commandment requires (marital, martial) faithfulness.

6. The boxer Mohammed Ali was known (formally, formerly) as Cassius Clay.

7. We had ice cream for (desert, dessert).

8. San Diego's (climatic, climactic) conditions are often described as ideal.

9. Put a stamp on that (envelop, envelope) and mail it for me.

10. The film director employed a variety of amazing special (affects, effects).

11. She was (all together, altogether) lovely.

12. The Bible warns us not to (avenge, revenge) a wrong done to us, but to return good for evil.

13. I will return (latter, later) to pick up my packages.

14. The fugitive was able to (allude, elude) the police for four days.

15. Chocolate syrup is the perfect (complement, compliment) for vanilla ice cream.

16. The children were (anxious, eager) to see their loving grandparents.

17. The climbers' (descent, decent) from the mountain was slow and treacherous.

Unit 7
Using Pronouns

Review Lesson 2, Lesson 35, and the information about pronouns in Lessons 31 through 33. As you learned in Lesson 2, *pronouns* are words that are used in place of nouns. Pronouns can be used in the same ways that nouns can be used; namely, as *subjects, direct objects, indirect objects, objects of prepositions, predicate nominatives,* and *appositives* (words that follow and re-name nouns or pronouns). Pronouns may be used singly or in compound groups in any of these ways.

There are several different types of pronouns: *personal, possessive, indefinite, relative, demonstrative, interrogative, reciprocal,* and *compound (intensive* and *reflexive).* In this unit, we will study all of these types of pronouns except relative pronouns. (*Relative pronouns* have a unique function in adjective clauses, the study of which is beyond the range of this unit.) Below is a chart listing many pronouns according to their type.

Personal	Possessive	Indefinite	Relative	Demon-strative	Interro-gative	Reciprocal	Com-pound
I	my	anybody	that	this	who	each other	myself
me	mine	anyone	which	that	whom	one another	ourselves
we	your	each, one	who	these	what		yourself
us	yours	many, most	whom	those	which		yourselves
you*	his	either	whose	such	whoever		himself
he	her	neither	whoever		whichever		herself
him	hers	nobody	whomever		whatever		itself
she	its	no one	whichever		whose		themselves
her	their	one, none	whatever				oneself
it	theirs	all, some	whosoever				
they	whose	any	whichsoever				
them		everybody	whatsoever				
		everyone					
		somebody					
		someone					
		both, few					
		several					

Note: *The singular and plural forms of "you" are the same. Do not use the illiterate form "yous" for the 2nd person plural of "you."

Choosing the correct pronoun is one of the most difficult problems in English grammar. The correct form of the pronoun is determined by how it is used in a sentence.

LESSON 43: USING PERSONAL PRONOUNS AS SUBJECTS AND SUBJECT COMPLEMENTS

Personal pronouns take different forms, depending upon whether they are used as subjects, subject complements, objects, or adjectives showing possession. The grammatical term describing these various forms is *case.* There are three cases: *nominative, objective,* and *possessive.* Nouns also have case, but they do not change forms unless showing possession. As subjects, subject complements, or objects, nouns use the same form. So the most difficulty with case comes when people use pronouns.

> CASE is the form that nouns or pronouns have signifying their relationship to other words in a sentence.

Only the subject form or *nominative case* (sometimes called *subjective case*) may be used for personal pronouns serving as *subjects* or *subjective complements* (predicate nominatives).

Here are the nominative-case forms of personal pronouns:

> **NOMINATIVE-CASE PRONOUNS**
> I, we, you, he, she, it, they

Note: Indefinite, demonstrative, and interrogative pronouns may also be used as subjects and subject complements.

PERSONAL PRONOUNS AS SUBJECTS

Selecting the correct form for single personal pronouns used as subjects comes quite naturally to most people familiar with the English language. For example, few people would naturally say, *"Me ate my supper"* or *"Him is a good friend."* Most of the problem comes when pronouns are used in *compound subjects*. For example, many people are inclined to say (incorrectly) such things as, *"Mary and her are sisters"* or *"John and them will be here soon."*

You can usually solve this problem by mentally saying each pronoun-subject by itself. The correct form normally will become clear by its natural sound. The most reliable way to solve the problem, however, is to memorize which pronouns are in the nominative case—those shown in the box above. Only these seven forms may be used as subjects when a personal pronoun is needed. *You* and *it* are seldom a problem because they use the same forms in both nominative and objective case. That leaves the first-person forms *I/me* (singular) and *we/us* (plural) and the third-person forms *he/him*, *she/her* (singular), and *they/them* (plural) as the main cause of confusion.

☞**EXAMPLES:**

WRONG: *Him* and *me* wear the same size of hat.

CORRECT: *He* and *I* wear the same size of hat.

WRONG: *Them* are the ones I wanted.

CORRECT: *They* are the ones I wanted.

WRONG: Audrey and *her* were the winners.

CORRECT: Audrey and *she* were the winners.

✎ **EXERCISE A** Write suitable nominative-case personal pronouns in the blanks in the following sentences. (HINT: Read the entire sentence first before trying to fill in the blanks.)

1. During the past few years, Kelly and _he_ have shared many great experiences.

2. _____ are both from Chicago.

3. _____ am happy to be a Christian.

4. Because _____ is an easy question, _____ will have no trouble passing your test.

5. Britt, Tonya, and _____ plan to sign up for the softball team.

6. Tom, _____ and _____ all enjoy history.

7. In my view, _____ and _____ are the best athletes in our school.

8. Was _____ the only one to understand me?

9. My mother and _____ look alike.

10. If your heart is humble, _____ will seldom offend others.

PERSONAL PRONOUNS AS SUBJECT COMPLEMENTS

A *subject complement* is a word that follows a linking verb and renames, describes, or explains the subject. Subjective complements can be predicate adjectives or predicate nominatives (nouns or pronouns).

Rule 7.1	**Personal pronouns used as *predicate nominatives* must be in the nominative case, just like the subjects they rename.**

☞**EXAMPLES:**

The chief *troublemaker* is **he**.

It was **they** who sent the gift.

The guilty *ones* are **she** and **I**.

Because the subject and predicate nominative refer to the same person, place, thing, idea, or quality, these two sentence parts can usually exchange places, and the sentence will still make good sense. Switching the subject and subject complement around may help you choose the correct pronoun in many cases.

☞**EAMPLES:**

The *man* of the hour is *(he, him)*.

He ~~Him~~ is the *man* of the hour.

The *person* speaking seemed to be *(her, she)*.

She ~~Her~~ seemed to be the *person* speaking.

The earliest *people* to arrive were Lisa and *(me, I)*.

Lisa and **I** ~~me~~ were the earliest *people* to arrive.

✎ **EXERCISE B** Write a suitable nominative-case personal pronoun in the blanks in each of the following sentences.

1. The next class secretary will be ___*she*___.

2. The man knocking on my door was _____.

3. The greatest beneficiaries were _____ and _____.

4. But for the grace of God, it could have been _____ and _____ in that situation.

5. In the upcoming election, the winner is likely to be _____.

6. This is _____ speaking.

7. The fastest runner was _____.

8. The loser will be _____, _____, or _____.

9. The people who started this organization were _____ and _____.

10. It was _____ calling us for dinner.

✎ **EXERCISE C** Underline the correct pronoun in parentheses in each of the following sentences.

1. (<u>She</u>, Her) and (<u>I</u>, me) are always late.

2. (He, Him) thought that Mary was (she, her).

3. When (they, them) asked who the author was, (he, him) replied, "(Me, I) am (him, he)."

4. Clarice and (she, her) are coming for a visit next week.

5. Was it you or (he, him) who ate the last five cookies?

6. It was both (he, him) and (I, me) who ate the cookies.

7. (They, them) are the songs (I, me) love to sing.

8. The telephone rang and a voice asked, "May (I, me) speak with Tina?" (I, me) replied, "This is (her, she)."

9. Why would (she, her) and (he, him) forget to call?

10. The first- and second-place finishers were (they, them) and (we, us).

LESSON 44: USING PERSONAL PRONOUNS AS OBJECTS

Like nouns, personal pronouns may be used as *direct objects, indirect objects,* and *objects of prepositions.* Unlike nouns, personal pronouns have unique forms when in the objective case.

Here are the objective-case forms of personal pronouns.

> **OBJECTIVE-CASE PRONOUNS**
>
> **me, us, you, him, her, it, them**

PERSONAL PRONOUNS AS DIRECT OBJECTS

Remember that a ***direct object*** is a noun or pronoun that receives the action of an action verb. Direct objects usually answer the questions *whom?* or *what?* about the verb.

Note: Direct objects never follow *linking verbs*. Linking verbs are followed by subject complements.

Again, *nouns* pose little problem as direct objects because nouns do not change form in the objective or nominative case. *Pronouns* in the objective case, however, do have distinct forms—those shown in the box above. Only these forms of personal pronouns may be used as direct objects when a pronoun is needed in that position in a sentence.

☞**EXAMPLES:**

Loud music annoys *her.* (*annoys whom?*)

She dislikes *it* intensely. (*dislikes what?*)

As with pronouns in the nominative case, most of the problem in choosing the correct form in the objective case comes with pronouns in *compound* direct objects and with pronouns in the first and third persons. The second-person, singular and plural personal pronoun *you* and the third-person, singular personal pronoun *it* use the same form for both nominative and objective cases.

☞**EXAMPLES:**

The team from Hope School defeated *(**him**, he)* and *(I, **me**)* in the finals.

The pastor invited *you* and *(she, **her**)* to the children's Sunday school class.

The Communist police beat *(they, **them**)* and the other prisoners unmercifully.

✎ **EXERCISE A** Write a suitable objective-case pronoun in the blanks in each of the following sentences.

1. Will you call ___*him*___ for me?

2. The teacher lectured Jake and _____ about our poor attendance.

3. Denise introduced _____ to her sister.

4. I saw neither _____ nor _____ at the concert.

5. They defeated _____ during the second round of our chess tournament.

6. She couldn't find her sunglasses because she lost _____ at the beach.

7. The witnesses reported _____ to the police.

8. Bob's father rewarded his brother and _____ for their good work.

9. The threat of disease did not worry _____ or _____.

10. He ate _____ without hesitating.

PERSONAL PRONOUNS AS INDIRECT OBJECTS

An *indirect object* is a noun or pronoun that shows *to who or what* or *for whom or what* the action of an action verb is done. It is the *receiver* of the direct object. Nouns do not change forms when used as indirect objects, but personal pronouns used as indirect objects must always be in the objective-case form.

☞**EXAMPLES:**

His parents gave *him* a compact-disc player for graduation. *(...gave [to] him...)*

The teacher told *them* an interesting account of the French Revolution. *(...told [to] them...)*

Mother bought *her* a new dress for the banquet. *(...brought [for] her...)*

✎ **EXERCISE B** Write a suitable objective-case pronoun in the blanks in each of the following sentences.

1. The waiter served ____us____ quickly and cheerfully.

2. The book gave _____ detailed instructions for assembling the machine.

3. She always cooks _____ a fine meal when we visit her.

4. They sold _____ a new one.

5. The organizers reserved _____ five seats for the game.

6. The company president offered _____ a promotion and extra benefits.

7. You told _____ a lie about their children's involvement in the incident.

8. Nellie gave Olivia and _____ two loaves of home-baked bread.

9. Who gave _____ the right to tell _____ what to do?

10. I have been informing _____ about his rights as a Christian.

PERSONAL PRONOUNS AS OBJECTS OF PREPOSITIONS

The nouns or pronouns that come after prepositions are called *objects of prepositions*, as you learned in Lesson 6 (see page 17). Because pronouns used in this way are objects, they must be in the objective-case form, just as pronouns used as direct and indirect objects must. Only the objective form of personal pronouns (those shown in the box at the beginning of this lesson) may be used as objects of prepositions.

☞**EXAMPLES:**

Jenny received a fine gift *from her.*

The bleachers *under them* collapsed.

The girl sitting *beside us* was crying.

The rule above applies even when the object of a preposition is a compound. Take special care in such cases, because most errors occur when pronouns are used in compound objects.

☞**EXAMPLES:**

Jake borrowed the tools *from Robert and me.*

Can you come *with the girls and us* to the coast next week?

To Rita and me, the wait seemed extremely long.

✎ **EXERCISE C** Write a suitable objective-case personal pronoun in the blanks in the following sentences.

1. I was talking to ___*her*___ for nearly an hour.

2. We saw everyone at the game except Will and _____.

3. Nan sat between _____ and _____.

4. They tried to put their troubles behind _____.

5. As the disciples met in an upper room, Jesus suddenly appeared among _____.

6. We Americans will long remember that the British and French fought alongside _____ during World War II.

7. Just between you and _____, I think Darcy deserves to win the contest.

8. "Thou shalt have no other gods before _____" (Exodus 20:3).

9. The school bus left without _____ and _____.

10. Mother warned the children to stay near _____ while they were in the mall.

LESSON 45: PERSONAL PRONOUNS AS APPOSITIVES AND OBJECTIVE COMPLEMENTS

> An APPOSITIVE is noun, pronoun, or other expression used as a noun, which is added to (usually after) another noun or pronoun to further identify or explain it.

☞**EXAMPLES OF APPOSITIVES:**

My father, a *doctor*, is often called out on emergencies late at night.

The thief, a young *man* wearing blue denim, was quickly apprehended.

Learn the meaning of the term *appositive* as it is given in the box above and study the two examples. An *appositive* signifies the *same thing* as the noun or pronoun it seeks to identify or explain. Therefore, the appositive *must be in the same case* as that noun or pronoun. If the word it renames is in the nominative-case form, the appositive must also be in the nominative case. If the word it renames is in the objective form, the appositive must also be in the objective case. Again, this is usually not a problem unless the appositive is a pronoun, because pronouns require different forms in each case. Special care must also be taken when the appositive is a compound.

☞**EXAMPLES OF PRONOUNS USED AS APPOSITIVES:**

One boy, *he*, will be selected to attend the competition. *("boy" is the subject)*

The judges selected one boy, *him*, to attend the competition. *("boy" is the direct object)*

The winners, *they* and *we*, were all given certificates. *("winners" is in nominative case)*

The judges gave awards to the winners, *them* and *us*. *("winners" is in objective case)*

Review what you learned about *objective complements* in Lesson 21 (see page 64). Because an objective complement renames a direct object, the complement must be in the same case form as the direct object it renames. Usually, this is not a problem, except in those *rare instances* when the objective complement is a personal pronoun.

☞**EXAMPLE:**

Mom mistakenly called Dick *me*.

✎ **EXERCISE** Underline the correct pronoun in parentheses in each of the following sentences.

1. "Our parents, (him, <u>he</u>) and (her, <u>she</u>), have set excellent examples for their children, Polly and (I, <u>me</u>)," I said, pointing to the couple across the room.

2. The co-captains, Francesca and (she, her), accepted the trophy.

3. They accepted the award on behalf of the other members of the team, Kathy, Carrie, Annie, and (I, me).

4. The nominees, Hernando and (him, he), were asked to leave the room during the voting.

5. Heather mistook her friend on the phone for another person whose voice was familiar to her, (I, me).

6. Affected citizens, (we, us) in Brownsville, will be most harmed by the change in policy and certainly have a right to voice objections.

7. The students with the highest scores, both (he, him) and (she, her), advanced to the finals.

8. The epidemic infected everyone, not only (they, them) but also (we, us).

9. There was no positive evidence against the defendants, neither (he, him) nor (she, her).

10. Either woman, Helen or (she, her), would do an excellent job of decorating the tables.

11. It will be up to (we, us), both you and (I, me), to set a good example for the younger children.

12. Thank you, Father in heaven, for making (I, me) (I, me).

Note: The pronoun in first parentheses is a *direct object* of "making," while the second pronoun is an *objective complement.*

---

13. Your guests, Gary and (me, I), are grateful.

LESSON 46: POSSESSIVE PRONOUNS

Personal pronouns can have three cases. You have already learned about the nominative and objective cases and the forms which personal pronouns take in those cases. The third case is *possessive.*

The possessive case is used to show ownership *(John's car)* or, in certain special uses, to show extent of time or space *(two days' journey).* Nouns in the possessive case usually add either an apostrophe (') alone or an apostrophe followed by an s ('s). Pronouns, however, have completely different forms in the possessive case. Only the following forms of personal pronouns may be used to show possession.

POSSESSIVE CASE PERSONAL PRONOUNS

**my, mine, your, yours, his, her, hers,
its, our, ours, their, theirs, whose**

The following possessive pronouns are used as *adjectives* before nouns: *my, your, his, her, its, our, their, whose.*

☞**EXAMPLES:**

This is *my* book.	This is *your* book.	This is *his* book.
This is *her* book.	This is *our* book.	This is *their* book.
The library loans *its* books.	Tell me *whose* book this is.	

The following possessive pronouns *stand alone* as pronouns: *mine, yours, his, hers, its, ours, theirs.*

☞**EXAMPLES:**

This book is *mine.*	This book is *yours.*	This book is *his.*
This book is *hers.*	This book is *ours.*	This book is *theirs.*
This book is *its.*		

Notice that the possessive personal pronouns *hers, its, ours, yours* and *theirs* are not spelled with apostrophes. Do not confuse the contraction *it's (it is)* with the personal possessive pronoun its or the contractions *you're (you are)* and *who's (who is)* for the personal possessive pronouns your and whose.

The following are not proper forms: *our's, ours', your's, yours', her's, hers', their's, theirs', his'.* Do not use such forms under any circumstances.

The possessive case pronoun *whose*, as noted earlier, can be used as an adjective; but it can stand alone *only in a question.* In such cases, it is classified as an *interrogative* pronoun, which we will study in a later lesson.

Note: *Whose* may also be used as a relative pronoun introducing adjective clauses, but you do not need to concern yourself with that use for now.

Be especially careful when using possessive pronouns in *compounds.*

☞**EXAMPLES:**

The teacher graded *his* and *her* papers. *(not: …him and her papers)*

These are *yours* and *ours.*

She washed Mary's and *my* car. *(not: …Mary and I's car)*

I baby-sat Mrs. Henson's and *their* children last night.

This is *your* and *my* only opportunity. *(not: ...yours and my only opportunity)*

The possessive case of *indefinite* and *reciprocal* pronouns is formed by adding *'s* or an apostrophe alone (') if the pronoun already ends with an *s*.

POSSESSIVE FORMS FOR INDEFINITE AND RECIPROCAL PRONOUNS

INDEFINITE (not a complete list)

one's, someone's, anyone's, no one's, each's,
another's, other's (plural: others')
either's, neither's, neither one's, either one's

RECIPROCAL

each other's, one another's

☞**EXAMPLES:**

Everybody's hope is to die happily.

They acted as if my property were *everyone's.*

You were supposed to get both of your parents' permission, but you obtained *neither's*.

We must all consider *one another's* best interests.

✎ **EXERCISE** Underline the correct word in each of the following sentences.

1. (Ours, Our's) is older than (their's, theirs).

2. (Yours, Your's) will last longer than (her's, hers).

3. (Its, It's) mother is building a nest.

4. The judges will determine (whose, who's) dog is the best.

5. (Ours', Ours) is a clean neighborhood.

6. (Its, It's) time (they're, their) serious about (their, they're) studies.

7. (Theirs, their's) was the best entry.

8. (Its, It's) leg was broken.

9. Is this necklace (hers, her's)?

10. (You're, Your) competing well today.

11. (Your's, Yours) is a good idea.

12. (You're, Your) answer is correct.

13. (It's, Its) a good thing we left early.

14. That tennis racket is (our's, ours).

15. (Hers, Her's) should be considered also.

16. When are (your's, yours) due?

17. (Its, It's) our chance to show good sportsmanship.

18. My brother and I often share (each others, each other's) clothes.

19. This stray cat seems to be (no one's, no ones).

20. Are you interested in either (Jerry's, Jerry) or (her's, hers, her) opinion?

LESSON 47: INDEFINITE AND RECIPROCAL PRONOUNS

INDEFINITE PRONOUNS

✎ **EXERCISE A** Review what you have learned about *indefinite pronouns* in Lessons 35 and 46. Make a list of indefinite pronouns below:

1. _____	8. _____	15. _____
2. _____	9. _____	16. _____
3. _____	10. _____	17. _____
4. _____	11. _____	18. _____
5. _____	12. _____	19. _____
6. _____	13. _____	20. _____
7. _____	14. _____	21. _____

■ *Everyone and Anyone*

Everyone and *anyone* are indefinite pronouns. Sometimes you may see sentences with *every one* and *any one* written as separate words. In these latter cases, one is a noun (meaning "a single individual") and every and any are adjectives. In most cases, these constructions are followed by a prepositional phrase beginning with *of.*

☞**EXAMPLES:**

> *Every one* of the basketball players was more than 6 feet 6 inches tall.

(In this sentence, "one" is a noun used as the subject of the sentence. It is modified by the adjective "every.")

> *Everyone* will be at the game tonight.

(In this sentence, "everyone" is an indefinite pronoun meaning "all persons.")

> *Any one* of the twenty players could become an outstanding athlete

(In this sentence, "one" is a noun used as the subject of the sentence. It is modified by the adjective "any.")

> *Anyone* interested in basketball may try out for the team.

(In this sentence, "anyone" is an indefinite pronoun meaning "any unspecified person.")

■ *One*

One may be an indefinite pronoun meaning "an indefinitely specified person or thing." It may also be a noun meaning "the number represented by the figure 1." The word *one* may also be an adjective with a variety of meanings, including "single in kind" or "existing alone." Study your dictionary for other meanings and uses of *one.*

☞**EXAMPLES:**

PRONOUNS:	*One* must be careful what *one* says in public.
NOUN:	Not *one* of the people I contacted knew the answer.
ADJECTIVE:	There was *one* apple in the basket.
ADJECTIVE:	He was *one* fine person.

■ *All*

All can be an indefinite pronoun. It can also be an adjective, a noun, or an adverb.

☞**EXAMPLES:**

PRONOUN:	*All* of us are your friends.
NOUN:	He was not the best athlete in the world, but he gave it his *all*.
ADJECTIVE:	*All* men are created equal.
ADVERB:	The girls were *all* excited about their upcoming slumber party.

In certain parts of the United States during the 1990's it became popular in colloquial usage to use the adverb "all" as a verb to mean "says" or "said," as in the following expression:

I told her I liked her dress, and she's *all*, "Thank you very much."

Such usage is completely substandard, faddish, and unacceptable. You should never use the word *all* in this way.

✎ **EXERCISE B** Consult a dictionary and write below what parts of speech the following words can be:

both _____

few _____

many _____

several _____

any _____

most _____

some _____

RECIPROCAL PRONOUNS

Reciprocal pronouns are noun substitutes indicating an *interchange of action*. There are only two reciprocal pronouns in the English language. They are *each other* and *one another*.

There are two simple rules to remember in order to make proper use of these two pronouns:

Rule 7.2	*Each other* is usually used to indicate interaction between *only two* persons or things.
Rule 7.3	*One another* is usually used to indicate interaction among *three or more* persons or things.

☞**EXAMPLES:**

My dad and mom always confer with *each other* before making any major decision.

Christians are expected to show love to *one another.*

Experts are divided about which to use when there is interaction between **groups** of persons or things, each group containing more than two individuals. When confronting such situations, choose the pronoun which seems to best express the intended idea.

☞**EXAMPLES:**

The boys and the girls [two distinct groups] in our school generally respect *each other.*

All boys and girls [all the students] in our school should respect *one another.*

Also, be sure to express the idea of *interaction* clearly when using a reciprocal pronoun.

QUESTIONABLE: We know what each other is thinking.

BETTER: We each know what the other is thinking.

✎ **EXERCISE C** Write each other or one another in the blanks in the following sentences.

1. It is sad that Jinni and Shari seem to hate _____.

2. England and the United States have come to cooperate with _____ despite their early history as enemies.

3. The 51 signers of the United Nations Charter agreed in 1945 to keep peace among _____, but that unrealistic dream has not always been fulfilled.

4. Bob and Carol always give _____ gifts on Valentine's Day.

5. The members of the band blend with _____ very well.

✎ **EXERCISE D** In the blanks, write which part of speech the italicized words are.

1. *Both* India and Sri Lanka are part of the subcontinent of Asia. _correlative conjunction_

2. *All* of the children weighed more than 50 pounds. _____

3. *None* of the deer had antlers. _____

4. Because Christ has redeemed us, we owe him our *all.* _____

5. *Few* people in the United States have seen a giraffe in the wild. _____

6. Almost *everyone* knows the tune to "Yankee Doodle." _____

7. *Each* must do his part. _____

8. *Several* made the same suggestion. _____

9. She invited *several* girls to her party, but *none* attended._____
   _____

10. *Most* states require that *anyone* hunting deer must have a license._____
    _____

11. Christians must carry *one another's* burdens. _____

LESSON 48: INTERROGATIVE AND DEMONSTRATIVE PRONOUNS

INTERROGATIVE PRONOUNS

> **An INTERROGATIVE PRONOUN is a pronoun which is used in asking a question.**

The following words can be used as interrogative pronouns. Some of them may be used in other ways, as well. However, if they are not used to ask a question and do not serve as a noun substitute, they are not interrogative pronouns.

> **INTERROGATIVE PRONOUNS**
>
> **who, whom, what, which, whoever,**
> **whomever, whatever, whichever, whose**

In some instances, the interrogative pronoun may be the subject of the sentence; in others, it may be the direct object; in still others, it may be an object of a preposition. *Who* and *whoever* are nominative-case forms; *whom* and *whomever* are objective-case forms.

☞**EXAMPLES:**

Who did that? *(subject)*

What did he say? *(direct object)*

Which will you select? *(direct object)*

Whoever would have expected that to happen? *(subject)*

For *whom* did you vote? *(object of a preposition — prepositional phrase used as adverb)*

The words *which, what,* and *whose* can also be used in questions as adjectives. Note that *whose* has the characteristic of showing possession. When used as adjectives, these words are not really being used as noun substitutes (pronouns).

☞**EXAMPLES:**

Whose jacket is this? *(modifies "jacket")*

What color is your favorite? *(modifies "color")*

Which one of the pies did you prefer? *(modifies "one")*

In *which* bus did they arrive? *(modifies "bus" in a prepositional phrase used as an adverb)*

Do not confuse the following question words for interrogative pronouns: *where, when, how, why, whence,* and *whither*. These are interrogative adverbs. They cannot be used in questions as noun substitutes, so they cannot be pronouns.

Do not mistake *relative pronouns* for interrogative pronouns. Relative pronouns serve a different function than interrogative pronouns, even if the sentence containing them is a question. Relative pronouns introduce dependent clauses that serve as adjectives.

☞**EXAMPLE:**

Is he the man **_who_ helped my brother**?

You will learn more about adjective clauses later in your study of grammar.

✎ **EXERCISE A** Some of the sentences below contain interrogative pronouns and some do not. Underline only the interrogative pronouns. Do not underline question words used as adjectives.

1. By what right does the king rule?

2. Are you the one whose voice I heard?

3. What can I do to help you?

4. When was the last time you wrote your grandmother a letter?

5. Which tie do you think looks best with this suit?

6. Under what circumstances would you accept the nomination?

7. Whose law is most basic: God's or man's?

8. Whatever made you say that about her?

9. Which of those two women is the one who wrote the book?

10. Whom do you wish to see?

11. Whose wallet is this?

12. Where can I buy the book which you recommended?

13. Whoever buys one ticket gets another one free.

14. Whatever would I do with a bagful of feathers?

15. When you buy a Bible, which translation should you select?

16. Who knows where to go next?

17. In which box did you store your winter clothes?

18. To whom should we address our questions about this product?

19. Who can catch the wind?

20. What was that strange noise I heard coming from your room?

DEMONSTRATIVE PRONOUNS

> **A DEMONSTRATIVE PRONOUN is a pronoun that points to, points out, identifies, or calls attention to something.**

There are five demonstrative pronouns in English: *this, that, these, those, and such.*

☞**EXAMPLES OF DEMONSTRATIVE PRONOUNS:**

This is my favorite program.

That is a fine car you have.

These are the best strawberries I have ever seen.

Those were my books.

Such is the fate of people who rebel against God.

This and *that* are singular pronouns and require singular verbs. *These* and *those* are plural pronouns and require plural verbs. *Such* may be either singular or plural.

These five words may *stand alone* as demonstrative pronouns, or they may be used as *demonstrative adjectives.*

☞ **EXAMPLES OF DEMONSTRATIVE ADJECTIVES:**

This book is one of my favorites.

I hope to read *that* book as well.

These shoes are too tight.

Don't give me *those* old excuses again.

Such things do not bother me.

Never use the personal pronoun **them** as a demonstrative adjective, as certain illiterate people often do.

WRONG: *Them* kites will never fly without a tail.

CORRECT: *Those* kites will never fly without a tail.

✎ **EXERCISE B** Write ten sentences using demonstrative pronouns. Be sure to use each of the five demonstrative pronouns twice. Remember not to use demonstrative words as adjectives.

1. _____

_____

2. _____

_____

3. _____

_____

4. _____

_____

5. _____

_____

6. _____

_____

7. _____

_____

8. _____

_____

9. _____

    _____

10. _____

    _____

LESSON 49: COMPOUND PRONOUNS

COMPOUND PRONOUNS

> **COMPOUND PRONOUNS are pronouns with the suffix *-self* (singular) or *-selves* (plural) attached.**

For this reason, they are sometimes called *"self"* pronouns. The following are compound pronouns:

> **COMPOUND PRONOUNS**
>
> myself, ourselves,
> yourself, yourselves,
> himself, herself, itself,
> themselves, oneself

USAGE OF COMPOUND PRONOUNS

There are two usage categories of compound pronouns: ***intensive*** and ***reflexive***. Pronouns in these two categories have exactly the same form, but they are distinguished by the way they are used in a sentence.

■ *INTENSIVE pronouns*

Intensive pronouns often appear in an appositive position after a noun or pronoun and are used merely to intensify or emphasize the noun or pronoun they follow. They are *not essential* to the meaning of the sentence and could be eliminated without destroying the thought of the sentence or clause.

☞EXAMPLE:

Bob *himself* gave the speech.

■ *Reflexive pronouns*

Reflexive pronouns usually follow a verb or preposition and direct or *reflect* back to the subject of the sentence or clause in which they are contained. Reflexive pronouns are *essential* to the meaning of the expression and cannot be eliminated without leaving the thought of the sentence or clause incomplete.

☞**EXAMPLE:**

Anne taught *herself* how to play the flute.

Rule 7.4	**Do not separate or hyphenate the suffixes *-self* and *-selves* from the rest of the compound pronoun.**
Rule 7.5	**Do not ever use the forms *hisself, ourself,* or *theirselves.* None of these are recognized English words.**
Rule 7.6	**Do not use a compound pronoun when it has NO antecedent* in the sentence.**

Note: *An *antecedent* is the noun or pronoun to which a pronoun refers.

☞**EXAMPLE:**

WRONG: Joel and *myself* will build the platform.

CORRECT: Joel and I will build the platform.

✎ **EXERCISE A** Underline the compound pronouns in the following sentences. In the blank, identify their use as either *intensive* or *reflexive*. Put an **X** in the blank if the compound pronoun is improperly used without an antecedent, as in the example immediately above.

1. He hurt <u>himself</u>. ____*reflexive*____

2. She herself did it. _____

3. I asked myself whether this would be a good idea. _____

4. He himself decided to apply for the scholarship. _____

5. Some friends, including yourself, are invited to my party. _____

6. Jill has been known to talk to herself when frustrated about something. _____

7. Speaking for myself, I think it's a good idea. _____

8. Perhaps you yourself could call for an appointment. _____

9. Perhaps you could call for an appointment yourself. _____

10. Perhaps you could call for an appointment for yourself. _____

11. A man who called himself a policeman was actually a thief. _____

12. No one should think too highly of himself. _____

13. Calm yourself. _____

14. The youngster calmly picked himself up after his fall. _____

15. My parents and myself attend church every Sunday. _____

16. People need to remind themselves daily about the importance of prayer. _____

17. This matter must be kept just between you and myself. _____

18. They can do it themselves. _____

✎ **EXERCISE B** In the following sentences, underline the *antecedent* of the compound pronouns in **dark print**. If the antecedent is implied, write it above the sentence and indicate with a caret mark (∧) where it goes.

      (You)
1.   ∧ Give **yourself** a break.

2.   When a hunter outfits **himself**, he should remember rain gear.

3.   We do **ourselves** a favor when we remember to show kindness to others.

4.   We enjoy eating lobster, but the lobster **itself** may not agree.

5.   They were grateful to have the place all to **themselves**.

6.   You can guess for **yourselves** what he **himself** might have meant by that remark.

7.   Special clothing helped the commandos disguise **themselves**.

8.   The cold **itself** was bad enough, but the addition of wind made the day unbearable.

9.   Brace **yourself** for some bad news.

10. I tried to tell **myself** that everything was all right.

LESSON 50: PRONOUN-ANTECEDENT AGREEMENT

PERSON, NUMBER, AND GENDER

Rule 7.7	Pronouns must agree with their *antecedents* in person, number, and gender.

An ANTECEDENT is a noun, pronoun, or other noun-like expression to which a pronoun refers.

■ *Person*

FIRST-PERSON pronouns refer to *first-person* antecedents.

SECOND-PERSON pronouns refer to *second-person* antecedents.

THIRD-PERSON pronouns refer to *third-person* antecedents.

■ *Number*

SINGULAR pronouns refer to *singular* antecedents.

PLURAL pronouns refer to *plural* antecedents.

■ *Gender*

FEMININE pronouns refer to *feminine* antecedents.

MASCULINE pronouns refer to *masculine* antecedents.

NEUTER pronouns refer to *neuter* antecedents.

☞**EXAMPLES:**

The *girl* found *her* book. *(third-person, singular, feminine antecedent)*

The *girls* found *their* books. *(third-person, plural, feminine antecedent)*

The *man* found *his* tools. *(third-person, singular, masculine)*

The *men* found *their* tools. *(third-person, plural, masculine)*

TWO ANTECEDENTS

In sentences where there are two antecedents and only one pronoun is used, the pronoun should agree with the antecedent which is *nearest* to it in the sentence.

☞**EXAMPLE:**

Either the car or the trucks can have *their* oil changed at a discount rate.

COLLECTIVE NOUNS

Collective nouns are nouns which name a group composed of individuals but considered as a unit. Among the most common collective nouns are the following: *group, class, team, audience, crowd, jury.* When a collective noun serves as an antecedent for a pronoun, the pronoun should be either singular or plural, depending upon whether the collective noun is considered as a group of individuals acting separately or as a group acting as a unified whole.

☞**EXAMPLES:**

The class sat quietly at *their* desks. *(Each individual class member sat quietly at his desk.)*

The class decided upon *its* motto. *(The class acted as a whole on its collective motto.)*

You must also be careful, in such cases, to ensure consistency in agreement with the verb.

INCONSISTENT:The team *was* agreed about *their* choice of a mascot.

CONSISTENT:The team *was* agreed about *its* choice of a mascot.

■ One & Oneself

A common problem with pronoun-antecedent agreement comes with use of the indefinite compound pronoun *oneself* or when the indefinite pronoun *one* is the antecedent.

☞**EXAMPLES:**

WRONG:	*One* must take care of *himself.*
BETTER:	*One* must take care of *oneself.*
WRONG:	Every *person* must remind *oneself* to be calm in a crisis.
BETTER:	*One* must remind *oneself* to be calm in a crisis.
OR:	Every *person* must remind *himself* to be calm in a crisis.

■ *The Fuzzy 'that'*

Be sure that there is a clear relationship between a pronoun and an antecedent. Many people make that relationship fuzzy when they use demonstrative pronouns without clear anteced-ents. In the sentence you have just read, for example, the word *that* is a demonstrative pro-noun. Its antecedent is found in the first sentence of this paragraph—either the word *"relationship"* or the phrase *"…relationship between a pronoun and an antecedent."* Below is an example of a doubtful case:

DOUBTFUL:

Your greeting gave me *that* happy-all-over feeling. *(no antecedent for pronoun "that")*

IMPROVED:

Your greeting gave me a happy-all-over feeling. *(pronoun replaced with indefinite article)*

ACCEPTABLE:

Your greeting gave me *that* happy-all-over feeling <u>which comes from communication with loved ones</u>. *(The antecedent of "that" is the underlined phrase.)*

✎ **EXERCISE** Underline the correct word in parentheses in the following sentences.

1. Mother groped blindly around the room until she found (<u>her</u>, their) own glasses.

2. The commission announced (their, its) final decision but did not disclose (their, its) individual opinions.

3. Our project was at (that, an) early stage of development.

4. One can learn to control (himself, oneself) with constant practice and prayer.

5. Neither the parents nor the boy had (their, his) rights protected by the social worker.

6. Neither the boy nor the parents had (their, his) rights protected by the social worker.

7. The class was assigned to turn in (their, its) compositions on Friday.

8. The class was assigned to clean (their, its) classroom before leaving.

9. The audience left (their, its) seats one by one.

10. The audience, in a unanimous vote, expressed (its, their) disapproval.

LESSON 51: UNIT REVIEW

✎ **EXERCISE A** Underline all the pronouns in the following passage from Acts 26:1-15 (NKJV), in which the Apostle Paul defends himself and his Lord before King Agrippa. Above the pronoun, identify it with one of the following abbreviations: **P** for personal pronoun, **S** for possessive pronoun, **D** for demonstrative pronoun, **I** for interrogative pronoun, **F** for indefinite pronoun, **R** for reciprocal pronoun, **C** for compound pronoun. (Do not underline words that introduce dependent clauses, such as relative pronouns or other clause signal words that may look like pronouns. Mark only the seven types you have studied if you find any of these types of pronouns.) CLUE: you should underline *66 pronouns*.

Then Agrippa said to Paul, "You are permitted to speak for yourself."

So Paul stretched out his hand and answered for himself:

"I think myself happy, King Agrippa, because today I shall answer for myself before you concerning all the things of which I am accused by the Jews, especially because you are expert in all customs and questions which have to do with the Jews. Therefore I beg you to hear me patiently."

"My manner of life from my youth, which was spent from the beginning among my own nation at Jerusalem, all the Jews know. They knew me from the first, if they were willing to testify, that according to the strictest sect of our religion I lived a Pharisee. And now I stand and am judged for the hope of the promise made by God to our fathers. To this promise our twelve tribes, earnestly serving God night and day, hope to attain. For this hope's sake, King Agrippa, I am accused by the Jews."

"Why should it be thought incredible by you that God raises the dead? Indeed, I myself thought I must do many things contrary to the name of Jesus of Nazareth. This I also did in Jerusalem, and many of the saints I shut up in prison, having received authority from the chief priests; and when they were put to death, I cast my vote against them. And I punished them often in every synagogue and compelled them to blaspheme; and being exceedingly enraged against them, I persecuted them even to foreign cities."

"While thus occupied, as I journeyed to Damascus with authority and commission from the chief priests, at midday, O king, along the road I saw a light from heaven, brighter than the sun, shining around me and those who journeyed with me. And when we all had fallen to the ground, I heard a voice speaking to me and saying in the Hebrew language, 'Saul, Saul, why are you persecuting Me? It is hard for you to kick against the goads.' So I said, 'Who are you, Lord?' And He said, 'I am Jesus, whom you are persecuting."

—From *The Holy Bible, New King James Version,* © 1982 by Thomas Nelson, Inc.

✎ **EXERCISE B** Cross out any pronoun that is used incorrectly and write the correct form above it. If a pronoun is correct in use and form, leave it as it is.

him
1.   The message was for Harley and ~~he~~.

2.   Could the girls who waved at us have been they?

3.   They should do the work theirselves.

4.   Him and Bob are on the same team.

5.   The government must protect the religious rights of we, the people.

6.   Was that them in the car that just went by?

7.   Behind Elise and I sat him and his brother.

8.   One should always keep himself pure from evil.

9.   If you have a problem with our products, address the problem to we ourself; and we will try to correct it.

10. Did the coach select yous and he for the varsity team?

11. To who did you speak this morning?

12. Whom did you speak to this morning?

13. Who did you say called me this morning?

14. Besides you and I, whom will be coming to the party?

15. Kaleb and myself will serve on the committee.

16. The three girls enjoy each other's company.

17. Our's is a land of opportunity and freedom.

18. "Your only as old as you feel," they're grandmother often says.

19. No one wants to have their own reputation smeared.

20. Jack and me realized too late that only us two were on the wrong bus.

21. The boat seemed to be coming closer to Mike and I.

✎ **EXERCISE C** All of the blanks in the following sentences represent missing pronouns. Indicate which *case* of pronoun should be used by writing **N** for nominative, **O** for objective, or **P** for possessive in the blanks. *(You may mentally consider which specific pronoun might fit the context, but do not write a pronoun itself.)*

1. _N_ was _P_ only brother.

2. Don't forget to add _____ to _____ list of people to invite to Jill's birthday party.

3. _____ am the tallest member of _____ family.

4. Columbus believed _____ had discovered the East Indies.

5. _____ arrived safely and gave _____ a hug.

6. Jesus' death was _____ means of paying for _____ sins.

7. In high school, _____ hopes to take courses in preparation for college.

8. _____ hope _____ will keep _____ in mind during _____ vacation trip.

9. Stephen gave _____ a pat on the back.

10. _____ was educated at home by _____ parents.

11. Let _____ pray.

12. _____ sister is shorter than _____ am.

13. "Put _____ money where _____ mouth is."

14. _____ mother bought _____ a new dress at a sale in the mall.

15. The policeman asked _____ for _____ driver's license and car registration.

16. Can _____ tell _____ where to find the library?

17. After _____ caught the hamster, _____ put _____ back into _____ cage.

18. _____ won _____ victory on Tuesday.

19. Next week, _____ and _____ plan to go camping.

20. "Would _____ pour _____ a glass of milk, Mommy?" the toddler asked.

21. _____ was a lot of work but well worth the effort.

Unit 8
Using Verbs

Review Lesson 3 (see page 7) concerning verbs. As you learned in that lesson, **verbs** are words that express action or a state of being or that help another verb complete its meaning. Verbs have many ways of expressing action or being. To do so, they take a variety of forms. These various forms are used to express differences in the *time* of the action (**tense**), to indicate from which *perspective* the action is done (**voice**), to indicate the *nature* of the action (**tone**), and to characterize the *state of mind* associated with the action (**mood**). These features of verbs make them one of the most important elements of the English language, and they show why English is such an expressive and detailed language, highly regarded by peoples all over the world. In this unit, we will begin to explore the tense, voice, and tone of verbs.

LESSON 52: PRINCIPAL PARTS OF VERBS

As noted in the introduction above, verbs have many different ways of expressing action or being; and they take different forms to express these differences. All of the forms are built around FOUR BASIC FORMS, known as the **four principal parts** of verbs.

> **The FOUR PRINCIPAL PARTS of verbs are: present, present participle, past, and past participle.**

By using one or another of these principal parts—with assistance from **helping verbs**, in some cases—it is possible to express:

❑ **past, present, and future time;**

❑ **progression and completion of action in various time settings;**

❑ **special emphasis and perspective; and**

❑ **various other fine points related to the nature of the action or condition.**

☞**EXAMPLES OF THE FOUR PRINCIPAL PARTS OF VERBS:**

PRESENT (to)+	PRESENT PARTICIPLE (am, are, is, was, were)+	PAST	PAST PARTICIPLE (have, has, had) +
go	going	went	gone
walk	walking	walked	walked
study	studying	studied	studied
eat	eating	ate	eaten

The *present* and *present participle* forms are easy to learn.

The *present* is the most basic form of any verb. It is the form used as the main entry for each verb in a dictionary. It is often expressed in what grammarians call the *present infinitive* form, introduced by the word *"to" (to go, to walk, etc.).*

You will notice from the chart above, that the *present participle* is very consistent—it always ends with *-ing*. It is formed by adding *-ing* to the present form. In a sentence, it often is preceded by a helping verb, which will be some form of the verb *to be (am studying, are studying, is studying,* etc.).

Most of the trouble people have with verbs is related to the *past* and *past participle* forms. This is because each verb has its own way of forming these two parts. For this reason, all verbs are classified as either **regular** or **irregular**.

> **REGULAR VERBS are verbs that make their past and past participle forms by adding -ed, -d, or -t to the present form.**
>
> **IRREGULAR VERBS are verbs that follow no pattern for making their past and past participle forms.**

Each *irregular verb* has its own form and spelling for the past tense and past participle. You must simply memorize the principal parts of irregular verbs. On the following page is a list of some **irregular** verbs. Study them carefully. Say each form with the first person, single pronoun *I* in front of it.

Note: The present participle form is not shown because it always ends with *-ing*. In addition, consult a dictionary on the alternate verb forms that have been marked with an asterisk (*).

PRESENT	PAST	PAST PARTICIPLE	PRESENT	PAST	PAST PARTICIPLE
arise	arose	arisen	lead	led	led
awake	awoke, awaked	awoken, awoke	lend	lent	lent
bear	bore	borne, born*	let	let	let
beat	beat	beaten	lie (recline)	lay	lain
become	became	become	lose	lost	lost
begin	began	begun	meet	met	met
bid	bid	bid (auction)	pass	passed	passed, past*
bid	bid, bade	bid, bidden (command)	pay	paid	paid
bite	bit	bitten	prove	proved	proved, proven
blow	blew	blown	put	put	put
break	broke	broken	rise	rose	risen
bring	brought	brought	ride	rode	ridden
build	built	built	ring (bell)	rang	rung
burst	burst	burst	run	ran	run
cast	cast	cast	say	said	said
catch	caught	caught	see	saw	seen
choose	chose	chosen	set	set	set
come	came	come	sit	sat	sat
cut	cut	cut	shine	shone	shone
deal	dealt	dealt	show	showed	shown, showed
dig	dug	dug	shrink	shrank, shrunk	shrunk
dive	dived, dove	dived	sing	sang	sung
do	did	done	sink	sank, sunk*	sunk
draw	drew	drawn	sleep	slept	slept
drink	drank	drunk, drunken*	speak	spoke	spoken
drive	drove	driven	spend	spent	spent
eat	ate	eaten	spring	sprang, sprung	sprung
fall	fell	fallen	stand	stood	stood
feel	felt	felt	steal	stole	stolen
find	found	found	swim	swam	swum
flee	fled	fled	swing	swung	swung
fly	flew	flown	take	took	taken
forecast	forecast (-ed)	forecast, forecasted	tear	tore	torn
forgot	forgot	forgotten, forgot	think	thought	thought
freeze	froze	frozen	throw	threw	thrown
get	got	got, gotten	understand	understood	understood
give	gave	given	undertake	undertook	undertaken
go	went	gone	wake	waked, woke	waked, woken
grow	grew	grown	wear	wore	worn
hang (object)	hung	hung	win	won	won
hear	heard	heard	wind	wound	wound
know	knew	known	wring	wrung	wrung
lay	laid	laid	write	wrote	written

The preceding list is not exhaustive. Altogether, there are about 200 irregular verbs in the English language.

Some **regular** verbs also may be troublesome. In some cases, the problem lies in the fact that they share some forms with irregular verbs having the same spelling but different meanings. In other cases, the confusion arises from the fact that certain illiterate usages have developed around these words. Here are a few examples:

PRESENT	PAST	PAST PARTICIPLE	PRESENT	PAST	PAST PARTICIPLE
burn	burned, burnt	burned, burnt	fly (baseball)	flied	flied
drown	drowned	drowned	hang (person)	hanged	hanged
drug	drugged	drugged	lie (falsehood)	lied	lied
flow	flowed	flowed	loose	loosed	loosed

Be careful not to omit the *-ed, -d, or -t* on certain regular verbs in the past or past participle forms, as some people commonly do.

☞**EXAMPLES:**

> **WRONG:**   They were *suppose* to go to bed by 10 p.m.
>
> Yesterday I *ask* for a ticket to the game.
>
> We *use* to go to the gym every day.
>
> Some people are *prejudice* against persons of a different race.
>
> **CORRECT:**   They were *supposed* to go to bed by 10 a.m.
>
> Yesterday I *asked* for a ticket to the game.
>
> We *used* to go to the gym every day.
>
> Some people are *prejudiced* against persons of a different race.

Following are some examples of how the four principal parts of verbs are used in sentences:

PRESENT:

> I *eat* breakfast before 7 a.m. every day.
>
> I *read* a few chapters in the Bible every night before bedtime.
>
> We *study* during our free time.

PRESENT PARTICIPLE:

> I *am reading* my book right now.
>
> His dog *is eating* your shoe.
>
> She *was studying* in her room.

Note: The *present participle* uses a form of "to be" as a helping verb.

PAST:

I *saw* your dog in the neighbor's yard yesterday.

My mother *read* to me every night when I *was* a child.

They *walked* over her flowers.

PAST PARTICIPLE:

I *have studied* English for most of my life.

We *had eaten* all of our food before we *had finished* our hike.

You *were bitten* by a mosquito.

Note: The *past participle* uses a form of "to have" or "to be" as a helper.

✎ **EXERCISE A** In the blank, indicate which principal part of the verb in **dark print** is used in each sentence. (NOTE: The past tense and past particple of a verb often have the same form; when this form appears below, be sure to indicate the correct principal part which is being used.)

_____*past*_____	1.	He **answered** the telephone.
_____	2.	I **see** you hiding behind the door.
_____	3.	Please **send** me a copy of your book.
_____	4.	I am **running** out of space on this paper.
_____	5.	We had **decided** to come before you called.
_____	6.	We **are** children of God in Christ.
_____	7.	She **turned** out the light.
_____	8.	The monkeys were **hanging** by their tails.
_____	9.	I **came** back from Chicago yesterday.
_____	10.	I **visited** my grandmother there.
_____	11.	She had **invited** me to come.
_____	12.	This dictionary **contains** a great deal of information.
_____	13.	Our band is **playing** the school song.
_____	14.	I sometimes **sing** in the shower.
_____	15.	She was **taken** to the hospital.

_____   16.   He **put** milk, sugar, and fruit on his cereal.

_____   17.   I have been **calling** you for an hour.

_____   18.   She **seems** like a nice lady.

✎ **EXERCISE B** Use the list in this lesson (page 163) or your dictionary, if necessary, to help you write the other three principal parts of the following verbs:

		Present Participle	**Past**	**Past Participle**
1.	(to) mean			
2.	(to) work			
3.	(to) choose			
4.	(to) fight			
5.	(to) laugh			
6.	(to) swim			
7.	(to) spread			
8.	(to) form			
9.	(to) climb			
10.	(to) pass			
11.	(to) gobble			
12.	(to) shiver			
13.	(to) participate			
14.	(to) telephone			
15.	(to) whistle			
16.	(to) lose			
17.	(to) loosen			
18.	(to) tie			
19.	(to) shine			
20.	(to) know			
21.	(to) drag			
22.	(to) drug			

LESSON 53: TENSE AND PERSON OF VERBS

Verbs express action or state of being in the context of time. That is to say that actions and existence always take place within some time frame—past, present, or future. The grammatical term used to describe this fact is *tense*.

> **TENSE is the time of the action or the state of being expressed by a verb.**

All English verbs have six tenses. Three of the tenses express *simple time—past, present,* and *future*. The other three tenses express *completed* or *perfected time—past perfect, present perfect,* and *future perfect*.

Rule 8.1	**Verbs express tense either by changing their form or by adding a helping verb—some form of *to have* or *to be*.**

Like nouns and pronouns, verbs also have *person*. Review Lessons 32 (page 94) and 33 (page 96) to refresh your memory about person and about how subjects and verbs must agree in *person*. Understanding the grammatical concept of person is important when studying *tense* because verbs use different forms in different tenses and persons. Verbs also have different forms when used with *singular* and *plural* subjects, so you should review Lesson 31 (see page 91) to refresh your memory about *number*. Below and on the following page is a chart illustrating the various tense, person, and number forms of the common irregular verb *"to go"*:

SIMPLE PRESENT TENSE	SINGULAR	PLURAL
1st Person	I go	we go
2nd Person	you go	you go
3rd Person	he, she, it goes	they go
SIMPLE PAST TENSE	SINGULAR	PLURAL
1st Person	I went	we went
2nd Person	you went	you went
3rd Person	he, she, it, went	they went
SIMPLE FUTURE TENSE	SINGULAR	PLURAL
1st Person	I shall go	we shall go
2nd Person	you will go	you will go
3rd Person	he, she, it will go	they will go

PRESENT *PERFECT* TENSE	SINGULAR	PLURAL
1st Person	I have gone	we have gone
2nd Person	you have gone	you have gone
3rd Person	he, she, it has gone	they have gone
PAST *PERFECT* TENSE	SINGULAR	PLURAL
1st Person	I had gone	we had gone
2nd Person	you had gone	you had gone
3rd Person	he, she, it had gone	they had gone
FUTURE *PERFECT* TENSE	SINGULAR	PLURAL
1st Person	I shall have gone	we shall have gone
2nd Person	you will have gone	you will have gone
3rd Person	he, she, it will have gone	they will have gone

Notice that in the future and future perfect tenses, a second helping verb has been added. Normally, *shall* is used with the first person and *will* is used with the second and third person. To stress determination or necessity, reverse the order and use *will* with the first person and *shall* with the second and third persons.

To express a verb in its six tenses—according to its various forms of first, second, and third person and singular and plural number—is to **conjugate** a verb, as we have done in the preceding chart.

Study the conjugation chart again to take note of which **principal parts** of the main verb *"go"* are used with each tense, person, and number. Notice that the first principal part *(present)* is used to form the *simple present* and *simple future* tenses. The third principal part *(past)* is used to form only the *simple past* tense. Notice also that the same pattern is followed with the helping verbs, where they are used: the first principal part *(present)* is used to express *present* and *future* time and the third principal part is used to express *past* time. The fourth principal part *(past participle)* of the main verb is used to form all of the *perfect* tenses. (The second principal part *[the present participle]* is not used to form any of the simple or perfect tenses. It is used to express *progressive tone [ongoing action]*, which we will study later.)

MEANING OF PERFECT TENSES
PRESENT PERFECT tense expresses action beginning in the past and ending just now or still in progress in the present.
PAST PERFECT tense expresses action beginning at a point in the past and ending at a later point in the past.
FUTURE PERFECT tense expresses action beginning in the present and reaching completion sometime in the future.

✎ **EXERCISE A** Conjugate the regular verb *walk* in all six tenses.

SIMPLE PRESENT TENSE	SINGULAR	PLURAL
1st Person		
2nd Person		
3rd Person		
SIMPLE PAST TENSE	SINGULAR	PLURAL
1st Person		
2nd Person		
3rd Person		
SIMPLE FUTURE TENSE	SINGULAR	PLURAL
1st Person		
2nd Person		
3rd Person		
PRESENT *PERFECT* TENSE	SINGULAR	PLURAL
1st Person		
2nd Person		
3rd Person		
PAST *PERFECT* TENSE	SINGULAR	PLURAL
1st Person		
2nd Person		
3rd Person		
FUTURE *PERFECT* TENSE	SINGULAR	PLURAL
1st Person		
2nd Person		
3rd Person		

✎ **EXERCISE B** In the blanks, identify the *tense* of the verbs or verb phrases in **dark print**.

1. _____*present*_____ She **is** her parents' only daughter.

2. _____ Erin **received** a gold bracelet from her grandmother.

3. _____ We **shall arrive** at your house before noon.

4. _____ Alex **has washed** the car.

5. _____ I **have** never **heard** of that brand before.

6. _____ Tessa **will have completed** her project before it is due.

7. _____ I **fail** to see your point.

8. _____ He **had finished** by the time the buzzer sounded.

9. _____ Jeff **will call** you in the morning.

10. _____ **Tell** Marianne to clean up her room.

11. _____ Mom **told** Marianne to clean up her room.

12. _____ How many times **have** I **told** you to clean up your room?

13. _____ Alabama **was** part of the Confederacy.

14. _____ Who knows all the things that **will happen** in the 21st century?

15. _____ Who **knows** all the things that will happen in the 21st century?

16. _____ Ben hopes he **will have passed** the test by this time tomorrow.

17. _____ We **shall see** you on Thursday.

18. _____ Schumann's "Rhenish Symphony" **has** always **been** one of my favorites.

19. _____ Michela **proved** that she was right all along.

20. _____ I **shall ask** Mr. Pierce if we may be on the committee.

21. _____ We hope the electrician **will restore** the power soon.

22. _____ Casey knew he **had seen** that dog before.

✎ **EXERCISE C** In the blank, write the correct form of the verb indicated for each sentence.

1. The sun ____*shone*____ brightly all last week. *(to shine - past)*

2. Do not believe everything you _____. *(to hear - present)*

3. The clerk _____ a notice on the bulletin board. *(to post - past)*

4. We _____ happy to lend you the money. *(to be - future)*

5. By the end of November, most of the leaves _____. *(to fall - future perfect)*

6. We could not tell what _____ to him. *(to happen - past perfect)*

7. The pond _____. *(to freeze - present perfect)*

8. Sam doesn't know what he _____ when he opens the box. *(to find - future)*

9. Carlos _____ into the swirling stream. *(to dive - past)*

10. God _____ my sins because of Jesus' sacrifice. *(to forgive - present perfect)*

11. This is the second time my younger sister _____ the cookies. *(to burn - present perfect)*

12. Some athletes _____ never _____ good coaches. *(to be - future)*

13. France once _____ the Louisiana Territory. *(to own - past)*

LESSON 54: VOICE OF VERBS

By changing the form of a verb you can indicate whether the subject of the verb is *doing* its action or receiving its action. This feature of verbs is called *voice*.

VOICE is the form or use of a verb indicating whether its subject is the *doer* or *receiver* of the verb's action.
ACTIVE VOICE indicates that the subject is the *doer* of the action.
PASSIVE VOICE indicates that the subject is the *receiver* of the action.

The conjugation table for the verb *to go* in Lesson 53 (page 167) gives examples of the *active voice* form of that verb. Likewise, all of the sentences in the exercises you completed in Lesson 53 have verbs in *active voice*. Study those sentences to take note of the fact that the subjects are the doers of the action.

PASSIVE VOICE

The *passive voice* is formed by placing a form of the helping verb *"to be"* before the *past participle* of the main verb.

☞**EXAMPLES:**

Their meal **was eaten** in haste. *(The subject, "meal," is the receiver of the action.)*

The painting **was hung** on the wall. *(The subject, "painting," is the receiver of the action.)*

The mailman **was bitten** by a dog. *(The subject, "mailman," is the receiver of the action.)*

In passive voice, the *doer* of the action is usually found in a prepositional phrase (either expressed or implied) beginning with the preposition *"by"* following the verb.

☞**EXAMPLES:**

The doorbell *was rung [by a visitor].*

The plane *was flown **by an experienced pilot.***

The tomatoes *were grown* in a hotbed *[by a nurseryman].*

Your point *is well taken [by me].*

The mailman *was bitten **by a dog.***

Below and on the following page is a table conjugating the irregular verb *to know* in **passive voice.**

SIMPLE PRESENT	SINGULAR	PLURAL
1st Person	I am known	we are known
2nd Person	you are known	you are known
3rd Person	he, she, it are known	they are known
SIMPLE PAST	SINGULAR	PLURAL
1st Person	I was known	we were known
2nd Person	you were known	you were known
3rd Person	he, she, it, was known	they were known
SIMPLE FUTURE	SINGULAR	PLURAL
1st Person	I shall be known	we shall be known
2nd Person	you will be known	you will be known
3rd Person	he, she, it will be known	they will be known

PRESENT *PERFECT*	SINGULAR	PLURAL
1st Person	I have been known	we have been known
2nd Person	you have been known	you have been known
3rd Person	he, she, it has been known	they have been known
PAST *PERFECT*	SINGULAR	PLURAL
1st Person	I had been known	we had been known
2nd Person	you had been known	you had been known
3rd Person	he, she, it had been known	they had been known
FUTURE *PERFECT*	SINGULAR	PLURAL
1st Person	I shall have been known	we shall have been known
2nd Person	You will have been known	you will have been known
3rd Person	he, she, it will have been known	they will have been known

WHEN TO USE PASSIVE VOICE

Passive voice may be used anytime the writer or speaker wishes to represent that the subject of the sentence is receiving the action of the verb, that the subject is not doing anything but is merely being "passive" in the sentence, or when the subject is somehow being "acted upon"—that is, something is being *done to* or *done for* the subject.

☞**EXAMPLES:**

The guests *were served* their meals. *(subject, "guests," is receiver of action)*

Some money *was given* to me by my rich uncle. *(subject, "money," is passive)*

The motion *was defeated*. *(subject, "motion," is acted upon)*

Passive voice may also be used effectively in *impersonal* writing or speaking—expressions which avoid any reference to people.

☞**EXAMPLES:**

The conclusion *was reached* after years of study.

The results of the balloting *were* never *disclosed.*

The facts *were obtained* through careful investigation.

WHEN TO USE ACTIVE VOICE

Active voice is generally considered the more direct and powerful means of expression. Therefore, it is usually preferable for most communications. Overuse of the passive voice will tend to weaken your writing and speaking, so use active voice unless one of the special purposes outlined above for passive voice is needed or preferred. Careful use of voice will give variety and interest to our written and oral expressions.

Note: When an expression is changed from active to passive voice, the direct object in active voice becomes the subject in passive voice. The doer of the action is the subject in active voice but is the object of the preposition *by* in an adverbial prepositional phrase in passive voice.

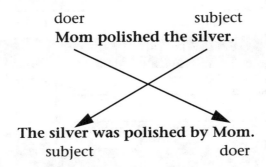

doer   subject
Mom polished the silver.

The silver was polished by Mom.
subject   doer

✎ **EXERCISE A** In the blanks, tell whether the verbs in **dark print** are *active* or *passive.*

1. _____*passive*_____   The bell **was wrung** for five minutes as a memorial.

2. _____   The United States **bought** Alaska from Russia in 1867.

3. _____   The door **was closed**.

4. _____   The keynote speech **will be delivered** by Senator Kline.

5. _____   Sue **invited** me to her house.

6. _____   The best contestant **was** Kaitlin.

7. _____   People entering the park **are given** a colorful guidebook.

8. _____   Crops cannot **be grown** without sufficient water.

9. _____   The tree **had been blown** over by the wind.

10. _____   The last piece of cake **has been eaten**.

11. _____   The program **will be** over at 10 p.m.

12. _____   I **am troubled** by your report.

13. _____   The employees **were given** a bonus.

14. _____   The company **gave** its employees a bonus.

15. _____   His business cards **were printed** in full color.

16. _____   The information **was** well **received** by the stockholders.

✎ **EXERCISE B** Rewrite the following sentences, changing all active-voice verbs to passive voice and all passive-voice verbs to active. Keep the verbs in their same tense.

1. Loren was asked by his teacher to reread the instructions.

   _____

   _____

2. Newcomers will be invited by our church to a reception following the service.

   _____

   _____

3. Because of the approaching storm, windows were boarded up by workmen.

   _____

   _____

4. The burro was led by a small boy.

   _____

   _____

5. Several speeches will have been given by the candidate by next week.

   _____

   _____

6. The composition was written by a ten-year-old girl.

   _____

   _____

7. The audience will choose the winner.

   _____

   _____

8. The wedding vows will be read by Pastor Edward Lawson.

    _____

    _____

9. William asked me to open the meeting with prayer.

    _____

    _____

10. The verb was changed to passive voice by the writer.

    _____

    _____

11. The story was told by an eyewitness.

    _____

    _____

LESSON 55: TONE OF VERBS

Verbs also have *tone* to indicate the nature of the action they express. There are three different verb tones in English: *simple*, *progressive*, and *emphatic*.

> **TONE is the characteristic of verb tenses to indicate
> progress, emphasis, or simple statement.**

SIMPLE TONE

Simple tone is the ordinary, straightforward way we make statements or ask many questions
using verbs in any of the tenses and in either voice.

☞**EXAMPLES:**

The price of liberty *is* vigilance.

We *will be* glad to see you.

The music *was* quite enjoyable.

Because you *are* my friend, I *feel* free to share my secrets with you.

PROGRESSIVE TONE

Progressive tone indicates *action in progress—on-going action*. It can be expressed in all tenses in active voice, but it is usually expressed only in the simple tenses in passive voice.

Note: In theory, the progressive tone can be expressed also in the perfect tenses in the passive voice, but the result is usually awkward and cumbersome: *have been being seen, had been being seen, shall have been being seen.* The same progressive idea can better be expressed in simple tone: *have been seen, had been seen, shall have been seen.*

■ *Progressive Tone—Active Voice*

The progressive-tone form of verbs in the *active voice* is created by using the **present participle** preceded by a form of the helping verb *to be*.

☞**EXAMPLES:**

We *are coming* to your house this afternoon.

The radio *was playing* my favorite song.

Katrina *has been studying* for her final exam.

We *shall have been traveling* for one month by this time tomorrow.

Study the following chart which conjugates the irregular verb *to see* in **progressive tone—** *active voice.* (NOTE: This chart continues on the next page.)

SIMPLE **PRESENT TENSE**	SINGULAR	PLURAL
1st Person	I am seeing	we are seeing
2nd Person	you are seeing	you are seeing
3rd Person	he, she, it is seeing	they are seeing
SIMPLE **PAST TENSE**	SINGULAR	PLURAL
1st Person	I was seeing	we were seeing
2nd Person	you were seeing	you were seeing
3rd Person	he, she, it, was seeing	they were seeing
SIMPLE **FUTURE TENSE**	SINGULAR	PLURAL
1st Person	I shall be seeing	we shall be seeing
2nd Person	you will be seeing	you will be seeing
3rd Person	he, she, it will be seeing	they will be seeing

PRESENT *PERFECT* TENSE	SINGULAR	PLURAL
1st Person	I have been seeing	we have been seeing
2nd Person	you have been seeing	you have been seeing
3rd Person	he, she, it has been seeing	they have been seeing
PAST *PERFECT* TENSE	SINGULAR	PLURAL
1st Person	I had been seeing	we had been seeing
2nd Person	you had been seeing	you had been seeing
3rd Person	he, she, it had been seeing	they had been seeing
FUTURE *PERFECT* TENSE	SINGULAR	PLURAL
1st Person	I shall have been seeing	we shall have been seeing
2nd Person	You will have been seeing	you will have been seeing
3rd Person	he, she, it will have been seeing	they will have been seeing

■ *Progressive Tone—Passive Voice*

The progressive-tone *passive voice* form of verbs is created by using the *past participle* preceded by a form of the helping verb to be.

☞**EXAMPLE:**

The artist's work *was being shown* at a local gallery.

Christians in Rumania *are being persecuted* for their faith.

The graduate *will be being interviewed* in the near future.

Study the following chart which conjugates the irregular verb *to see* in **progressive tone—** *passive voice*. (NOTE: This chart continues on the next page.)

SIMPLE PRESENT TENSE	SINGULAR	PLURAL
1st Person	I am being seen	we are being seen
2nd Person	you are being seen	you are being seen
3rd Person	he, she, it is being seen	they are being seen
SIMPLE PAST TENSE	SINGULAR	PLURAL
1st Person	I was being seen	we were being seen
2nd Person	you were being seen	you were being seen
3rd Person	he, she, it was being seen	they were being seen

SIMPLE FUTURE TENSE	SINGULAR	PLURAL
1st Person	I shall be being seen	we shall be being seen
2nd Person	you will be being seen	you will be being seen
3rd Person	he, she, it will be being seen	they will be being seen

EMPHATIC TONE

The emphatic tone has two main uses: to emphasize and to ask questions. It is used only in the present and past tenses, active voice. It is formed by placing a form of the helping verb "do" (do, did, does) before the first principal part (present) of the main verb.

☞**EXAMPLES:**

He *does wish* to see you.

I *did study* the lesson.

Do you *want* this hot dog?

Did he *explain* his reasons?

Yes, he *did explain* his reasons.

Below is a conjugation table for the verb "to see" in the emphatic tone.

PRESENT TENSE		PAST TENSE	
SINGULAR	PLURAL	SINGULAR	PLURAL
I do see	we do see	I did see	we did see
you do see	you do see	you did see	you did see
he, she, it does see	they do see	he, she, it did see	they did see

✎ **EXERCISE A** In the blank, write **S**, **P**, or **E** to indicate whether the verb or verb phrase in **dark print** is in the *simple, progressive,* or *emphatic* tone.

_____1. I **have been thinking** about you.

_____2. He **did** not **accuse** you of anything.

_____3. Karen **wants** to learn how to play golf.

_____4. I **am wondering** how I will pay for this.

_____5. I am wondering how I **will pay** for this.

_____6. **Do** you **hear** what I hear?

_____7. **Does** she **understand** the consequences of her actions?

_____8. **Are** you **going** to the school play tonight?

_____9. Kayla **has been reading** a novel by Louisa May Alcott.

✎ **EXERCISE B** In the blanks, write the correct progressive form of the verbs in parentheses. Look for clues from other words in the sentence showing which tense and voice to use. In some cases, there will be no such clues, so any tense or voice may be acceptable.

1. The sand castle (*to break*) _____*was breaking*_____ apart.

2. It was good to hear that the buses (*to run*) _____ on time.

3. When he left, he said, "I'll (*to see*) _____ you."

4. What (*to happen*) _____ to our country?

5. The painter (*to climb*) _____ the ladder.

6. When we last saw him, he (*to drive*) _____ his car on Haskell Street.

7. The river (*to rise*) _____ rapidly after a week of heavy rainfall.

8. Listen to what I (*to say*) _____.

9. My sister thinks she (*to fall*) _____ in love.

10. It seems as though I (*to forget*) _____ something.

✎ **EXERCISE C** Write five sentences using verbs of your choice written in *emphatic tone.*

1. _____

    _____

2. _____

    _____

3. _____

    _____

4. _____

_____

5. _____

_____

LESSON 56: UNIT REVIEW

✎ **EXERCISE A** Fill in the blanks below:

1. The form verbs take to express time of action or state of being is _____.

2. The form verbs take to express whether the subject is the doer or receiver of the action is _____.

3. The characteristic of verbs indicating progress, emphasis, or simple time is known as _____.

4. The six tenses are: _____ _____ _____

_____ _____ _____

5. The two voices of verbs are: _____ _____

6. The three tones of verbs are: _____ _____ _____

7. Verbs have _____ principal parts.

8. The principal parts of verbs are called: _____ _____

_____ _____

9. Write the principal parts of the irregular verb *"to arise."*

_____ _____ _____ _____

10. Verbs that always form their past and past participle parts by adding *-ed, -d,* or *-t* are called _____ verbs. Verbs that follow no set pattern in forming their past and past-participle parts are called _____ verbs.

11. *Underline the correct word in parentheses in this sentence*: In the future and future perfect tenses, the helping word (shall, will) is used with the first person while (shall, will) is used with the second and third persons in ordinary speech.

12. To express a verb in its six tenses—according to its various forms of first, second, and third person and singular and plural number—is to _____ a verb.

13. When the doer of the verb's action is the subject, the verb is in _____ voice.

✎ **EXERCISE B** In the chart below, conjugate the irregular verb *"to begin"* in the *active voice* only. NOTE: This exercise continues at the top of the next page.

SIMPLE PRESENT TENSE	SINGULAR	PLURAL
1st Person		
2nd Person		
3rd Person		
SIMPLE PAST TENSE	SINGULAR	PLURAL
1st Person		
2nd Person		
3rd Person		
SIMPLE FUTURE TENSE	SINGULAR	PLURAL
1st Person		
2nd Person		
3rd Person		
PRESENT *PERFECT* TENSE	SINGULAR	PLURAL
1st Person		
2nd Person		
3rd Person		
PAST *PERFECT* TENSE	SINGULAR	PLURAL
1st Person		
2nd Person		
3rd Person		

FUTURE *PERFECT* TENSE	SINGULAR	PLURAL
1st Person		
2nd Person		
3rd Person		

✎ **EXERCISE C** In the blanks, identify the *tense* of the verbs or verb phrases in **dark print**.

1. _____ I **saw** you at church yesterday.

2. _____ My mother **loses** sleep whenever we stay out too late.

3. _____ We **will tell** you our plans later.

4. _____ You **have come** a long way since you began your lessons.

5. _____ His condition **was** well **known** by his doctors.

6. _____ **Take** heed, all you who pass by.

7. _____ They **will have given** away all of our secrets.

8. _____ Please **set** the table for dinner.

9. _____ Yesterday, he **set** out on his journey.

10. _____ You **have run** a good race.

11. _____ The captain **runs** a tight ship.

12. _____ Today we **bid** you a fond farewell.

✎ **EXERCISE D** In the blanks, identify the *voice* of the verbs or verb phrases in **dark print**.

1. _____ Your reputation **is known** far and wide.

2. _____ We **caught** our limit of fish.

3. _____ The girls **were driven** to their youth meeting by Laurel's mom.

4. _____ She **is** a good rider.

5. _____ His condition **was** well **known** by his doctors.

6. _____ The house **was shown** to us by a real estate agent.

7. _____   They **will have given** away all of our secrets.

8. _____   God **laid** on Jesus the sins of the world.

9. _____   We **were chosen** in Christ before the foundation of the world.

10. _____   You **have run** a good race.

Unit 9
Using Modifiers

In Lessons 4 and 5 you learned the basic grammatical facts about the two kinds of modifiers in the English language—adjectives and adverbs. You have also learned that groups of words, such as prepositional phrases, can be used as modifiers. Review Lessons 4 and 5 and Lessons 25 and 26. In this unit, we will learn some additional facts about adjectives and adverbs.

LESSON 57: MODIFIERS FOLLOWING VERBS

Most of the time, people have little difficulty in deciding when to use an adjective and when to use an adverb. Adjectives modify only nouns or pronouns. Adverbs modify only verbs, adjectives, or other adverbs. However, there are certain situations and certain types of modifiers which sometimes cause confusion.

Sometimes, the *location* of a modifier in a sentence is a source of confusion over whether the modifier should be an adjective or adverb. This is a particular problem when the modifier comes after the verb.

Usually, an adjective is placed right before the noun or pronoun it modifies. However, when the adjective is a predicate complement it follows a *linking verb* and is therefore separated from the word it modifies. Adverbs can be placed in various locations, including after verbs; but they can never be predicate complements modifying the subject.

The best solution is to consider carefully which word is being modified. If it is a noun or pronoun, the modifier is an adjective. If it is an verb, adjective, or adverb, the modifier is an adverb. The *location* is *not* always a sure indicator of which kind of modifier is needed.

Rule 9.1	Do not use an adjective to modify a verb.

☞**EXAMPLE**

> WRONG: The stream was flowing quite ***rapid***.
>
> Our teacher writes ***neat***.
>
> Everyone should take the law of God very ***serious***.

CORRECT:	The stream was flowing quite *rapidly*.
	Our teacher writes *neatly*.
	Everyone should take the law of God very *seriously*.

Rule 9.2	**Do not use an adjective to modify another adjective or an adverb.**

WRONG:	This is a *real* bad idea.
	That jar is *plenty* full.
	His essay is a *tight* written piece of literature.
CORRECT:	This is a *really* bad idea.
	That jar is *very* full.
	His essay is a *tightly* written piece of literature.

Rule 9.3	**Do not use an adverb as a predicate complement following a linking (state-of-being) verb or verb form (see page 8).**

WRONG:	He feels *badly* about the outcome.
	Her new perfume makes her smell *wonderfully*.
CORRECT:	He feels *bad* about the outcome.
	Her new perfume makes her smell *wonderful*.

✎ **EXERCISE** Cross out any adjectives or adverbs that are used incorrectly and write the correct word in the blank. If the modifier is used correctly, leave it as it is.

1. ___*uneventfully*___ The morning passed ~~uneventful~~.

2. _____ Some people do not watch careful when they cross a street.

3. _____ I don't need near that many nails for this project.

4. _____ She seems spry for a woman of her age.

5. _____ I still believe as strong as I always have in the American way.

6. _____ You must look more deep into that subject.

7. _____ She was behaving quite selfish when she refused to share.

8. _____Kelsey is a real good friend of mine.

9. _____I feel sadly about your loss.

10. _____One boy was hurt bad in the car accident.

LESSON 58: MODIFIERS ENDING IN -LY

Another source of error in the use of modifiers is found in the fact that some *adjectives* end with -*ly*, which is a common ending for *adverbs*. On the other hand, there are some adverbs which do *not* end with -*ly* and look very much like adjectives. Some other adjectives and adverbs have exactly the same form.

The key to selecting the correct modifier, again, is to determine which word it is modifying in the sentence.

EXAMPLES OF ADJECTIVES ENDING WITH -LY				
holy	manly	friendly	goodly	lovely
timely	womanly	neighborly	godly	kindly
heavenly	sprightly	slovenly	portly	comely
scraggly	costly	gangly	shapely	ghostly

EXAMPLES OF WORDS NOT ENDING WITH -LY THAT MAY BE EITHER ADJECTIVES OR ADVERBS (As adverbs, the words marked with an asterisk [*] also have -ly forms)				
fast	cheap*	deep*	far	wrong*
sure*	quick*	sharp*	late*	early
little	well	less	more	close*
hard*	long	straight*	strong*	slow*

☞**EXAMPLES:**

You run the risk of accident if you drive *slowly (adverb)* in the *fast (adjective)* lane.

Hold *fast (adverb)* to the beliefs you have received from your parents' teaching.

Grandma is moving a *little (adverb) slow (adverb)* today because of her arthritis.

Be thoughtful of *little (adjective)* children.

The prodigal son left for a *far (adjective)* country.

This is a *far (adverb) better (adjective)* approach.

The engine runs *better (adverb)* since the mechanic worked on it.

✎ **EXERCISE** In the blanks, write *adj.* or *adv.* to indicate whether the modifier in **dark print** is an *adjective* or *adverb.* (CLUE: Determine what kind of word is being modified.)

adv.   1. I spoke as **plainly** as I could.

_____   2. We had a **hard** winter last year.

_____   3. The girls' team played **hard** but lost the game.

_____   4. We could **hardly** believe our ears.

_____   5. They arrived **early** for Sunday school.

_____   6. We attended the **early** service at church.

_____   7. I have **more** work than I can handle.

_____   8. They seem **more** open to our suggestions than they were before.

_____   9. He is **surely** wrong about that.

_____   10. The Word of God is a **sure** foundation for one's life.

_____   11. **Sure,** I will be happy to help you.

_____   12. David ran a **close** race with his rival.

_____   13. The frightened child sat **close** to his mother.

_____   14. Their plans were a **closely** guarded secret.

_____   15. The prince and princess lived **happily** ever after.

_____   16. That story had a **happy** ending.

_____   17. Helping the old woman next door was a **neighborly** thing to do.

_____   18. The hobo's clothes were **slovenly** and his hair **scraggly.**

_____   19. The boy wrote **slovenly.**

_____   20. We had **less** time than we expected.

_____   21. Her words were **less** angry than the look in her eye.

_____   22. I am thankful for my **godly** parents.

_____   23. She **richly** deserves the reward she was given.

_____   24. Please give us a **clear** indication of your intentions.

_____ _____   25. We can hear you **loud** and **clear.**

_____   26. Stand up and speak **clearly** into the microphone.

_____   27. She ran **straight** to her mother with the sad tale.

LESSON 59: DEGREES OF COMPARISON (ADJECTIVES)

Adjectives have three degrees of comparison. If there is no comparison implied in the use of the adjective, the degree of comparison is called *positive*. If two things are compared, the degree of comparison is called *comparative*. If three or more things are compared, the degree of comparison is called *superlative*.

☞**EXAMPLES:**

POSITIVE	COMPARATIVE	SUPERLATIVE
tall	taller	tallest
shrewd	shrewder	shrewdest
fast	faster	fastest
dark	darker	darkest

☞**EXAMPLES OF COMPARISONS IN SENTENCES:**

POSITIVE:

This is a *large* box.

This is a *good* apple.

COMPARATIVE:

This box is *larger* than that box.

This apple is *better* than that apple.

SUPERLATIVE:

Of the three boxes, this is the *largest*.

This is the *best* apple of all those in the basket.

Adjectives that are one-syllable words (and some that are two-syllable words) form their "upward" comparative degree by adding *-er* to the positive form and their superlative degree by adding *-est* to the positive. For "downward" comparisons, use *less* and *least*.

☞**EXAMPLES:**

slow	slower, less slow	slowest, least slow
able	abler, less able	ablest, least able

One-syllable adjectives and some two-syllable adjectives that end with the letter *-y* form their "upward" degrees of comparison by changing *y* to *i* and adding *-er* for the comparative and *-est* for the superlative. For "downward" comparisons, use *less* and *least*.

☞**EXAMPLES:**

cozy	cozier, less cozy	coziest, least cozy
funny	funnier, less funny	funniest, least funny

Most two-syllable or multi-syllable adjectives form their degrees of comparison by using *more (or less)* in front of the positive to form the comparative degree and *most (or least)* in front of the positive to form the superlative degree.

☞**EXAMPLES:**

competent	more competent	most competent
violent	less violent	least violent

Rule 9.4	**A few adjectives undergo changes in their spellings when their degrees of comparison are formed.**

☞**EXAMPLES:**

free	freer	freest
big	bigger	biggest
bad	worse	worst

Notice that the second *e* was dropped from *free* before the endings were added and a second *g* was added to *big* before the endings were added.

✎ **EXERCISE** Write the second and third degrees of comparison of the following adjectives. Check a dictionary if you are not sure.

	POSITIVE	COMPARATIVE	SUPERLATIVE
1.	dense	*denser*	*densest*
2.	fierce		
3.	gentle		
4.	magnificent		
5.	green		
6.	sad		
7.	silly		
8.	soft		
9.	lovely		
10.	cheap		
11.	ugly		
12.	outrageous		
13.	jubilant		
14.	popular		
15.	easy		
16.	obedient		
17.	generous		

LESSON 60: DEGREES OF COMPARISON (ADVERBS)

Adverbs also have three degrees of comparison. The rules for forming the comparative and superlative degrees for adverbs are the same as those for forming degrees of comparison for adjectives. Because most adverbs end with -ly, making them multi-syllable words, the introductory words *more, most, less* and *least* are more commonly used with adverbs.

☞**EXAMPLES:**

POSITIVE	COMPARATIVE	SUPERLATIVE
quickly	more (less) quickly	most (least) quickly
cautiously	more (less) cautiously	most (least) cautiously
closely	more (less) closely	most (least) closely
early	earlier (less early)	earliest (least early)

☞**EXAMPLES OF COMPARISONS IN SENTENCES:**

POSITIVE:

The horse came *quickly*.

Henry works *cautiously*.

COMPARATIVE:

This horse came *more quickly* than that one.

Henry works *more cautiously* than his co-worker.

SUPERLATIVE:

Of the three horses, this one came *most quickly*.

Of all the employees, Henry works *most cautiously*.

The superlative adverb *most* has a special informal use in English when no particular comparison is intended, as in such expressions as: "He is a *most* generous person." Used in this way, *"most"* is an intensifier with the same meaning as *"very"* (see Lesson 5): "He is a *very* generous person."

✎ **EXERCISE** Write the second and third degrees of comparison for the following adverbs. Check a dictionary if you are not sure. NOTE: This exercise continues on the next page.

POSITIVE	COMPARATIVE	SUPERLATIVE
1. loudly	*more loudly*	*most loudly*
2. fiercely	_____	_____
3. gently	_____	_____
4. efficiently	_____	_____
5. noticeably	_____	_____

	POSITIVE	COMPARATIVE	SUPERLATIVE
6.	sadly	_____	_____
7.	unpredictably	_____	_____
8.	softly	_____	_____
9.	lovingly	_____	_____
10.	cheaply	_____	_____
11.	painfully	_____	_____
12.	outrageously	_____	_____
13.	jubilantly	_____	_____
14.	deeply	_____	_____
15.	easily	_____	_____
16.	obediently	_____	_____
17.	generously	_____	_____
18.	fearfully	_____	_____
19.	late	_____	_____
20.	fast	_____	_____

LESSON 61: GOOD AND WELL

Many people have trouble with the correct use of the two modifiers *well* and *good*. Memorize the following to help you remember how and when to use these two words:

Rule 9.5	*Good* is usually an adjective. It is used to modify a noun or pronoun.

☞**EXAMPLE:**

"We had a *good* time at the party."

Rule 9.6	*Well* can be either an adjective or an adverb, but in each case it has a different meaning.

Adjective meaning: "in good health, condition, or standing"

   EXAMPLE: "I feel *well* today."

Adverb meaning: "ably"

   EXAMPLE: "He performed *well* in the race."

Adverb meaning: "thoroughly"

   EXAMPLE: "He is *well* known around here."

Note: For various other meanings of *well*, check your dictionary.

Rule 9.7	In a few informal uses, *good* may serve as an adverb. Combined with "*and*" it is an intensifier.

☞**EXAMPLE:**

We got *good and* wet. = We got *very* wet.

I'll go when I am *good and* ready. = I'll go when I am *fully* ready.

Rule 9.8	Combined with "*as...as*" it means "approximately," "nearly," or "practically."

☞**EXAMPLE:**

The plant was *as good as* dead.

Note: The phrase, *as good as,* can also be a preposition: He is *as good as* his word.

DEGREES OF COMPARISON

Both *good* and *well* form their degrees of comparison in the same way.

POSITIVE	COMPARATIVE	SUPERLATIVE
good	better	best
well	better	best

☞**EXAMPLES:**

Adjective:	This is a *good* book.
	This is a *better* book than that one.
	This is the *best* book of all.
Adjective:	I feel *well* today.
	I feel *better* today than I did yesterday.
	I feel *best* after resting a few minutes.
Adverb:	I perform *well* under a deadline.
	He performs *better* without a deadline than with one.
	She performs *best* of all when left to herself.

Remember, comparative degree is used to show relationships between only two items; superlative is used to show relationships among three or more. This rule is often forgotten, and we therefore hear people say such things as: *The Dodgers and the Giants are both good baseball teams, but I think the Giants are best.*

☞**OTHER EXAMPLES:**

WRONG:	Both of you should now shake hands, and may the ***best*** man win.
CORRECT:	Both of you should now shake hands, and may the ***better*** man win.
	In this three-way contest, may the ***best*** man win.
WRONG:	You should vote for the ***better*** of the five candidates.
CORRECT:	You should vote for the ***best*** of the five candidates.
	You should vote for the ***better*** of the two candidates.

✎ **EXERCISE A** Write *good* or *well* in the blank.

1. The team played _____*well*_____ during the tournament.

2. That was a _____ meal.

3. My dad made a _____ deal on a new car.

4. I have been sick for several days, but I hope to be _____ by tomorrow.

5. That bit of _____ news gives me a _____ feeling.

6. The facts are _____ established.

7. A glass of ice-cold lemonade tastes _____ on a hot day.

8. You would do _____ to learn your lessons.

9. Tyler has always been a _____ boy.

10. Mother is a _____ cook.

11. I like my steaks _____ done.

12. All of the election returns were not counted yet, but we considered our candidates to be as _____ as elected.

13. Mom told the children to be _____ for the babysitter.

14. If you want a _____ performance, you must attend all rehearsals.

15. We hope all is _____ with you.

✎ **EXERCISE B** Write *better* or *best* in the blanks.

1. Some people think one cola tastes ____*better*____ than another.

2. Which of these three pies do you think is _____?

3. All five of you have good ideas, but Jennifer's is _____.

4. In the Super Bowl game, the 49ers proved to be the _____ of the two teams.

5. Cassie made the _____ flower arrangement of all.

6. "It is _____ to have loved and lost than never to have loved at all."

7. "_____ late than never."

8. I have been ill for a week, but I feel much _____ today.

9. I have many friends, but Angie is my _____ friend.

10. Whose music do you like _____, Bach's or Beethoven's?

11. Whose music do you like _____, Bach's, Beethoven's, or Mozart's?

12. Tatiana was the _____ gymnast in the eight-way competition.

13. I like swimming, but I like bicycling _____.

14. I like hiking, camping, and hunting; but of the three I like hunting _____.

15. Running is good exercise, but some people think fast walking is _____ for your leg joints and back.

16. Of all the famous landmarks we saw in Europe, I enjoyed viewing the Leaning Tower of Pisa _____.

LESSON 62: OTHER PROBLEMS WITH MODIFIERS

FARTHER VS. FURTHER

For many people, one of the most difficult comparisons to understand and use are those associated with the word *far: farther/farthest* and *further/furthest.*

It was once taught that there is a strict distinction between these two pairs. Some writers preferred *farther/farthest* to indicate "space" or "measurable distance" and *further/furthest* to indicate more abstract "extent" or "degree."

☞**EXAMPLES:**

> We walked two miles *farther* than they did. *(distance)*
>
> I do not want to discuss this matter any *further*. *(degree)*

Today's grammarians, however, mostly agree that the two forms are pretty much interchangeable in most uses.

In this workbook, we will consider *farther/farthest* and *further/furthest* to be interchangeable when referring to *"measurable distance."* Use only *further/furthest* to mean *"additional"* in other respects.

> ACCEPTABLE: We walked *farther* than they did. OR
>
>   We walked *further* than they did.
>
> DOUBTFUL: They took the idea *farther* than we did.
>
> PREFERRED: They took the idea *further* than we did.
>
> NONSTANDARD: I want no *farther* consideration of this matter.
>
> STANDARD: I want no *further* consideration of this matter.

DOUBLE COMPARISON

Rule 9.9	**Avoid the use of the so-called *double comparison*.**

This means you should not use *-er* and *more* together or *-est* and *most* together.

> WRONG: Winters are *more colder* in Minnesota than in Texas.
>
>   The Bible is the *most widest* read book of all time.
>
> CORRECT: Winters are *colder* in Minnesota than in Texas.
>
>   The Bible is the *most widely* read book of all time.

INCOMPLETE COMPARISONS

Rule 9.10	Do not omit important words in making comparisons unless the comparisons are perfectly clear without the implied or omitted words.

UNCLEAR:	The teacher had to help John more than Jane.
CLEAR:	The teacher had to help John more than *she had to help* Jane. OR
	The teacher had to help John more than Jane *had to help him*.
UNCLEAR:	This pie is the best. *(Best compared to what?)*
CLEAR:	This pie is the best *I have ever eaten*. OR
	This pie is *superior*.
CLEAR:	Bob is taller than she.
UNNEEDED:	Bob is taller than she *is tall*.

ILLOGICAL COMPARISONS

Rule 9.11	Avoid illogical comparisons that may result from omission of certain words.

ILLOGICAL:	Carla's clothes are more stylish than Beth.
LOGICAL:	Carla's clothes are more stylish than Beth*'s clothes*. OR
	Carla's clothes are more stylish than Beth*'s*. OR
	Carla's clothes are more stylish than *those of* Beth.

MEMBERS OF GROUPS

Rule 9.12	Be careful when comparing a group with one of the members of that same group.

Avoid confusion by using words such as *other* or *else*.

WRONG:	Tiffany is faster than any runner on her track team.
	(Tiffany is one member of the team. She cannot run faster than herself.)
	Jeff gets higher grades than anyone in his class.
	(Jeff is one member of the class. He cannot get higher grades than his own.)
CORRECT:	Tiffany is faster than any *other* runner on her track team.
	Jeff gets higher grades than anyone *else* in his class.

DOUBLE NEGATIVES

Rule 9.13	Avoid combining two modifiers with negative meanings.

Some negative modifiers are *not (n't)*, *no*, *hardly*, *scarcely*, *barely*, *but* (meaning *only*).

WRONG: They did*n't hardly* have enough to eat.

Randy had*n't scarcely* started his project.

They do*n't* have *no* money.

This project will *not* take *but* a little effort.

CORRECT: They *hardly* had enough to eat.

Randy had *scarcely* started his project.

They have *no* money. OR They do*n't* have *any* money.

This project will take *but* a little effort.

✎ **EXERCISE** Rewrite the following sentences, correcting any errors they contain.

1. The Wilsons' doghouse is smaller than their neighbor.

    _____*The Wilsons' doghouse is smaller than that of their neighbor.*_____

2. Mr. Jenkins sings louder than anyone in his church.

    _____

3. Next week, we will debate these suggestions farther.

    _____

4. Redwoods generally grow more taller than Douglas firs.

    _____

5. His music is the best!

    _____

6. Some people don't want no more foreigners in our country.

    _____

7. Is the Missouri River the most longest in the United States?

_____

8. Ten-year-old Marissa is smaller than her class members.

_____

9. You never give me no attention.

_____

10. Tony gave me more time than Tom.

_____

LESSON 63: COMPARING ABSOLUTES

Some adjectives and adverbs cannot be compared because they have **absolute** meanings. For example, the adjective **dead** is an absolute, because one cannot be more dead, most dead, less dead, or least dead. Something or someone is either dead or not dead. Logically, there are no degrees of deadness.

Here are some other absolute adjectives (many have adverbial counterparts):

ABSOLUTE ADJECTIVES				
perfect	round	impossible	unique	normal
average	horizontal	vertical	parallel	perpendicular
accurate	absolute	final	fatal	current
destroyed	finished	original	correct	flawless

To suggest comparisons when using absolutes, you may use such introductory words as **more nearly, most nearly,** or **almost.**

☞**EXAMPLES:**

His idea was **more nearly original** than Rachel's.

Your test score was the **most nearly perfect** one in the class.

The diseased plant appeared to be **almost dead.**

Never use adverbs such as *perfectly* or *completely* before an absolute. Absolutes are already "complete" by definition. Adding "completely" is *redundant (unnecessarily repetitive or wordy)*. Read the following sentences without the words "completely" or "perfectly," and you will see that the meaning does not change.

WRONG: The house was *completely destroyed* by fire.

             This job is *completely impossible*.

             He drew a figure that was *perfectly square*.

             Her answer was *perfectly accurate*.

✎ **EXERCISE** Write the degrees of comparison for all of the absolutes listed on the previous page.

POSITIVE	COMPARATIVE	SUPERLATIVE
dead	*more nearly dead*	*most nearly dead*

LESSON 64: UNIT REVIEW

✎ **EXERCISE A** In the blanks, write the comparative or superlative degree of the word in parentheses needed to fit the context of each sentence.

most nearly perfect 1. Of the four competitors, which had the (perfect) performance?

_____ 2. A (far) explanation was needed.

_____ 3. That machine gave us a (accurate) reading than the one we read yesterday.

_____ 4. When the two cars were driven in a test, the (large) car had

_____   the (quiet) engine.

_____ 5. Which of the two cars has the (low) selling price?

_____ 6. The (far) distance anyone ran was 25 miles.

_____ 7. Of the two animals, the dog is the (noisy).

_____ 8. My Dad purchased a new machine part that was (correct) than the first one he was given.

_____ 9. We are encouraged that our test scores are (average) this month than they were last month.

_____ 10. The new players are (cautious) than the old players.

_____ 11. Which of the two pieces of equipment is the (good) buy?

_____ 12. Of the two bicyclists competing, the (fast) one finished only two inches ahead of the other.

_____ 13. It is an encouraging sign that our pet's fever is (normal) today than it was yesterday.

_____ 14. The sound we heard just now is (distinct) than the one we heard a minute ago.

_____ 15. The (courteous) person I have ever met is my brother.

_____ 16. The (gentle) horse of the two is my choice.

_____ 17. Have you ever met a (polite) person than she?

_____ 18.   The students were (free) to speak their minds than they thought.

_____ 19.   The (original) project of all the entries in the science fair will re-
                                ceive the first-place award.

✎ **EXERCISE B** Write sentences using the degree of the adjective specified. Some of the words
shown on the left are also capable of being used as adverbs. However, be sure that in your sentences
you use them as *adjectives*, modifying nouns or pronouns.

bad — superlative

1. _____ *This is the worst case of poison ivy I have ever seen.* _____

current — comparative

2. _____

   _____

friendly — comparative

3. _____

   _____

hearty — positive

4. _____

   _____

lame — superlative

5. _____

   _____

late — comparative

6. _____

   _____

much — superlative

7. _____

   _____

pretty — comparative

8. _____

_____

wise — superlative

9. _____

_____

worthy — comparative

10. _____

_____

polite — superlative

11. _____

_____

✎ **EXERCISE C** Cross out any adjectives or adverbs that are used incorrectly and write the correct word in the blank. Some sentences may have more than one incorrect modifier. If a modifier is used correctly, however, leave it as it is.

1. _____*badly*_____ As a child, I wanted to be a fireman very ~~bad~~.

2. _____ I washed my hands real good.

3. _____ My brother's motorcycle is running terrible.

4. _____ Some drivers panic more easy than others.

5. _____ To prevent breakage, open the package careful.

6. _____ Speak as loud and plain as you can.

7. _____ I couldn't get out of there quick enough.

8. _____ I feel badly about the fact that I forget your birthday.

9. _____ He's the one who was primary responsible for the fight.

10. _____ Of the three, I like this one better.

11. _____ Snow was falling heavy in the mountains.

Unit 10
Using Punctuation
& Capitalization

Our written expressions, as we have learned, consist of words. Words are grouped into sentences to express complete thoughts. Words, however, are not the only building blocks used to make sentences. Sentences also include *punctuation* (and *capitalization* which is discussed at the end of this unit).

Punctuation is a system of written marks by which we make our sentences more meaningful and clear. In a sense, we use punctuation in our oral speech as well by including certain types of pauses and voice inflections (rising and falling tones) in our speaking. These pauses and inflections are represented by several types of marks in written communications. The most common are *commas* and *periods*. Others include *semicolons, colons, question marks, exclamation marks, apostrophes,* and *quotation marks*. Some punctuation marks are used at the **end** of sentences to indicate where one sentence ends and another begins. Others are used only **within** sentences or within words.

Proper punctuation is extremely important for correct, clear, and effective communications. It is often as important as the words we choose if we hope to express our meaning exactly to those who listen to us or read what we write.

LESSON 65: USING COMMAS TO SEPARATE

> **The COMMA (,) is a mark of punctuation used for separating, introducing, and enclosing words, phrases, and clauses within a sentence.**

A comma is only used *within* sentences, never as an ending mark. Because it is used in such a wide variety of ways, the comma is one of the most difficult punctuation marks to learn how to use correctly. In writing, it represents the weak, brief pauses we make in speech.

Rule 10.1	Use commas to separate items in a series.

A *series* is three or more items (words or groups of words) written or spoken one after another. Commas are used to separate each item in the series from the others. By placing commas between the items, we avoid confusion.

CONFUSING: He was studying *English math history economics* and *geography*.

CLEAR: He was studying *English, math, history, economics,* and *geography*.

Notice that the last two items in the series in the previous example are connected by the conjunction *and*. In addition, recognize that the conjunction is *precede*d by a comma.

Note: The conjunctions *or* and *nor* are used in some series to indicate that the items in the series are alternatives to one another. The conjunction *but* can also be used to show contrast.

Rule 10.2	**DO NOT put a comma *after* a conjunction in a series.**

Some writers, especially those who write in newspapers, do not use a comma before the conjunction in a series.

A series may consist of nouns, pronouns, verbs, adjectives, adverbs, or phrases.

Series of nouns:

He planted *corn, oats, alfalfa,* and *soybeans*.

Series of verbs:

She *hopped, skipped,* and *jumped* all the way.

Series of pronouns:

He, she, it, and *they* are all third-person personal pronouns.

Series of adjectives:

She has a *quiet, meek, humble,* but *happy* disposition.

Series of adverbs:

Make your point *quickly, concisely,* and *clearly*.

Series of phrases:

They could not find the missing item *in the closet, under the bed,* or *behind the sofa*.

Sometimes, for special emphasis, *all* the items in a series are joined by conjunctions. In such cases, DO NOT use commas.

☞**EXAMPLE:**

He seems to have no love or joy or patience or kindness in his heart.

When the series consists of adjectives preceding a noun, DO NOT use a comma between the last adjective in the series and the noun modified.

▼ *(remove comma below)*

WRONG: She has a quiet, meek, humble, but happy, disposition.

Rule 10.3	**Use a comma to separate independent clauses in a compound sentence when they are joined by a simple coordinating conjunction.**

☞**EXAMPLES:**

I enjoy going to school, but summer vacation is always welcome.

He has never used alcohol or drugs, nor does he ever intend to do so.

You can do you homework now and have the evening free, or you can put it off and work late into the night.

If the clauses in a compound sentence are especially short, no comma is needed.

☞**EXAMPLES:**

Dogs bark but cats meow.

God loves you and so do I.

Make sure the sentence is truly a compound sentence before using a comma. DO NOT use a comma to separate two items in a compound subject or compound verb in a simple sentence.

WRONG: He wakes up early, and reads his Bible every morning before school.

CORRECT: He wakes up early and reads his Bible every morning before school.

He wakes up early, and he reads his Bible every morning before school.

Rule 10.4	**Use a comma to separate certain introductory expressions from the rest of the sentence.**

☞**EXAMPLES:**

If you arrive before I do, make the arrangements for our visit.

When you pray, do not be like the heathen.

In order to get high grades in school, you must study hard.

During the second day of our vacation, we visited the park's Visitors' Center.

Well, that was an interesting experience.

Some introductory expressions that are especially short do not always need a comma unless the writer believes a comma would add to the clearness of the sentence.

☞**EXAMPLES:**

In 1492 Columbus discovered the New World.

Without exception everyone passed the test.

OR

Without exception, everyone passed the test.

Rule 10.5	**Use a comma to separate two or more adjectives that equally modify the same noun or pronoun.**

☞**EXAMPLES:**

There is a ***tall, stately*** tree in front of the courthouse.

The material had ***red, white,*** and ***blue*** stripes.

Rule 10.6	**DO NOT use commas, if two or more adjectives *do not* modify the same word *equally*.**

One way to tell if adjectives are equal is to insert the word *and* between them. If the word *and* fits logically, the adjective are most likely equal. If it does not fit logically, the adjectives are not equal.

EQUAL:

Lettuce is a ***tasty, healthy*** vegetable. (Lettuce is a *tasty [and] healthy* vegetable.)

UNEQUAL:

We bought a ***new leather*** sofa. (We bought a *new [and] leather* sofa.)

Rule 10.7	**Use a comma to separate numbers consisting of four or more digits.**

☞**EXAMPLES:**

More than ***25,000*** people attended the game.

The business sold for ***$3,250,500***.

Rule 10.8	**EXCEPTIONS: *Do not* use commas in numbers indicating years, telephone numbers, or house numbers.**

☞**EXAMPLES:**

She was born in 1983.

I live at 3547 Avon Drive, and my telephone number is 555-7928.

| Rule 10.9 | **Use commas to separate different elements in addresses and dates.** |

Use commas to separate the names of cities (towns, etc.) from the names of states (or provinces) and countries when they are written together in a sentence. Separate elements of complete dates with commas. When a date includes only a month and a year, *do not* use a comma.

☞**EXAMPLE:**

They lived at 145 Coralwood Street, Modesto, California, USA.

Her address was: P.O. Box 123, Memphis, TN 38104.

Note: DO NOT place a comma between a state abbreviation and the local postal code.

He was born on Sunday, April 30, 1944.

He was born in April 1944.

✎ **EXERCISE** Insert commas where they are needed in the following sentences. Put an **X** through any commas that should not be included.

1. Basketball, baseball, and volleyball are some of my favorite sports.

2. If he could have his way, he would eat ice cream for breakfast, lunch, and dinner.

3. They sat around a warm, cozy fire during the long, cold night.

4. The Protestant Reformation is said to have begun in A.D. 1,517.

5. Grass, trees, unripened apples, and frogs are all green.

6. More than 5,000 men, women, boys, and girls were fed from the five loaves and two fishes.

7. The White House is located at 1,700 Pennsylvania Avenue, Washington D.C.

8. Alligators, and crocodiles seem similar to many people, but they have distinctive features.

9. She bought a bagful of red, green, yellow, purple, blue, and orange candies.

10. The story appeared in *The New York Times*, *The Washington Post*, *USA Today*, and *Newsweek*.

11. In this unit of your workbook, you will learn about commas, periods, and semicolons.

12. He walked down a long, dark, narrow corridor to find the exit door.

13. At dawn, he awoke, got dressed, and fixed breakfast.

14. At nightfall, he lit a candle, and worked for a short time by its light before brushing his teeth, washing his face, blowing out the candle, and going to bed.

15. He received money, or credits to pay his rent, electricity, gas, and telephone, bills.

16. He can sleep in bed, on the floor, in a car, on a plane, and sometimes even while standing.

17. Philip can play, the piano, the violin, the flute, and the clarinet.

18. Many Europeans can speak English, French, German, and several other languages.

19. Half-hidden in the darkness, the stranger went unnoticed.

20. Having completed all his requirements for graduation, he was awarded his diploma.

LESSON 66: USING COMMAS TO INTRODUCE OR ENCLOSE

Rule 10.10	Use a comma to introduce a word or a phrase.

☞**EXAMPLES:**

He had one goal, *to do his best in all circumstances*.

She lacked one thing, *patience*.

I had a big decision to make, *whether or not to attend college*.

Rule 10.11	Use a comma to introduce a short quotation.

☞**EXAMPLE:**

Mother said, "Thank you for your help."

If the quotation comes first, use a comma *after* it (but inside the quotation marks).

☞**EXAMPLE:**

"Thank you for your help," Mother said.

If the quotation is interrupted by its *attribution*, use commas to enclose the attribution.

☞**EXAMPLE:**

"I am grateful to all of you," Mother said, "for the help you have given me."

When material in quotation marks is a title, slang, or some other type of special-use quotation, do NOT enclose the quoted material with commas.

☞**EXAMPLES:**

He was "burned" by their trickery once before.

The "me first" attitude is not a Christian one.

She sang "He Leadeth Me" at the funeral.

When he said "over my dead body" to you, he did not mean it literally.

Note: The *comma* in the previous sentence is included because it separates an *introductory expression* from the rest of the sentence. See previous lesson.

Rule 10.12	Use commas to enclose "interrupters."

Use two commas to enclose words or expressions that merely interrupt a sentence that would otherwise be complete without them. If such words or expressions come at the beginning or end of the sentence, only one comma is needed.

☞**EXAMPLES:**

They promised, *however,* that they would not do it again.

Of course, one can never know what will happen in the future.

It might rain tomorrow, *for example*.

We must, *on the other hand,* expect anything to happen.

Rule 10.13	Use commas to enclose appositives.

An **appositive** is an expression that means the same thing as the word it follows. An appositive may be a word or group of words. If the appositive is only a *single word*, especially a name, it usually is NOT enclosed by commas.

☞**EXAMPLES:**

Uncle Todd, *the man in the blue suit,* is my mother's brother.

George Washington's wife *Martha* was the nation's first "First Lady."

Mercury, *the planet closest to the Sun,* is very hot.

| Rule 10.14 | **Use commas to set off words used in direct address.** |

Use two commas if the words are in the middle of a sentence. Use one comma if the words are at the beginning or end of the sentence.

☞**EXAMPLES:**

Thank you, ***ladies and gentlemen,*** for attending our banquet tonight.

Mrs. Brewer, may we be excused now?

We are proud, ***Mom,*** to have you for our mother.

What do you want us to do next, ***Mr. Foster?***

✎ **EXERCISE** Insert commas where they are needed in the following sentences. If no comma is needed, leave the sentence the way it is written.

1. The song they were singing, I believe, was "Onward Christian Soldiers."

2. My brother, the tallest boy in his class, loves to play basketball.

3. The United States, on the other hand, did not enter World War II until December 1941.

4. Mother answered, "Well, I am really surprised by your attitude."

5. "But as for me," Patrick Henry said, "give me liberty, or give me death!"

6. And now, friends and neighbors, we have a special treat for you.

7. To tell you the truth, I don't know who that was.

8. "This is one of my favorite songs," she said.

9. Most people, generally speaking, are friendly toward their neighbors.

10. My brother, Bob, is older than I am.

11. "Ashlee, don't touch that dial," she warned me, "or you might damage the machine."

12. Of course, I heeded the warning.

13. They were in fact, the only people to recognize me.

14. In my opinion, Christians should not say such things about others.

15. Ted Whitman the station's helicopter pilot reports traffic conditions every hour.

16. What is your name young man?

17. "I would be happy madam to help you across the street" the lad offered.

18. At the exact moment 12 noon on Friday May 1 the bells began to ring in commemoration.

19. King Richard the Lion-Hearted left England for a Crusade in the Holy Land.

20. His cruel treacherous tyrannical brother John villain of the Robin Hood legend was forced to sign one of the first great documents granting democratic freedoms the Magna Carta.

LESSON 67: SEMICOLONS AND COLONS

> A SEMICOLON (**;**) is a mark of separation that is somewhat "stronger" than a comma, indicating a longer pause in speech. It is also used when the words it separates are not as closely related to each other as those which might otherwise be separated by a comma.
>
> A COLON (**:**) is usually a mark of introduction.

SEMICOLONS IN COMPOUND SENTENCES

Rule 10.15	Use a semicolon to separate independent clauses that ARE NOT joined by a simple coordinating conjunction.

☞**EXAMPLES:**

I cannot come to your party; I have a previous commitment.

Please hurry; you have two minutes to get ready.

Rule 10.16	Use a semicolon to separate independent clauses that ARE joined by simple coordinating conjunctions *when there are commas within one or more of the clauses.*

☞**EXAMPLES:**

He was, in fact, a good athlete; but he had a poor record this season.

She taught first, second, and third grade; and she was comfortable with all three.

Rule 10.17	Use a semicolon to separate independent clauses joined by a conjunctive adverb or a phrase that serves as a conjunctive adverb.
a.	If the conjunctive adverb has *two or more syllables,* follow it with a comma.
b.	If the conjunctive adverb has *one syllable,* do NOT follow it with a comma.

☞**EXAMPLES:**

I was ill yesterday; *otherwise,* I would have gone to school.

I was ill yesterday; *so* I could not go to school.

SEMICOLONS IN SIMPLE SENTENCES

Rule 10.18	Use a semicolon to separate items in a series when one or more of the items in the series have internal commas.

☞**EXAMPLES:**

The children included Annie, age 2; Brett, age 3; and Timothy, age 5.

He cited the several literary works, including *A Christmas Carol,* a story by Charles Dickens; *The Gift of the Magi,* a short story by O. Henry; and *The Homecoming,* a novel by Earl Hamner, Jr.

COLONS USED TO INTRODUCE

Rule 10.19	Use a colon *after* an introductory statement when it is clear that something is to follow: a series, a list, a tabulation, etc.

Use a **colon** for such purposes only when there is a clear break between the introductory statement and the items that follow. The usual signals for such a break are words like *the following* or *as follows.* NEVER use a colon after the expression *such as.*

WRONG:

I enjoy eating: ice cream, cake, and cherry pie.

We visited cities such as: Paris, London, Rome, and Berlin.

CORRECT:

Please bring the following: a main dish, a salad, and a dessert.

I will interview each of you in the following order: Mona, Dick, Angela, and Chris.

Mom needs these items from the store: sugar, salt, ketchup, and milk.

Rule 10.20	Use a colon *after* the greeting of a formal or business letter.

☞**EXAMPLES:**

Dear Sir:

Dear Mr. Welles:

Greetings:

Rule 10.21	Use a colon to introduce a long or formal quotation.

☞**EXAMPLES:**

Saint Augustine once wrote: "Thou madest us for Thyself, and our heart is restless, until it repose in Thee."

According to the author Francis Schaeffer: "Just as one is born or not born, married in God's sight or not married, so one has accepted Christ as Savior, and thus is declared justified by God, or not. There is no halfway, no degrees."

Rule 10.22	Use a colon to introduce a word or phrase when emphasis is desired.

☞**EXAMPLE:**

I have one serious problem: no money!

There is only one option: to quit.

Note: When emphasis is *not* needed, use a comma after the introductory statement.

COLONS USED TO SEPARATE

Rule 10.23	Use a colon to separate hour, minute, and second figures in writing time.

☞**EXAMPLE:**

He will arrive at 10:45 a.m. Her time was 1:02:35.

Rule 10.24	Use a colon to separate a title of a book, article, etc. from a subtitle.

☞**EXAMPLE:**

He subscribed to *Crosswinds*: *The Reformation Digest.*

Rule 10.25	Use a colon to separate chapter and verse in the Bible.

☞**EXAMPLE**

My favorite passage in the Bible is John 3:16.

✎ **EXERCISE** Punctuate the following sentences with commas, semicolons, and/or colons.

1. We have little time; therefore, we shall have to hurry.

2. Here's something typical: I can never remember the punch line of jokes.

3. If you visit Barclay's Restaurant, you should make reservations; otherwise you may not get a table.

4. Pack the following items: a toothbrush, a towel, soap, a comb, and other toiletries.

5. Education is very important; you may not succeed in life without it.

6. I am allergic to poison oak, poison ivy, and poison sumac; and I hope I never encounter any of these again.

7. Camping is one of my favorite activities; it seems to challenge my skills and instincts.

8. About two hours before the play began, I was asked to substitute for one of the cast members.

9. The Fifth Commandment says: "Honor thy father and thy mother."

10. He began his letter as follows: "Dear Sir, I would like to order one of the introductory kits you advertised in the newspaper."

11. Please send my order to the following address: P.O. Box 567, Helena, MT 59601. It would be appreciated if the order could arrive before 10:30 a.m., Tuesday, August 11.

12. We left early; thus we did not see the end of the program.

13. Of course, I finished my assignment; however I did not get a good grade.

14. What I am saying is this: always use your time wisely.

15. The article was entitled, "Home Education: An Innovation For a Literate Future."

LESSON 68: ENDING MARKS

> English has three punctuation marks to indicate the end of a sentence: the PERIOD (.), the QUESTION MARK (?), and the EXCLAMATION POINT (!).

THE PERIOD

Rule 10.26	The period (.) is used at the end of a declarative sentence or an imperative sentence that makes a mild command or request.

☞**EXAMPLES:**

There is a growing interest in classical music. *(declarative)*

Please print your name clearly. *(mild imperative)*

Rule 10.27	Use a period at the end of declarative sentences which state an indirect question.

☞**EXAMPLE:**

She asked me where I had laid the scissors.

OTHER USES FOR THE PERIOD:

Besides ending sentences, the period has these other uses:

| Rule 10.28 | Use a period after an abbreviation. If a declarative sentence ends with an abbreviation, only one period is needed. |

☞**EXAMPLES:**

Mr. Jones

Carl Benning, M.D.

Dec. 15

12 lbs. etc.

| Rule 10.29 | Use a period as a decimal point in fractions and to separate dollars and cents. |

☞**EXAMPLES:**

5.25 percent (or 5.25%)

$5.25

$ .25

QUESTION MARK

| Rule 10.30 | Use a question mark at the end of every direct question. |

☞ **EXAMPLES:**

Where do we go from here?

Who knows the answer to this question?

| Rule 10.31 | If a sentence which is already a question ends with a quoted question, use only one ending question mark. |

☞**EXAMPLE:**

Who asked, "What shall we do next?"

Rule 10.32	If a question comes at the end of a declarative sentence, end the sentence with only a question mark (no period).

☞**EXAMPLE:**

It is polite to ask each customer: May I help you**?**

Rule 10.33	Use a question mark to indicate a series of questions in the same sentence.

☞**EXAMPLE:**

Who will be coming**?** you**?** your brother**?** your parents**?**

Rule 10.34	Use a question mark, enclosed in parentheses, to express uncertainty or doubt.

☞**EXAMPLE:**

He seemed sincere (**?**) by the look on his face.

EXCLAMATION POINT

Rule 10.35	Use an exclamation point at the end of an exclamatory or forceful imperative sentence.

☞**EXAMPLES:**

What a wonderful time we had at Disneyland**!**

Come here at once**!**

Rule 10.36	Use an exclamation point at the end of any forceful expression or interjection, even if it is not a complete sentence.

☞**EXAMPLES:**

Ouch**!** Help**!**

Stop**!** Oh dear**!**

Introducing the winner**!**

Rule 10.37	**Use an exclamation point in parentheses to express sarcasm or sly meanings.**

☞**EXAMPLE:**

What a fine friend (!) you turned out to be.

She is such a humble (!) person.

✎ **EXERCISE** Punctuate the following sentences correctly.

1. What a pleasant surprise!

2. Who was the first president of the organization?

3. Can you come before 7:30 p.m.?

4. Four of life's most basic questions are the following: Who am I? Where did I come from? Where am I going? and Why am I here?

5. Stop! You must never, ever touch that switch!

6. Wow! What a magnificent view!

7. Don't men ever open doors for women anymore?

8. Do you plan to go to college after high school?

9. I would like to ask you two questions.

10. The heat wave has finally ended. What a relief!

11. The article tried to answer the question, should Christians be involved in politics?

12. The article concluded that Christians should be involved in politics.

13. Do you agree that Christians should be involved in politics?

14. Absolutely. Christians certainly MUST be involved in politics!

15. The subject of Christians in politics is entirely noncontroversial (!).

16. He seemed certain (?) of the answer.

17. Did she ask, "When are we leaving?"

18. Oh! How I regret that remark!

19. Always use a period at the end of a declarative sentence.

20. This is the last sentence in this exercise.

LESSON 69: APOSTROPHES AND QUOTATION MARKS

> An APOSTROPHE (') is a mark of spelling more than a mark of punctuation.
>
> QUOTATION MARKS (" ") enclose quotations and a variety of other words with special uses.

APOSTROPHES

The **apostrophe** has several uses, but all of them are *within* words. Thus the apostrophe is more a mark of spelling than a mark of sentence punctuation.

Rule 10.38	Use an apostrophe to show possession. An apostrophe and an *s* is used to form the possessive of any noun *not* ending in *s*.

☞**EXAMPLES:**

the man's shirt

the doctor's office

the children's behavior

Rule 10.39	Use an apostrophe alone to form the possessive of *plural* nouns ending in *s* and some *singular* nouns (usually proper names) ending in *s*.

☞**EXAMPLES:** (Examples continued on the top of the next page.)

the boys' room

the students' attitudes

the dogs' howling

☞**EXAMPLES: (cont.)**

Socrates' philosophy

Jesus' resurrection

the class' idea

Rule 10.40	Use an apostrophe to indicate that letters or figures have been omitted, such as in contractions.

☞**EXAMPLES:**

won't

eatin' goober peas

Class of '96

Rule 10.41	Use an apostrophe and *s* to indicate the plurals of figures, letters, and words used as words.

☞**EXAMPLES:**

She was carving figure *8's* in the ice.

Cross your *t's* and dot your *i's*.

I will accept no *if's*, *and's*, or *but's*.

The Civil War was fought during the *1860's*.

QUOTATION MARKS

Quotation marks come in two varieties: double (" ") and single (' '). They are always used in pairs—at the beginning and end of the material they enclose. Ending commas and periods always go *inside* ending quotation marks. Semicolon and colons usually go *outside*. Question marks and exclamation marks go inside the quotation marks only if the question mark or exclamation mark is part of the quoted material.

Rule 10.42	Use double quotation marks to enclose every direct quotation—complete or partial.

☞**EXAMPLES:**

Jerry said, "I would be happy to take part in your discussion."

Lincoln spoke of government "of the people, by the people, and for the people" in his Gettysburg Address.

| Rule 10.43 | **Use double quotation marks to enclose the titles of articles, short stories, poems, and songs.** |

Note: Underline or *italicize* titles of books, plays, films, magazines, and newspapers.

☞**EXAMPLES:**

My article, "Student Council Meets Tuesday," was published in the school newspaper.

He read Robert Frost's poem, "The Mending Wall."

| Rule 10.44 | **Use single quotation marks to enclose quotations or titles within quotations.** |

☞**EXAMPLES:**

"He yelled, 'I'm coming' when I called," Jack's brother said.

"Have you read the poem 'Hiawatha'?" our teacher asked.

✎ **EXERCISE A** Write contractions for the following words.

1. he is   _he's_
2. cannot   _can't_
3. they are   _they're_
4. we shall   _we'll_
5. have not   _haven't_
6. you would   _you'd_
7. they have   _they've_
8. let us   _let's_
9. who is   _who's_
10. is not   _isn't_

11. what will   _what'll_
12. Jenny is   _Jenny's_
13. were not   _weren't_
14. she will   _she'll_
15. you have   _you've_
16. they will   _they'll_
17. there are   _there're_
18. here is   _here's_
19. could not   _couldn't_
20. should not   _shouldn't_

✎ **EXERCISE B** Write the possessive form of the nouns in parentheses.

1. the (cat) meow   _the cat's meow_

2. (Megan) bedroom   _Megan's bedroom_

3. the (children) story hour _the children's story hour._

4. the (child) toy dishes _the child's toy dishes_

5. the (class) motto _the class' motto_

6. the (classes) competition _the classes' competition_

7. (Jesus) miracles _Jesus' miracles_

8. the teddy (bear) ears _the teddy bear's ears_

9. the (family) future _the family's future_

10. the (families) homes _the families' homes_

11. the (people) choice _the people's choice_

✎ **EXERCISE C** Punctuate the following sentences correctly.

1. Kayla replied, "We can do it together."

2. Try to recite the first six lines of Longfellows poem Paul Reveres Ride our teacher said

3. My favorite hymn is What a Friend We Have in Jesus my grandmother said

4. I wonder said Michele whether we did the right thing

5. Do you think we did the right thing she asked.

6. She smiled and said Would you care to join me for lunch

7. Maybe you should rest for a while the nurse suggested

8. Her exact words were I wont be there until 8 p m tomorrow Barry reported

9. I thought I would never see you again his mother gasped

10. Are we there yet the children asked every two minutes

11. My Old Kentucky Home is a song by Stephen Foster

12. The teachers last question was Can you name the capital of Michigan Johnny told his mother

LESSON 70: CAPITALIZATION

The English language has 26 letters. Each of these letters can be written in two different ways: *small* (a, b, c, d, etc.) and **capital** (A, B, C, D, etc.). In English writing, certain words must always begin with a capital letter. Certain other words may begin with a capital or small letter, depending on how they are used. It is therefore important for good communication that you learn when and how to use capital letters properly. This lesson is a guide to some of the most important rules for using capitals.

SENTENCES BEGIN WITH CAPITALS

Rule 10.45	**In written English, the first word of every sentence must begin with a capital letter.**

☞**EXAMPLES:**

For clear and accurate writing, always capitalize the first word of a sentence.

Capitals help readers understand what the writer is saying.

PROPER NOUNS ARE CAPITALIZED

Rule 10.46	**Names of *specific* people, places, or things are called proper nouns. All proper nouns must be capitalized.**

☞**EXAMPLES:**

Europe	New Hampshire	Statue of Liberty
Herman Bavinck	Liberty Bell	George Washington

Rule 10.47	**Capitalize the names of businesses, government agencies, and organizations, including common nouns which are part of the name of the business or organization.**

☞**EXAMPLES:**

Microsoft Corporation	General Mills	Addison High School
Gideons International	United Nations	Hope Reformed Church
The Salvation Army	Utah Legislature	U.S. Department of State

Rule 10.48	Capitalize the names of particular places or defined regions, including names that have directions of the compass in them.
Rule 10.49	DO NOT capitalize directions of the compass when they are used in a general way and not part of a name.

☞**EXAMPLES:**

the **A**merican **S**outhwest	**C**edar **R**apids, **I**owa	**G**obi **D**esert
the **E**ast **C**oast	The lake is **n**orth of town.	**Y**osemite **N**ational **P**ark

Rule 10.50	Capitalize the names of nations, tribes, races, nationalities, languages, and religions.

☞**EXAMPLES:**

the **A**pache nation	**I**slam	**S**paniards
Caucasians	**N**orwegian language	**C**hristianity

Rule 10.51	Capitalize the names of holidays, special historic events, and other calendar elements.

☞**EXAMPLES:**

Thanksgiving **D**ay	the **B**attle of the **B**ulge	the **C**ivil **W**ar
Fourth of **J**uly	10th **A**nnual **I**rish **D**ays	**P**rotestant **R**eformation

Rule 10.52	DO NOT capitalize the names of school subjects, unless they are the names of languages or unless they are followed by a number indicating they are the name of a specific course of study.

☞**EXAMPLES:**

history	social studies	**A**lgebra **I**
science	**H**istory 101	**L**atin, **F**rench, **S**panish

Rule 10.53	Capitalize words that refer to the true God, the god of any monotheistic (one-God) religion, and the names of specific deities of other religions. Do not capitalize the word god in other references.

☞**EXAMPLES:**

Jesus **C**hrist	**A**llah	the **L**ord
Jehovah	the **H**oly **S**pirit	**G**od

PROPER ADJECTIVES ARE CAPITALIZED

An adjective that is formed from a proper noun is called a *proper adjective.*

☞**EXAMPLES:**

American flag	**B**uddhist temple	**F**rench pastry
Chinese history	**S**wedish pancakes	**I**rish setter

Rule 10.54	**DO NOT capitalize a noun that is modified by a proper adjective unless the noun and adjective are both part of a proper name.**

☞**EXAMPLES:**

two **C**atholic churches	**I**ndian beadwork	**F**rench **R**evolution
Republican **P**arty	**F**irst **P**resbyterian **C**hurch	**E**nglish toffee

TITLES ARE CAPITALIZED

Rule 10.55	**Capitalize the first and every important word in the titles of books, magazines, newspapers, poems, films, articles, stories, songs, etc.**
Rule 10.56	**DO NOT capitalize small words such as *the, a, an, and, of, with,* etc. when used in titles unless such words are part of an official name.**

☞**EXAMPLES:**

Gone with the **W**ind	**T**he **N**ew **Y**ork **T**imes	the **T**en **C**ommandments
Amazing **G**race	**O**liver **T**wist	**N**ewsweek
Holy **B**ible	**O**de to a **N**ightingale	**K**nowing **G**od

Rule 10.57	**Capitalize a person's title when it comes before his or her name or when the title takes the place of the person's name in direct address.**
Rule 10.58	**DO NOT capitalize a title that comes after a name or a general title that stands alone. The word *president* is usually capitalized when it refers to the president of a country.**

Rule 10.59	**DO NOT capitalize general occupations that are not titles.**

☞**EXAMPLES:**

Governor Stanley Durban	—	Stanley Durban, governor of the province
Treasurer Margie Steen	—	Margie Steen, treasurer of the club
"How will you vote, **S**enator?"	—	It was not known how the senator would vote.
The **P**resident was inaugurated.	—	Carl is the president of our class.
Professor Thomas Moore	—	He was appointed to be professor of history.
Attorney **G**eneral Mark Sontag	—	attorney Marvin Amador; Mr. Amador, attorney-at-law

Rule 10.60	**Capitalize words signifying a family relationship "title" when used before a name or when used alone in place of a name.**
Rule 10.61	**Generally DO NOT capitalize words referring to relatives when they are modified by a possessive pronoun unless the word is considered to be a title and part of the person's name.**

☞**EXAMPLES:**

We visited **G**randpa **H**erman during Christmas vacation.

Yes, **M**om, I will clean my room.

What shall we buy for **F**ather for his birthday?

I saw my cousin Ryan yesterday.

Her sister Rachel is older than she.

My **U**ncle **N**ed and **A**unt **L**ois live in Georgia.

✎ **EXERCISE** Put a line through the letters that need to be capitalized, and write the correct capitalized letter above them in the following sentences.

55/58
95%

1. ~~M~~rs. ~~M~~c~~I~~ntosh makes the best ~~S~~cottish shortbread and ~~G~~erman strudel.

2. ~~U~~ncle ~~E~~d and ~~A~~unt ~~L~~oretta moved from the south side of ~~C~~hicago years ago.

3. ~~I~~n ancient times, the ~~G~~reeks believed in a god of the ~~U~~nderworld called ~~H~~ades.

4. during the crusades, armies of devout christians fought to end islamic rule in the holy land.

5. this summer we will study jude and revelation, the last two books in the new testament.

6. william holmes mcguffey was an american educator who edited a series of school readers.

7. lars johnson toured the former yugoslavia under the auspices of the university of florida.

8. the so-called terrestrial planets are as follows: mercury, venus, earth, mars, and pluto.

9. the classical architect john russell pope designed the jefferson memorial in washington, d.c.

10. the secretary of state met with representative-elect harold p. jones to discuss federal policies.

LESSON 71: UNIT REVIEW

✎ **EXERCISE A** Fill the blanks below:

1. Written punctuation marks represent certain types of __pauses__ and voice __inflections__ in spoken language.

2. The comma serves three purposes. These are:

   __seperating__   __introducing__   __enclosing__

3. A __series__ is three or more items (words or groups of words) written or spoken one after another. Usually, a __comma__ is used to separate these items.

4. If items in a series have internal commas, a __conjuctions__ is used to separate them.

5. Use a comma to separate independent clauses in a compound sentence when they are joined by __simple coordinating conjuction__

6. Use a __comma__ to separate certain introductory expressions from the rest of the sentence.

7. Use a __comma__ to introduce a short quotation. Use a __comma__ to introduce a long or formal quotation.

8. Use a __semi colon__ to separate independent clauses that *are not* joined by a simple co-ordinating conjunction.

9. English has three punctuation marks to indicate the end of a sentence. They are:

    period   _exclamation mark_   _question mark_

10. When are single quotation marks used? _to enclose quotation or_

    titles in a quotation.

✎ **EXERCISE B** Punctuate the following sentences correctly.

1. The sun was warm and the surf was calm so we had a pleasant day at the beach.

2. After you have completed your first draft correct your errors and rewrite your paper.

3. I enjoyed reading Chapter 6 How to Make Friends.

4. The messenger reported Sir I am sorry to tell you that President Lincoln is dead

5. The Bible exalts faith hope and love but it says that the greatest of these is love.

6. She asked him how he did on his exam.

7. How did you do on your exam she asked him.

8. Galatians 5 22-23 lists the fruits of the Spirit as the following love joy peace long-suffering kind-
    ness goodness faithfulness gentleness and self-control.

9. We couldn't find Elm Street consequently we had to ask for directions.

10. Oh how I hate to see you go.

11. Our schools colors are green yellow and white.

12. Are you glad you were born and raised on a farm she asked.

13. The morning air was crisp and the birds were singing merrily.

14. We do not have a table at the moment but we will be happy to put your name on our waiting
    list the head waiter said.

15. Eric and Alicia asked What time should we come?

16. Dinner will be served at 7 p.m. Melanie replied but there will be a social hour between 6 p.m. and 7 p.m.

17. A roll of that film costs $10.95 but there is no extra charge for developing it.

18. Whos going to tell him his entry did not win a prize

19. This mornings newspaper carried a story about the extent of the earthquakes damage

20. It is extremely rare for a comet to pass through the earths orbit but arent meteor showers quite common

---

✎ **EXERCISE C** Put a line through the letters that need to be capitalized, and write the correct capitalized letter above them in the following sentences.

1. dr. robert rogers preached at the new park street chapel on sunday morning.
   (D R R N P S C S)

2. wasn't the crusade of a.d. 1147 encouraged by the preaching of bernard of clairvaux?
   (W A D B C)

3. by the early fourteenth century, not only had the bohemians, poles, and hungarians adopted christianity, but also the wends, pomeranians, lithuanians, prussians, and the baltic peoples.
   (B B P H C W P L P B)

4. patrick was a great missionary to ireland, and his priority was evangelizing the celtic peoples.
   (P I C)

5. augustine was born to african parents of berber origin in tagaste, numidia, in a.d. 354.
   (A A B T N A D)

6. about 1445 johann gutenburg began to pioneer with moveable metal type in mainz, germany.
   (A J G M G)

7. john of wesel foreshadowed the german reformers by declaring the bible alone as authoritative.
   (J W G B)

8. wessel gansfort, a dutch theologian, wrote against indulgences and other church errors.
   (W G D)

9. john chrysostom, bishop of constantinople, attacked evil empress eudoxia from the pulpit.
   (J C B C E E P)

10. nestorius was condemned for heresy at the council of ephesus in a.d. 431, because he essentially denied that jesus christ was concurrently god and man.
    (N H C E A D J C G)

11. in 1519 martin luther posted his *95 theses* on the church door at wittenberg.
    (I M L W)

12. in an ongoing debate with erasmus, luther argued that salvation is entirely in the hands of god.

13. the great awakening in america began in 1735 under the preaching of jonathan edwards.

14. the scotttish reformer john knox, who spent several years as a french galley-slave, studied under

    john calvin in geneva before returning to scotland in 1559.

15. after refuting catholicism, calvin fled france and lived as an exile in basel, switzerland, where he

    formulated his theology and published the first edition of *the institutes of the christian religion*.

Unit 11
Writing Skills

In Units 1-10 you have learned the basic building blocks of the English language. First you learned about words, the smallest unit of thought. You learned that words are classified according to their use in larger units of expression called phrases and clauses. Words, phrases, and clauses are, in turn, combined into complete-thought expressions called sentences. You learned that sentences can be designed in a variety of ways, and that capitalization and various punctuation marks help you to make your sentences more clear and meaningful. In this unit, you will learn some basic skills for combining sentences into even larger compositions by which people share knowledge with one another.

Writing will always be an important part of your life. It will be needed in your personal life as you write letters to friends and relatives. It will be needed in your business or professional life as you communicate ideas necessary for productivity and accomplishment. If you are a lawyer, for example, your skill in writing legal documents and court arguments may mean the different between life or death, freedom or its loss, a favorable or unfavorable verdict for your client. If you are a businessman or businesswoman, your skill in advancing business proposals and making sales presentations may mean the difference between success or failure, advancement or sluggishness in your career. Scientists, engineers, journalists, doctors, nurses, computer software experts, teachers, ministers, housewives, technicians, researchers, professional consultants, and almost all other professions or occupations need good writing skills.

Furthermore, the personal joy and satisfaction you get in being able to express your ideas and influence the course of your life and the lives of others is an important reason for developing good writing skills.

LESSON 72: FORMING PARAGRAPHS

> **A PARAGRAPH is a group of sentences developing one topic.**

Perhaps the most important word in the above definition of a paragraph is the word *one*. A good paragraph combines sentences in such a way that only *one main idea or topic* is presented. The following is an example of a poorly written paragraph.

One of the most enjoyable and important parts of our church service is the music. We have a wide variety of musicians in our church. My mother is a pianist. My father studied piano when he was young, but he never became an accomplished player. He is now in the export business. On a recent business trip to Asia he visited Hong Kong, which is one of the most prosperous cities in the Far East. Hong Kong is also densely populated. Some people believe the whole world has too many people. In parts of the world, however, there are vast areas with almost no human inhabitants. One such area is the Sahara Desert in North Africa. During World War II, many important battles were fought in North Africa.

Notice that this paragraph mentions a wide range of topics. It begins with a statement about church music and ends somehow with a statement about World War II battles in North Africa. This is a rambling paragraph that is badly confused and fails to communicate any single idea effectively. Its failure to communicate is obvious when the reader asks himself: what is the point of this paragraph? what central idea is being communicated?

Now reread the paragraph immediately above. Notice that it has one central idea: *the shortcomings of the paragraph at the top of the page*. It develops this central idea in four sentences. Each of the sentences expresses some aspect of the central idea.

TOPIC SENTENCES

The central idea of a paragraph is usually expressed in one key sentence in the paragraph. This important sentence is called the **topic sentence**. In many cases, the topic sentence is the first sentence of the paragraph. This gives the reader a clue as to what he will be reading in the paragraph. The topic sentence helps him to focus his thoughts on the central idea the writer is trying to get across.

The topic sentence does not always have to be the first sentence in the paragraph, however. The writer may wish to place the topic sentence in the middle or at the end of the paragraph, building the reader's anticipation about the central idea. A topic sentence at the end of a paragraph may be like the last page of a mystery novel—the reader is eager to get to the end to find the solution to the mystery.

Read the following paragraph written by the great English preacher Charles H. Spurgeon. The topic sentence is printed in dark type. Notice how all of the other sentences develop the central idea expressed in the topic sentence.

If we are begotten of God we must love all those who are also born of God. It would be an insult to you if I were to prove that a brother should love his brother. Does not nature herself teach us that? Then those who are born of God ought to love all those of the same household. And who are they? They are all those who have believed that Jesus is the Christ, and are resting their hopes where we rest ours, namely, on Christ the Anointed One of God. We are to love all such. We are to do this because we act as those who are of the Divine family. Let us count it our privilege that we are received into the household, and rejoice to perform the lovely obligations of our high position. We look around us and see many others who have believed in Jesus Christ; let us love them because they are of the same kindred.

INDENTATION

The most notable characteristic of a good paragraph is that all of the sentences fit together in discussing a single topic. In English writing we have one other helpful device to show where one paragraph ends and another begins. In standard writing style, this device is *indentation*. The first line of the paragraph begins a few spaces to the right of the left margin of the page. The margin is the blank space between the edge of the paper and the area where the writing or print is placed on the page.

In some styles of writing—usually in business or professional writing and reports—the *block* style is used. In this style, the first line of the paragraph is *not* indented. Instead, a space equal to the height of one line of writing is left blank between each paragraph.

STANDARD PARAGRAPH STYLE: BLOCK PARAGRAPH STYLE:

```
    XXXXXXXXXXXXXXXXXXXXXXXXXXXXXX        XXXXXXXXXXXXXXXXXXXXXXXXXXXXXXXXXX
XXXXXXXXXXXXXXXXXXXXXXXXXXXXXXXXXX        XXXXXXXXXXXXXXXXXXXXXXXXXXXXXXXXXX
XXXXXXXXXXXXXXXXXXXXXXXXXXXXXXXXXX        XXXXXXXXXXXXXXXXXXXXXXXXXXXXXXXXXX
XXXXXXXXXXXXXXXXXXXXXXXXXXXXXXXXXX        XXXXXXXXXXXXXXXXXXXXXXXXXX
XXXXXXXXXXXXXXXXX
    XXXXXXXXXXXXXXXXXXXXXXXXXXXXXX        XXXXXXXXXXXXXXXXXXXXXXXXXXXXXXXXXX
XXXXXXXXXXXXXXXXXXXXXXXXXXXXXXXXXX        XXXXXXXXXXXXXXXXXXXXXXXXXXXXXXXXXX
XXXXXXXXXXXXXXXXXXXXXXXXXXXXXXXXXX        XXXXXXXXXXXXXXXXXXXXXXXXXXXXXXXXXX
XXXXXXXXXXXXXXXXXXXXXXXXXXXXX             XXXXXXXXXXXXXXXXXXXXXXXXXXXXXXXX
    XXXXXXXXXXXXXXXXXXXXXXXXXXXXXX
XXXXXXXXXXXXXXXXXXXXXXXXXXXXXXXXXX        XXXXXXXXXXXXXXXXXXXXXXXXXXXXXXXXXX
XXXXXXXXXXXXXXXXXXXXXXXXXXXXXXXXXX        XXXXXXXXXXXXXXXXXXXXXXXXXXXXXXXXXX
XXXXXXXXXXXXXXXXXXXXXXXXXXXX              XXXXXXXXXXXXXXXXXXXXXX
```

✎ **EXERCISE** Read the following paragraphs. Underline the topic sentence. Each paragraph contains one sentence which does not belong because it is not related to the topic expressed in the topic sentence. Cross out the sentence that does not belong.

Paragraph 1

This is the story of King Gold. Wherever King Gold is thought to be, there men run to find him. He weighs heavier and he calls louder than any of the other kings. My mother has a gold ring. King Gold has his throne in the banks—the banks are his palaces. But he can never make men eternally happy or peaceful.

Paragraph 2

Once a young settler boy went to live with the Indians and learn their ways. His name was Henry—Henry Spelman. He went to live with the Indians because he was hungry, and knew that the Indians had plenty to eat. The English settlers lived at Jamestown. Henry Spelman lived with the Indians a long time. He learned how to talk with them, and he learned how they did their work. He saw them plant corn, hunt ducks and deer, and make boats; and he saw them catch fish.

Paragraph 3

Robert E. Lee loved his mother and tried to do all he could to make her happy. His mother was sick nearly all the time. For several years Mrs. Lee could not walk, but by the time Robert was seventeen he was strong enough to carry her around in his arms. She liked to go out driving; so Robert would hurry home from school in the evening and take her out for a drive. The big old coach would come up in front of the door. Then Robert would take his mother up in his arms, carry her out, and tuck her in among the cushions. Then he would get in himself, and they would take a long drive. Sometimes he would put old newspapers over the cracks in the curtains to keep out the cold. He did not mind the cold, but his mother did. Robert E. Lee, who enjoyed fox hunting as a youth, later led the Confederacy in the Civil War.

Paragraph 4

One day in September, almost six hundred years ago, a young man climbed to the top of a mountain. The Indians had told him that he could see from the mountaintop a great water. This man was not disappointed. As he stood on the height and looked southward, he saw a great ocean stretching away and away, far beyond the reach of his keen eyes. He called it the South Sea, because he saw it as he looked toward the south. The young man on the mountaintop was Vasco Balboa, a Spaniard who was the first European to set eyes on the Pacific Ocean. The Panama Canal now allows ships from Europe to reach the Pacific Ocean. The mountain from which Balboa first saw the Pacific Ocean was on the Isthmus of Panama.

Paragraph 5

One day, more than two hundred years ago, five men were appointed to write a letter to the world. One of the five men was old—seventy years old. His name was Benjamin. Two of them were middle-aged. Their names were John and Roger. The other two were young men, and their names were Robert and Thomas. Most of the letter was written by one of the young men—by the one named Thomas. The letter they wrote to the world was known as the Declaration of Independence, and it was signed in Philadelphia on July 4, 1776. It told the world why the United States wished to be free. The Liberty Bell is located in Philadelphia. The young man named Thomas was Thomas Jefferson, who later became president of the United States.

Paragraph 6

The white Easter lily is often called the flower of light. White is the color of perfect light. It is the color of the snow. It is the color that stands for virtue and purity. The right kind of conduct we call white conduct. White robes and white snow give forth white light. White lilies love light and give light. They smile forth most sweetly in the beautiful white light of dawn. For some people Easter means fine clothes, the Easter bunny, and Easter egg hunts.

The above paragraphs were adapted from *History Stories for Children*, Arlington Heights, IL: Christian Liberty Press, 1991.

LESSON 73: SELECTING A SUBJECT

For many people, one of the hardest parts of writing a paragraph or composition is selecting a subject to write about. It is, however, one of the most important steps in writing. Selecting a subject and properly focusing on that subject will make the difference in whether your paragraph or composition is interesting or uninteresting—both to you, as the writer, and also to your readers. You should choose a subject about which you have something new and concrete to say. People are not interested in reading about information that is already common knowledge to them. Since a good writer has something to contribute to the world of knowledge, you should also strive to do the same. Make it your goal not to waste your time or your reader's time.

There are two important steps in selecting a subject:

■ *Select a general subject that is familiar to you*
Choose a subject area about which you have firsthand knowledge. Your knowledge might come from your personal life experience or from your own study and research into a subject which is of interest to you.

■ *Narrow your subject*
Choose a specific topic within your general subject area so that you can properly focus your information. This will generate more interest. Make sure the topic is not so broad that your paragraph or composition could go off into any or all directions. On the other hand, do not make the subject so narrow that nothing can be said about it beyond the mere statement of your topic.

Consider the following two topic sentences:

1. **Electricity has many uses.**

2. **The light switch on the wall of my room is made of white plastic.**

The first topic sentence is too broad. Almost anything could be included in a paragraph which begins with such a sentence. The paragraph would probably be very dull. The second topic sentence may be too narrow. There would not be much more to say in a paragraph which begins with such a sentence. This paragraph would also likely be quite uninteresting.

Study the diagram below illustrating an example of how to select and narrow a subject. The general subject of "SPORTS" is far too big to fit into one paragraph, one composition, or even one book. The specific subject on the right would be an interesting topic about which something new and useful could be told to the reader, based on the writer's knowledge, personal research, or experience.

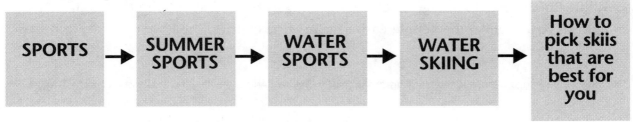

✎ **EXERCISE** Below are several groups of topics for paragraphs. Some topics in each group are too broad and some are two narrow. Put a check mark (✔) in the blank next to the topic that would be best suited for developing in a paragraph.

A.

_____ 1. The Protestant Reformation

_____ 2. How Many Nails Did Luther Use to Post His "95 Theses" to the Church Door?

_____ 3. Why Martin Luther Opposed John Tetzel

B.

_____ 1. Hobbies

_____ 2. Building Model Boats and Airplanes

_____ 3. Building a Ship in a Bottle

C.

_____ 1. The Origin of the Tune "Yankee Doodle Dandy"

_____ 2. Patriotic Folk Songs in America

_____ 3. The Role of Music in History

D.

_____ 1. Extracurricular Activities at School

_____ 2. The Difficulties of Playing in a School Band

_____ 3. Which Valve to Push to Play a B-flat on a Cornet

E.

_____ 1. What's Right and Wrong with the Entertainment Industry, 1960-1990?

_____ 2. The History of Films in the 20th Century

_____ 3. Are G-Rated Films Financially Profitable for Movie Studios?

F.

_____ 1. Skunks and Opossums

_____ 2. How the Skunk Uses Its Scent to Defend Itself

_____ 3. Animals that Prowl About at Night

G.

_____ 1. The Travel Industry

_____ 2. Interesting Places to Visit in South America

_____ 3. The Best Kept Travel Secret of Patagonia

H.

_____ 1. Being a Teacher in a Christian School

_____ 2. Miss Anderson's Life Story

_____ 3. Miss Anderson's Most Embarrassing Moment at Wayland Christian School

LESSON 74: DEVELOPING YOUR TOPIC

Once you have chosen a general subject and narrowed it down to workable size, you should begin to think about how you might develop your chosen subject in a paragraph or composition. If it is a subject with which you are familiar, you may find that it is easy to use too much material. This often happens also when you begin to research the subject for additional facts that you might not know without study. Many writers fear that they will not be able to think of enough material to write a complete paragraph or composition. Most find, however, that the bigger problem is "boiling down" the information they accumulate so that the composition remains focused on the specific subject.

1. CONSIDER THE PURPOSE

The first step in developing your subject is to *consider the purpose* of your proposed composition. Understanding your purpose will help you pick and choose from all your available information which items will be "to the point." In fact, deciding upon your specific purpose ahead of time will save you time during your research. You will then tend to collect only the material that is needed to serve your purpose and not all sorts of wide-ranging material. *Keeping your central purpose in mind throughout the writing process is one of the best guarantees of successful communication.*

2. RESEARCH SUBJECT

Unless the subject is one with which you are completely familiar or fully experienced, you will likely find it necessary to gather some additional information. This can be done by reading books, encyclopedias, and articles; watching videos sources; interviewing experts; conducting "field" studies; etc. Make well-focused notes while you do your research and information gathering. Using separate note cards for each item of information is useful. Organize your notes by arranging them according to logical categories or by eliminating information that does not fit your specific topic and purpose.

3. WRITE A TOPIC SENTENCE

The next step is to begin writing. The best place to start is to write a topic sentence. The topic sentence should be narrow enough so that the paragraph which contains it will remain focused on your central idea and purpose. It should be just broad enough to allow you opportunity to develop several points related to the specific topic. Usually one, two, or three words in the topic sentence will tell the reader what the main subject of the paragraph is. The rest of the words give the reader clues about how the main subject will be developed.

☞**EXAMPLE:**

Study again the paragraph from Lesson 72 about Robert E. Lee. It is reproduced below.

Robert E. Lee loved his mother and tried to do all he could to make her happy. His mother was sick nearly all the time. For several years Mrs. Lee could not walk, but by the time Robert was seventeen he was strong enough to carry her around in his arms. She liked to go out driving; so Robert would hurry home from school in the evening and take her out for a drive. The big old coach would come up in front of the door. Then Robert would take his mother up in his arms, carry her out, and tuck her in among the cushions. Then he would get in himself, and they would take a long drive. Sometimes he would put old newspapers over the cracks in the curtains to keep out the cold. He did not mind the cold, but his mother did. ~~Robert E. Lee, who enjoyed fox hunting as a youth, later led the Confederacy in the Civil War.~~

Notice the topic sentence (printed in bold type on the previous page). The topic sentence tells the reader that the paragraph is going to be about Robert E. Lee and his relationship with his mother. The topic sentence also tells the reader that these main subjects will be developed in such a way as to tell what Robert did to make his mother happy. Everything in the paragraph should be somehow related to Robert, his mother, and the ways he tried to make her happy. As we study the paragraph, we can see that all of the sentences do indeed relate to the ideas stated in the topic sentence—EXCEPT the last sentence. The last sentence does not deal with the main subject of Robert's loving assistance to his mother. It tells us something unrelated about Robert's youth and his later life. The final sentence should be eliminated from the paragraph because it is not focused on the main idea of the paragraph.

4. CHOOSE SUBPOINTS

As we have noted, the main subject of the paragraph about Robert E. Lee is Robert and his love and assistance to his mother. The paragraph includes several *subpoints* which develop this theme:

❏ **Why his mother needed Robert to make her happy (she was sick).**

❏ **What the nature of her problem was (she could not walk or get around on her own).**

❏ **Robert was strong enough to solve this problem (he could carry her).**

❏ **What would make his mother happy (she liked going for carriage rides).**

❏ **How Robert met this desire (he carried her to the carriage and made her comfortable).**

❏ **How Robert had to sacrifice his own interests for his mother (hurried home from school and "went the extra mile" for her beyond his own needs).**

While these are all separate and additional points, they all relate in some way to the information stated in the topic sentence: *Robert's love and care for his mother.* Bringing in this additional information and relating it to the topic is called *developing the subject.*

✎ **EXERCISE** Below are some main topics and some possible subpoints for developing the main topic in a paragraph. One of the subpoints in each case is not related or somewhat off the point of the main topic. Put a check mark (✔) next to the subpoint that should be eliminated.

1. **The spiritual significance of the Old Testament high priest's garments**

    _____ the meaning of the breastplate

    _____ the meaning of the colors on the apron

    _____ why the tassels on the priest's garments were important

    _____ why only Levites could be priests

    _____ the significance of the ephod

2. **How to prevent breakage of dishes when moving household goods**

    _____ pack dishes only in specially designed boxes made of heavy material

    _____ wrap each dish in soft paper

    _____ make sure the wrapping is bulky enough to prevent dishes from making contact

    _____ pack mirrors and picture frames carefully

    _____ label dish boxes "fragile"

    _____ exercise care in carrying and placing dish boxes in the moving vehicle

3. **Assembling a bicycle**

    _____ obtain the necessary tools as outlined in the instruction sheets

    _____ remove all parts from the carton

    _____ inventory parts to make sure none are missing

    _____ wear a safety helmet when riding a bicycle

    _____ review all assembly instructions before starting the assembly process

    _____ assemble the parts in the order stated in the instructions

    _____ recheck all connections for secureness.

4. **The Christian's responsibility toward believers who are suffering persecution**

    _____ remember them in prayer

    _____ learn names of specific individuals suffering oppression

    _____ write letters to oppressive government leaders

    _____ be kind to your neighbors and attend church every Sunday

    _____ support organizations which provide relief or intervention

    _____ travel to restricted countries to provide personal encouragement, if possible

    _____ encourage your own government leaders to develop foreign policies upholding religious freedoms throughout the world

5. **Moral decline in the Roman Empire**

    _____ emperor worship

    _____ persecution of Christians

    _____ emphasis on pleasure and games

    _____ perverted relationships between the sexes

    _____ bloody spectacles in the arenas

    _____ how Julius Caesar rose to power in the early days of Rome

    _____ final conquest by barbarians

6. **Corruption in professional, major-league sports**

    _____ overemphasis on extremely high salaries

    _____ drug use and immoral behavior by professional athletes

    _____ labor strikes showing indifference to the interests of fans

    _____ illegal recruitment of high school students into college athletic programs

    _____ more interest in product endorsements than in the game itself

7. **Why I like deer hunting**

_____   good source of meat

_____   enjoy getting outdoors

_____   improves my survival skills and knowledge of safety

_____   motorboating is also an enjoyable outdoor activity

LESSON 75: BLUEPRINT FOR A GOOD PARAGRAPH

Once you have carefully planned your paragraph or composition by selecting a topic, re-searching it, and considering your topic sentence and subpoints, the hard work of actually designing and writing your ideas begins. A good paragraph design includes not only a topic sentence but some other ingredients as well.

1. GRAB YOUR READER'S ATTENTION

One of the most effective devices in grabbing your reader's attention is the opening sentence of your paragraph. Usually this is the topic sentence, but that is not always the case. Whether or not the first sentence is the topic sentence, great thought and care should be given to this sentence. The opening or "lead" sentence could take one or another of the following forms or approaches:

A QUESTION:	Put the question in your reader's mind that you hope to answer in your writing.
AN EXAMPLE:	Give an illustration of the matter which you will discuss.
A QUOTATION:	Find appropriate or well-known words which someone has spoken or written in the past that relates to your subject.
AN INCIDENT OR ANECDOTE:	Tell a small story which relates to or introduces your topic.
DIALOGUE:	A bit of conversation may introduce the subject.

These devices may prove interesting, but they should not be overused. Too much cleverness or cuteness is often the sign of amateur writing ability. Professional writers tend to take a more straightforward, factual approach when writing informative pieces or they make a forthright statement of opinion when writing to influence people.

Professional journalists follow a formula for the "lead" sentences of their news stories. The formula is known as "the 5 W's and the H." The five "W's" are who? what? where? when? and why? The "H" is how? News writers try to answer all of these questions with a word or two, combining them into one powerful opening sentence. This gives readers who merely skim newspapers a good, full idea about the content of the news story right at the start. While not all writing is like that, writers of other types of literature often profit by taking a similar _summary_ approach to their leading sentences.

2.   DEVELOP THE BODY OF THE PARAGRAPH

After you have written an effective leading sentence, you must proceed to develop the rest of your paragraph. In the *body* of the paragraph, you will discuss the main subject and the sub-points which are stated or implied in your topic sentence. There are two main considerations when "backing up your ideas" in the body of the paragraph:

■ *Support your ideas in a variety of ways*

You might use facts. You might use arguments or reasoning. You might use illustrations or examples. You might use quotations or figures of speech. You might use questions or dialogue. What approach you take will usually be influenced by the type of writing you are doing: **story telling** *(narrative)*; **explaining how** *(expository)*; **describing or "painting a picture"** *(descriptive)*; or **influencing, reasoning, or giving opinions** *(argumentative)*. Sometimes a composition will be a combination of these approaches.

■ *Arrange the body of the paragraph in an order that best suits your purpose*

You might summarize first and then give details. You may start with details and then summarize. You may take the "mystery story" approach and save the most important revelation until last. You may tell things in the order in which they happened or in reverse order. You may start in the present and "flashback" to the past and work back to the present. You may offer your supporting material in ascending or descending order of *importance*. You may alternate facts and reasons—or reasons and examples. You may alternate statements of fact with dialogue or quotations to illustrate or prove the facts. In summary, use your imagination and creativity to accomplish your central purpose.

3.   STATE YOUR CONCLUSION

Some paragraphs end with a *concluding sentence*, but not all paragraphs do. A conclusion is a statement summarizing or drawing a final thought from the material that has gone before. Often the conclusion will be a restatement, in different words, of the topic sentence. In some paragraph designs, the concluding statement will actually *be* the topic sentence. After you have written the body of the paragraph, consider whether it would be wise to reinforce your communication by finishing with a formal concluding statement. Sometimes repeating a central idea will help the reader remember the main purpose of your paragraph. Never introduce new material in a sentence that is supposed to be stating a conclusion, because a conclusion is, by definition, a statement that takes into account or summarizes all the *preceding* steps of your reasoning.

4.   COMPOSE A TRANSITIONAL STATEMENT

When a composition consists of more than one paragraph, one of the best devices for making your writing logical and easy to read is the *transitional sentence*. **A transitional sentence is one that connects what has been written with what will follow.** Writing good transitional sentences will give smoothness, unity, and logical flow to your writing.

Where should transitional devices be placed? There are several possibilities.

1. Sometimes transitional *words* or *phrases* may be used *within* paragraphs to lead the reader from one subpoint to another.

2. A transitional *sentence* will usually be the first sentence of a succeeding paragraph. As such, it may also set the theme for the new paragraph and therefore double as the topic sentence for that new paragraph.

3. Sometimes, however, a writer may use the last sentence in a paragraph as a transitional sentence, connecting what has already been written with what will follow in the next paragraph. When the last sentence of a paragraph is a *transitional sentence*, it will not likely be the *conclusion* of that paragraph even though it comes at the physical end.

4. Sometimes, writers put a transitional sentence in a paragraph of its own, as in the paragraph at the very top of this page.

Study the following example, again from the writings of Charles H. Spurgeon. (The transitional devices are in dark type. Notice also how the writer uses dialogue with himself and with Christ for interest, variety, and effective communication of his purpose.)

> If you are at all like me, you will at times feel your inner life to be sadly declining. I am ashamed to confess it, but even when I seek to live nearest to God, I still feel an evil heart of unbelief struggling within me…. **At such times** we are apt to say, "I must try to make myself somewhat better than this by some means before I dare hope in God." **Then** we go off to our own selves and our own works, and we sink in the deep mire where there is no standing.

> **At such moments it is a happy thing to turn again to Christ and say, "O my Master, unworthy as I am to be Your follower, although the vilest of all those whose names are written on Your roll, yet I still do believe in You.** I will cling to Your cross; I will never let go my hope, for You have come to save sinners, even such ones as I am, and on You I will continue to trust." You will find that while **this** restores your peace, at the same time it excites you to seek after higher degrees of holiness….

Notice how the transitional sentence (the first one in paragraph two) connects what has gone before it with what follows. The words *"At such moments"* refer to the times of unbelief which the author was discussing in the first paragraph. The rest of the words in the transitional sentence introduce ideas which are discussed further in the second paragraph. In this way, the transitional sentence ties the two paragraphs together, creating unity and encouraging the reader to continue reading what the writer has to say.

✎ **EXERCISE** Read the following paragraphs from Washington Irving's book, *The Alhambra*, and answer the questions at the end.

The Spanish muleteer has an inexhaustible stock of songs and ballads, with which to be-guile his incessant wayfaring. The airs are rude and simple, consisting of but few inflec-tions. These he chants forth with a loud voice, and long, drawling cadence, seated sideways on his mule, who seems to listen with infinite gravity, and to keep time, with his paces, to the tune. The couplets thus chanted, are often old traditional romances about the Moors, or some legend of a saint, or some love-ditty; or, what is still more fre-quent, some ballad about a bold contrabandista, or hardy bandolero, for the smuggler and the robber are poetical heroes among the common people of Spain. Often, the song of the muleteer is composed at the instant, and relates to some local scene, or some inci-dent of the journey. This talent of singing and improvising is frequent in Spain, and is said to have been inherited from the Moors. There is something wildly pleasing in listen-ing to these ditties among the rude and lonely scenes they illustrate; accompanied, as they are, by the occasional jingle of the mule bell.

It has a most picturesque effect also to meet a train of muleteers in some mountain-pass. First you hear the bells of the leading mules, breaking with their simple melody the still-ness of the airy height; or, perhaps, the voice of the muleteer admonishing some tardy or wandering animal, or chanting, at the full stretch of his lungs, some traditionary ballad. At length you see the mules slowly winding along the cragged defile, sometimes descend-ing precipitous cliffs, so as to present themselves in full relief against the sky, sometimes toiling up the deep arid chasms below you. As they approach, you descry their gay deco-rations of worsted stuffs, tassels, and saddle-cloths, while, as they pass by, the ever-ready trabuco, slung behind the packs and saddles, gives a hint of the insecurity of the road.

1. Which type of writing does the author mainly use to develop his ideas? *(check one)*

_____ **narrative**   _____ **expository**   _____ **descriptive**   _____ **argumentative**

2. Write the sentence in the first paragraph which you believe is the topic sentence.

_____

_____

3. How does the author develop his topic in the first paragraph? *(check all that apply)*

_____ **facts** _____ **examples** _____ **reasons/arguments** _____ **dialogue** _____ **questions**

4. Read the last sentence in the first paragraph and answer the following two questions:

    a.) Which words in that sentence do you think might be considered a conclusion for the first paragraph?

    _____

    _____

    b.) Which words in that sentence do you think might be considered as transitional material tying the first and second paragraphs together?

    _____

    _____

5. What *order* does the author use to develop his ideas in the second paragraph? *(check one)*

    ____ **order of time (chronological order or sequence in which things happen)**

    ____ **order of importance (order of significance, most important first, etc.)**

6. Write the sentence in the second paragraph which you think is the topic sentence.

    _____

    _____

7. *How* does the author develop his ideas in the second paragraph? *(check all that apply)*

    ___ **description**   ___ **narrative**   ___ **facts**   ___ **dialogue**   ___ **questions**   ___ **quotations**

LESSON 76: WRITING PROJECT

It is now time to put into practice what you have learned about writing. Choose a subject of interest to you and write a paragraph of approximately 200-400 words (the number of words is not as important as *how well* you do). Use separate sheets of white lined paper for your *first* draft and your *final* version.

Follow the steps you have learned in this unit in selecting a subject and narrowing it down, researching and reading, making notes, writing a topic sentence, writing a powerful and effective lead sentence, considering and developing subpoints in your paragraph, using transitional words and phrases effectively, writing a conclusion as needed, etc.

After you select a well-focused subject and before you start writing, consider which type of writing will best communicate your ideas: **story telling** *(narrative)*; **explaining how** *(exposi-*

tory); **describing or "painting a picture"** *(descriptive)*; or **influencing, reasoning, or giving opinions** *(argumentative)*. Consider which facts, quotations, examples, illustrations, arguments, or other supporting information you will need for each of these types of writing. Of course, as you have learned, sometimes a composition will be a combination of these approaches; but your subject will likely require you to take one main approach.

After writing your first draft, read it over with the following concepts in mind:

■ *Meaning*

Have you carefully chosen precise and appropriate words and phrases? Are your main ideas clearly stated in the topic sentence? Is the meaning made clear with appropriate details in the body of the paragraph? Is there logical order in the presentation of your ideas?

■ *Sentence structure*

Is there variety or are all of your sentences pretty much alike? Are your sentences grammatically correct? Have you used transitional devices to create unity, progress, and smoothness?

■ *Mechanics*

Is your punctuation correct? Have you spelled your words correctly? Did you capitalize the first word of every sentence? Do verbs and subjects agree? Do pronouns have antecedents and do they agree? Are modifiers used and placed correctly?

After writing and reviewing your first draft, make corrections and write a second version. Keep reviewing and rewriting until you are satisfied that your paragraph is as good as it can be. It will be acceptable when it is *correct*, *clear*, *effective*, and *appropriate*.

Glossary

Absolutes

Adjectives and adverbs that are logically incapable of comparison because their meanings are absolute. Such words include: *unique, perfect, perpendicular, horizontal, parallel, excellent, accurate, absolute, round, square, final, fatal, impossible, correct, current, normal, original, average.* Comparison may be achieved only by the addition of qualifying adverbs, such as *nearly, more/most nearly, almost.*

Active voice

The form of an action verb which tells that the subject is the doer of the action.

EXAMPLE:

George *mowed* his lawn.

Adjective

A part of speech that modifies or limits the meaning of a noun or pronoun.

They usually answer one of the following questions about the noun or pronoun they modify: *which one? what kind? how much? how many?* Simple adjectives are generally located immediately before the word they modify. Predicate adjectives are usually located after a linking verb and modify the subject of that verb.

EXAMPLES:

the *happy* people (simple adjective)

The eggs are *rotten*. (predicate adjective.)

Adjective clause

A dependent clause used to modify a noun or pronoun.

EXAMPLE:

The car *which you rented* must be returned tomorrow.

Adverb

A part of speech that modifies a verb, adjective, or another adverb. Adverbs used as transitional devices in sentences may modify the entire thought of the sentence.

EXAMPLE:

We are, *however*, planning to visit you shortly.

Adverb (adverbial) clause

A dependent clause that modifies a verb, adjective, or adverb.*

NOTE: *Examples begin at the top of the column.

EXAMPLES:

Mary quit her job *because she preferred her role as a mother*. (Modifies verb.)

The test was harder *than most others were*. (Modifies adjective.)

I think more sharply after a good *night's rest*. (Modifies adverb.)

Agreement

Sameness in number, gender, and person. Agreement in number is required between a subject and predicate. Pronouns must agree with their antecedents in person, number, and gender.

Antecedent

The substantive (noun or pronoun) to which a pronoun refers.

Antonyms

Pairs of words that have the opposite or negative meanings.

Appositive

A noun or noun clause added to (usually following) another noun or pronoun to further identify or explain it. The appositive signifies the same thing as the noun or pronoun it seeks to identify or explain.

EXAMPLES:

One economic system, *socialism*, is a proven failure.

A basic socialist premise, *that all people deserve an equal share of the world's material substance*, is a false assumption.

Auxiliary verb

Also called a ***helping verb***. A verb used to "help" another verb in forming voices, tenses, and other grammatical ideas. The most common are forms of *be, have, do, can, could, may, might, shall, should, will, would, must, ought, let, dare, need,* and *used.*

Case

The forms that nouns or pronouns have (nominative, objective, possessive) signifying their relationship to other words in a sentence.

EXAMPLES:

The *car* was new. (Nominative.)

The subject of the *speech* was crime. (Objective.)

The *children's* story hour was always popular. (Possessive.)

Clause
A group of words including a subject and a predicate and forming a part of a sentence. All words in a sentence must be part of a clause. Clauses are classified as to their *use* (adjective, adverb, noun), their *character* (dependent, independent, elliptical), and their *necessity* (essential [restrictive], non-essential [non-restrictive]).

Comparative degree
The form of an adjective or adverb used when comparing two entities. The comparative form is created by adding *-er* to one-syllable and some two-syllable adjectives and adverbs or by preceding adjectives and adverbs of two or more syllables with the word *more*.

> EXAMPLES:
>
> That painting is *prettier* than the other one.
>
> Robert seems to learn *more easily* than Sally.
>
> (See also Absolutes.)

Comparison, degrees of
A change in the form of adjectives and adverbs signifying greater or smaller degrees of quantity, quality, or manner. The three degrees of comparison are: *positive, comparative,* and *superlative.*

> EXAMPLES:
>
> small, smaller, smallest; beautiful, more beautiful, most beautiful

Complement
A word or expression used to *complete* the action or idea indicated by a verb. Predicate *complements* include predicate nominatives (noun or pronoun) and predicate adjectives following linking verbs and describing, identifying, or modifying the subject.

Complex sentence
A sentence consisting of one independent clause and one or more dependent clauses.

> EXAMPLE:
>
> When Jesus came, He preached a message of salvation to all who would believe.

Compound sentence
A sentence consisting of two or more independent clauses.

> EXAMPLE:
>
> The battle was won, but the war was lost.

Compound-complex sentence
A sentence consisting of two or more independent clauses and one or more dependent clauses.

> EXAMPLE:
>
> Since Mike was artistic, he designed the brochure; but Jennifer, who was a better writer, wrote the text.

Compound pronoun
A pronoun with the suffix *-self*. There are two types: reflexive and intensive. (See entries for *reflexive pronoun* and *intensive pronoun*).

Conjugation
Changes in the form and use of a verb to signify *tense, voice, number, person,* and *mood.*

Conjunction
A part of speech used to connect words or groups of words such as phrases and clauses. Conjunctions are classified as *coordinating* when they link equal elements or *subordinating* when they link unequal elements.

> EXAMPLES:
>
> I like apples *and* bananas. (Coordinating conjunction linking two direct objects.)
>
> My hair is brown, *whereas* Mary's is blonde. (Subordinating conjunction linking an independent clause with a dependent clause.)
>
> (See also Conjunctive adverb.)

Conjunctive adverb
An adverb used as a coordinating conjunction connecting two independent clauses.

> EXAMPLE:
>
> The picnic was cancelled; *nevertheless,* we had a pleasant afternoon in the park.

Coordinating conjunction
A conjunction linking words, phrases, or clauses of equal grammatical rank, importance, or value.

> EXAMPLE:
>
> Do your duty, *or* turn in your badge.

Correlative conjunction
Coordinating conjunctions used in pairs. Each member of the pair must be followed by words of equal grammatical value. The most common are: *either...or, neither...nor, both...and,* and *not only...but also.*

> EXAMPLE:
>
> *Neither* my grandfather *nor* my grandmother was born in America.

Declarative sentence
A sentence that states a fact, possibility, or condition.

Demonstrative pronoun
A pronoun pointing to, pointing out, identifying, or calling attention to: *this, that, these, those, such.*

Dependent (or subordinate) clause
A clause that does not express a complete thought in itself but which depends for its full meaning upon an independent clause in the same sentence. The three use-related classifications of dependent clauses are: *adjective, adverb,* and *noun.*

Direct quotation
Stating the exact words (all or part) of a writer or speaker.

Exclamatory sentence
A sentence or sentence fragment expressing strong feeling or surprise.

Future perfect tense
The time of a verb's action beginning in the present and reaching completion sometime in the future.

> EXAMPLE:
>
> He *will have finished* his work by this time tomorrow.

Future tense
The time of a verb expressing action or state of being after the present time.

> EXAMPLE:
>
> She *will be* 10 years old next Tuesday.

Gender
The classification of nouns or pronouns indicating sex: *masculine, feminine, neuter,* or *common.*

Homographs
Two or more words that are spelled alike but which have different meanings and may have different pronunciations.

Homonyms
Pairs of words that sound alike but are spelled differently and have different meanings.

Imperative sentence
A sentence expressing a command or declaring a request.

Indefinite pronoun
A pronoun with an implied antecedent but referring to no specific person, place, or thing: *one, someone, everyone, somebody, everybody, each, none, no one, nobody, everything, nothing,* etc.

Independent clause
A clause that expresses a complete thought in its context and could, if necessary, stand alone as a complete sentence.

> EXAMPLE:
>
> If she is chosen next Friday night, *Kim will be the first Chinese homecoming queen in the school's history.*

Indirect object
A noun or pronoun preceding a direct object of a verb and indicating a recipient of the object of the verb. An indirect object usually could have the prepositions *to* or *for* placed before them.*

NOTE: *Example begins at the top of the column.

EXAMPLE:
I sent *Mother* a birthday card. (i.e., I sent (to) *Mother* a birthday card.)

Infinitive
A verb form which is the first principal part of a verb, equivalent to the first person present tense. The infinitive has the function of a verb (as part of the predicate) but is also a verbal or in a verbal phrase, commonly used as a noun, adjective, or adverb. As a verbal it is preceded by an introductory *to,* either expressed or implied. The infinitive may also serve as the predicate of an infinitive "clause."

Intensive pronoun
A pronoun ending with -*self,* usually non-essential to the sentence but added for emphasis or intensification of its antecedent.

> EXAMPLE:
>
> I will make the announcement *myself.*

Interjection
An exclamatory word expressing strong feeling or surprise and having little or no grammatical connection with other words in a sentence.

> EXAMPLES:
>
> *Ouch!* That hurts.
> *Oh,* what a lovely day!

Interrogative pronoun
A pronoun used in a question: *who, which, what, whoever, whatever.*

Interrogative sentence
A sentence asking a question. A question mark is used as its closing punctuation.

Irregular verb
A verb whose past and past participle forms are different in spelling from the present (infinitive) form and do not follow the regular pattern of having the last two principal parts formed by the addition of the letters -*d,* -*t,* or -*ed.*

> EXAMPLES:
>
> see, seeing, saw, seen
> drive, driving, drove, driven
> lose, losing, lost, lost
> set, setting, set, set

Linking verb
A non-action verb that expresses a state of being or fixed condition. It "links" a subject to a noun or adjective (or equivalent phrase or clause) in the predicate. The most common linking verbs are forms of *be, look, seem, appear, feel, smell, sound, become, grow, remain, stand, turn, prove.*

> EXAMPLES:
>
> She *is* small. His theory *proved* correct.
> You *look* better today. That dog *smells* bad.
> The word of the Lord *stands* secure.

Modifier

Words that describe or limit. Adjectives and adverbs modify other words.

> EXAMPLES:
>
> sang *happily* (describes), the *only* child (limits)

Nominative case

The case of nouns or pronouns used as subjects or predicate complements.

> EXAMPLES:
>
> *He* is Lord.   This is *he*.

Non-restrictive or non-essential

A modifier, usually a phrase or clause, that does not limit but describes or adds information.

Noun

A part of speech that names a person, place, thing, idea, action, or quality.

> EXAMPLES:
>
> *John, sky, table, capitalism, eating, ugliness*

Number

The form of a noun or pronoun showing whether one or more than one is indicated. Nouns and pronouns are either *singular* (one) in number or *plural* (two or more) in number. Verbs have singular or plural forms corresponding to the number of the nouns or pronouns that perform their action or state of being.

> EXAMPLES:
>
> The *boy sings*. (Singular noun and verb.)
> The *children sing*. (Plural noun and verb.)

Object

The noun, pronoun, or noun clause following a transitive verb or preposition.

> EXAMPLES:
>
> Larry ate the *cake*.
> (Noun as object of a transitive verb.)
> Put the cake on the *table*.
> (Noun as object of a preposition.)
> She gave him *what he wanted*.
> (Noun clause as object of a transitive verb.)

Objective case

The *case* of nouns or pronouns used as objects of prepositions or as direct or indirect objects of verbs.

> EXAMPLES:
>
> I gave *him* some advice. Tell your problems to *me*. She loves *us* very much.

Participle

A verb form functioning either as a verb in a predicate or as an adjective. Participles have three forms: *present participle, past participle,* and *perfect participle.**

NOTE: *Examples begin at the top of the column.

> EXAMPLES:
>
> I am *enjoying* my lunch.
> (Present participle in a predicate.)
> I have *finished* my lunch.
> (Past participle in a predicate.)
> A *steaming* bowl of soup would make a good lunch. (Present participle as adjective.)
> *Having finished* my lunch, I returned to work.
> (Perfect participle used as adjective.)

Part of speech

A classification for every word in a language. In English, the primary parts of speech are: *noun, pronoun, adjective, verb, adverb, preposition, conjunction,* and *interjection.*

Passive voice

The form of a verb telling that the subject is not the doer of the action but the entity which is acted upon.

> EXAMPLE:
>
> The song *was performed* by the choir.

Past participle

The fourth principal part of a verb used as part of a predicate or an adjective.

> EXAMPLE:
>
> I have *eaten* my breakfast. (Fourth form of the verb *eat, eating, ate, eaten.*)

Past perfect tense

The time of a verb beginning at a point in the past and ending at a later point in the past.

> EXAMPLE:
>
> She *had said* the same thing before.

Past tense

The time of a verb before now. The third principal part of a verb.

> EXAMPLE:
>
> She *baked* a cake. (Third form of the verb: *bake, baking, baked, [have/had] baked.*)

Perfect infinitive

Formed by the auxiliary to have and the past participle.

> EXAMPLE:
>
> *to have loved*

Perfect participle

Formed by the auxiliary having and the past participle.

> EXAMPLE:
>
> *having loved*

Person

The form of a pronoun (and corresponding form of a verb) indicating whether the "person" or "thing" represented by the pronoun is the one speaking or writing (*first person*: I/we worship), the one spoken or written to (*second person*: you worship), or one spoken or written about (*third person*: he/she/it/they worship).

Personal pronoun

A pronoun referring to the speaker or writer, the person spoken or written to, or the person spoken or written about.

EXAMPLES:

I, you, he, she, it, we, they, me, him, her, she, us, them

Phrase

A group of related words not containing a subject and predicate.

EXAMPLE:

The sound *of the old church bell* brought back many memories.

Plural

The classification of nouns, pronouns, subjects, and predicates indicating a number of two or more.

EXAMPLES:

cows, they
The animals graze.

Positive degree

The simple form of an adjective or adverb expressing no comparison.

EXAMPLES:

The *blue* sky. The *old* woman.
The *beautiful* words of the psalm.

Predicate

The verb or verb phrase in a sentence that makes a statement about the subject. A *simple predicate* is the verb or verb phrase alone. A *complete predicate* is the verb or verb phrase plus its object(s), indirect object(s), and all of their modifiers. A *compound predicate* consists of two or more verbs or verb phrases in a single sentence.

EXAMPLES:

She *wrote the letter yesterday*.
(*Wrote* is the simple predicate. *Wrote the letter yesterday* is the complete predicate.)
She *sealed* the envelope and *stamped* it.
(Compound predicate.)

Predicate adjective

An adjective placed in a predicate after a linking verb and used to modify the subject of a sentence or clause.

EXAMPLE:

Children are *happiest* when they are *loved*.

Predicate nominative

A noun, pronoun or equivalent clause used in a predicate after a linking verb to identify the subject.

EXAMPLES:

God is our *Father*.
This is not *what it seems to be*.

Preposition

A part of speech "positioned before" a noun or pronoun showing the relationship of that noun or pronoun (object) to some other word in the sentence.

EXAMPLES:

at school, *under* the couch, *behind* the house, *across* the ocean

Prepositional phrase

A preposition plus its object and related words. The preposition usually precedes, but sometimes follows, its object in the phrase.

EXAMPLES:

They crawled {*through the dark and damp tunnel*} {*to the other side*} {*of the cave*}.
What is the world coming *to*?

Present participle

The second principal part of a verb. The present participle is the *-ing* form of a verb and is used as part of a predicate or as an adjective.

EXAMPLES:

He is *working* at a local factory.
(Part of predicate.)
This is the *working* part of the engine.
(Adjective.)

Present perfect tense

The time of a verb beginning in the past and ending just now or still in progress in the present.

EXAMPLE:

I *have been studying* all morning.

Present tense

The time of a verb showing action or state of being now.

EXAMPLE:

God *loves* me.

Principal parts

The four primary forms of verbs—*present (infinitive)*, *present participle*, *past*, *past participle*—from which all other forms and uses (tense, mood, tone, voice) of verbs are created.

EXAMPLES:

(to) love, loving, loved, (have/had) loved; (to) burst, bursting, burst, (have/had) burst; (to) swim, swimming, swam, (have/had) swum
(See also Irregular verbs and Regular verbs.)

Progressive tone

A verb form, sometimes referred to as *progressive tense* and sometimes referred to as *progressive tone*, expressing on-going action or state of being. The progressive tense or tone consists of an appropriate form of the auxiliary verb *to be* plus the present participle.

EXAMPLES:

Jody *is going* to the store.

Bill *was playing* golf this morning.

Darlene *will be helping* her mother clean the house.

Pronoun

A part of speech used to replace a noun, often to prevent undue repetition of a noun. Pronouns include: *I, me, you, he, him, she, her, it, they, them, who, whom, which, that,* etc. Pronouns are classified as: *personal* (he), *relative* (which), *reflexive* (she gave herself), *interrogative* (Who?), *demonstrative* (these), *intensive* (he himself), *indefinite* (all), and *reciprocal* (each other).

Reciprocal pronoun

A pronoun indicating interchange. English has only two: *each other* (interchange between two) and *one another* (interchange among more than two).

Reflexive pronoun

A pronoun ending in *-self* and referring back to the subject. It usually comes after the verb and is essential to the meaning of the sentence.

EXAMPLE:

She told *herself* not to be afraid.

Regular verb

The most common verbs in English, they form their past and past participle forms by adding *-d, -t,* or *-ed* to the present form.

EXAMPLES:

move, moved, (have/had) moved; mean, meant, (have/had) meant; laugh, laughed, (have/had) laughed

Relative pronoun

A pronoun connecting or *relating* an adjective clause to its antecedent. They include *who, whom, which,* and *that*.

Restrictive or essential

A modifier, usually a phrase or clause, that limits or identifies the word modified.

Simple sentence

A sentence containing one subject (simple or compound) and one predicate (simple or compound); tantamount to one independent clause.*

NOTE: *Examples begin at the top of the column.

EXAMPLES:

The weather was ideal for working outdoors. (One simple subject and one simple predicate.)

Rock music is loved by some people but hated by others. (One simple subject and one compound predicate.)

Singular

The number classification of nouns, pronouns, verbs, subjects, and predicates indicating a quantity of *one*.

EXAMPLES:

a *girl,* the *cowboy,* a *truck*

One *game* of tennis *makes* me tired.

Subject

The noun, pronoun, noun phrase, or noun clause about which a sentence or clause makes a statement. A *simple subject* is the noun or pronoun alone.

EXAMPLE:

The *president* of the United States spoke on television.

A *complete subject* consists of a simple subject and all its modifiers.

EXAMPLE:

The *president of the United States* spoke on television.)

A compound subject consists of two or more subjects in a single sentence.

EXAMPLE:

George Washington and *Abraham Lincoln* are two well-known presidents.

Subordinating conjunction

A conjunction connecting a dependent clause to an independent clause.

EXAMPLES:

because, that, since, if, although.

I have been lonely *since* you left.

Superlative degree

The form of an adjective or adverb comparing three or more entities. It is formed by adding *-est* to one-syllable and some two-syllable adjectives or adverbs, or by preceding an adjective or adverb of two or more syllables with the word *most*.

EXAMPLES:

sharpest, loudest, heaviest, most peculiar, most unpredictable

Synonyms

Words that have the same or similar meanings.

Tense

The time of action or state of being expressed in a verb: *present, past, future* (simple tenses), *present perfect, past perfect, future perfect* (perfect tenses). The *progressive* form of a verb is sometimes called a *tense* and sometimes a *tone* within some of the other six primary tenses.

Tone

A characteristic of verb tenses indicating *progress, emphasis,* or *simple* time.

EXAMPLES:

eat (simple tone)

did eat (emphatic tone)

am eating (progressive tone)

Topic sentence

A sentence which expresses the central idea in a paragraph.

Transitional sentence

A sentence which serves as a link between one paragraph and another. It connects what has already been expressed with what will follow.

Verb

A part of speech expressing *action* or *state of being,* or *helping* another verb complete its meaning.

EXAMPLES:

construct (action verb)

is (state of being or linking verb)

have built (helping verb).

Verb phrase

A group of words consisting of a verb and its helpers.

EXAMPLES:

has spoken, did speak, will have been spoken

Verbal

Verb forms used as other parts of speech: *participles, gerunds,* and *infinitives.*

Voice

The form or use of a transitive verb indicating whether its subject is the doer (*active voice*) or receiver (*passive voice*) of the verb's action.

EXAMPLES:

The buck *stops* here. (Active voice.)

The book *was written* in the 19th century. (Passive voice.)

Index